YEAR
OF
TRIAL

YEAR OF TRIAL

KENNEDY'S CRUCIAL DECISIONS

Helen Fuller

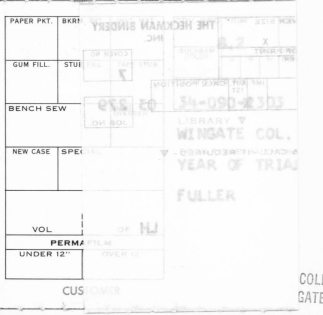

NEW YORK
HARCOURT, BRACE
& WORLD, INC.

Foreword

It was in a spirit of being equal to the task that John F. Kennedy and his comrades in politics met in the Fish Room at the White House on the morning after his swearing-in as President. They had appraised the position of the United States in the world and had made some general plans to strengthen it. They had taken the measure of the opposition in Congress and worked out initial strategy for meeting it. And they had assembled the best team they could bring together.

A highly competent group of men was eager to begin making the improvements in government that Kennedy had called for. But the preliminaries, they found, took time. It took time for the President and his chosen associates to master their new jobs. It took time to draft legislation and executive orders. It took time to clear away the accumulation of commitments and problems that the former Administration had left behind.

In his definitive study, *Presidential Transitions,* Laurin Henry of the Brookings Institution observes: "It seems to take about a year for an administration to put its stamp on basic policies and institutions and settle down to its characteristic modes of behavior."

This historical rule held for the Kennedy Administration even though it set a record for speed and order in the transfer of power; and the Kennedy style was discernible by midsummer of 1961. One reason was that the circumstances did not permit President Kennedy the leisurely period of settling in that both Truman and Eisenhower enjoyed—Truman as a result of the surrender of Germany and Japan in 1945 and Eisenhower as a result of Stalin's death in 1953. Kennedy was forced at once into the main stream, and the daily burden of great and possibly irreversible decisions brought his Administration to an early maturity. By the end of its first year, the character and personality of the new Administration emerged with considerable clarity.

The record of a single year is, of course, far from sufficient evidence on which to judge Mr. Kennedy's performance as President. That judgment must be reserved to the historians. But the decisions

20754

of his first year in office, together with one decision he made immediately after his nomination—the choosing of Lyndon B. Johnson as his running mate—do provide important indications of how President Kennedy is likely to deal with the succession of crises that almost surely lies ahead in the remaining years of his term.

The modern Presidency, as Mr. Kennedy has observed, is largely a matter of judgment. He spoke of this aspect of the office in a prerecorded interview that was broadcast in England the day after the failure of the Cuban invasion. "I sometimes think," he said, "we overstate the administerial difficulties of the Presidency. I think really in many ways it is a judicial function where alternatives are suggested which involve great matters, and finally the President must make a decision. That is really the most onerous and important part of the burdens of being President."

This book deals with some of John F. Kennedy's crucial decisions and the circumstances under which he made them.

Contents

CONTENTS

YEAR
OF
TRIAL

· I ·

The Choosing of L.B.J.

The man who was phoning Senator John F. Kennedy from Lyndon B. Johnson's suite in the Biltmore Hotel in Los Angeles was excited. "Jack," he said, "Bobby is down here telling the Speaker and Lyndon that there is opposition and Lyndon should withdraw." It was midafternoon of July 14, 1960, the day after the Democratic Party had nominated its candidate for President, and the nominee was now about to choose his running mate.

"Oh, that's all right." Kennedy's voice came back calmly. "Bobby's been out of touch and doesn't know what's been happening."

"Well, what do you want Lyndon to do?"

"I want him to make a statement right away. I have just finished making mine."

The first big decision of the Kennedy regime had been made by the President-to-be, alone, before most of those closest to him knew what was happening. Since it was a choice that would affect not only the outcome of the election but also his relations with Congress and possibly the succession to the Presidency in 1968, it is interesting to see how Kennedy came to make it.

On Monday, July 11, 1960, the day before the Democratic National Convention opened, two national newspapermen, both friends of John F. Kennedy, were enjoying the sound of their own voices as they conversed about what the week ahead might hold. Bored with the seeming certainty of Kennedy's nomination, they turned to the Vice Presidency. And when they found themselves arguing the case for Lyndon Johnson with equal ardor, they telephoned Kennedy headquarters to ask for five minutes of the Senator's time. Moments later they were in the reception hall of his ninth-floor headquarters at the Biltmore. And when the Senator

3

brought them into his sitting room, the two took turns presenting
their arguments for Johnson for Vice President: his region; his
religion; the difficulty of running a campaign, and later a Congress,
with a vanquished and embittered Johnson to contend with; and
last and most important, Johnson's exceptional ability.

When they had finished, Kennedy, to their amazement, told
them quietly that he had considered the same factors and had come
to the same conclusion. To be certain there was no misunderstanding, his visitors made their speeches over again, adding the plea
that if Kennedy did offer Johnson second place he do it so persuasively that Johnson could not refuse. Kennedy replied emphati-
cally that this was his intention. Johnson, he said, would help the
ticket not only in the South but with important segments of the
party all over the country.

The two newsmen left, still puzzled by Kennedy's positiveness,
for Bobby Kennedy had assured one of them just as positively only
a few days before that Johnson would not even be considered for
Vice President.

Behind the seeming contradiction was what has become a traditional effort every four years to read the South out of the Democratic Party. In 1960 the case for it was even more plausible than
usual. Would-be experts who could count up to 269, the number
of electoral votes required to win, argued that the Democrats
would lose the Presidency unless they piled up huge majorities in
the industrial cities of the North and that this could be done only
with the enthusiastic support of labor and minority groups. A
policy of no compromise with the South's position on civil rights
was essential; and to put Lyndon Johnson, "Mr. Compromise" himself, on the national ticket would probably be fatal. The wise
course, the argument ran, was to pick a liberal running mate from
the Midwest or West—Senator Stuart Symington of Missouri or
Senator Henry M. Jackson of Washington—concentrate on those
regions plus the Northeast, and forget about the South.

Kennedy figured differently. By convention time the Kennedy
camp was again deeply conscious of the religious issue. After the
primary victory over Hubert H. Humphrey in Protestant West
Virginia in April, Kennedy and his strategists believed that anti-
Catholicism of the virulent sort was definitely on the wane. Since
then, their eyes and ears and a fresh batch of private polls had
been telling them otherwise. They still did not suspect how much
the religious issue would hurt, but the Senator's strategists were
convinced that intense prejudice against the Church was largely

centered in the South. At the moment, therefore, when Kennedy was choosing his running mate, he believed that the South was the region most desperately in need of shoring up. This was reason enough for turning to the South for a partner on his ticket—and for turning not to Senator Albert Gore of Tennessee or Senator George A. Smathers of Florida, both of whom were panting for the honor, but to Senator Lyndon B. Johnson, who was strong enough to force skittish Southern politicians back into line for the national ticket and persuade them it would be unsafe not to stay there.

Senator Kennedy must also have been thinking ahead to the short "rump" session of Congress that would convene in August. At that session, Majority Leader Johnson could make or break Kennedy's chance of carrying out some of his campaign promises in advance of election. And Kennedy must surely have considered the unpleasing prospect of trying, as President, to get along with a Congress ruled in the Senate by a disgruntled, defeated opponent and in the House by that opponent's campaign manager, Speaker Sam Rayburn. Kennedy had served in the Senate long enough to know that life can be beautiful with Johnson as your friend and hideous with him as your enemy. There was much to be said for finding the Majority Leader another place in the sun.

But it is clear from what has followed that Kennedy saw more in a Kennedy-Johnson ticket than a regional coalition to hold Southern votes in the election and help persuade Southern leaders to go along with the Kennedy program in Congress. The evidence suggests that what led Kennedy to offer Johnson the nomination for Vice President over strong objection, and in turn led Johnson to accept the offer, was the basic respect the two men have for each other.

Early in the primary campaign Kennedy made the statement that if he could not be President himself, his choice would be Lyndon Johnson. And an interviewer reported Kennedy as saying a year before that he considered himself as well qualified as any of the other candidates "except probably Lyndon"—but he didn't think Lyndon could get the nomination. As Majority Leader, Johnson, in his turn, had repeatedly showed high regard for the Junior Senator from Massachusetts, even assigning him to a much-sought-after seat on the Foreign Relations Committee in preference to men with greater seniority.

Senator Johnson never stated an explicit preference for Kennedy over the rest of the Democratic candidates, but, months before the nominating convention, intimates of Johnson confidently predicted that Johnson would support Kennedy if he himself were out of the race.

For all their outward differences, the reserved young New Englander and the back-slapping cajoler from Texas have many traits and values in common. Unlike most elected officials, who come out of the law, business, or some other way of life, neither Kennedy nor Johnson has ever been trained for or worked seriously at anything but politics; politics is their profession. Both are enthralled by the political art and proud of their skill in the practice of it. Both are self-confident men of tremendous energy who instinctively reach for the position of power in any situation. They share an aversion for "extremists" and for the doctrinaire. They demand excellence in those around them and cannot abide sloppiness (at work, that is—both "slop" around at home in off-hours) or less than absolute loyalty. Both, moreover, have been able to contain their driving ambition "within a framework of reality." That was why Kennedy was graceful in defeat for the Vice Presidency against Estes Kefauver in 1956 and why Johnson, as one Senate colleague pointed out after the Los Angeles convention, didn't suffer from psychological shock when he failed to get the Presidential nomination. ("He just coolly moved into the next best spot. And he plans to brand it forever with LBJ.") Neither man would have respected the other had he failed to do everything in his power to achieve the top job in his profession—the Presidency of the United States.

THE SECOND-BEST MAN

For second place on the ticket Kennedy picked his second choice for President in 1960. And Johnson, knowing that he could work with another professional whom he respected, and confident that his powers of personal leadership would not be diminished by changing jobs, chose to accept the second place as another step on his way to the top.

The inner logic of Kennedy's choice of Johnson is clear enough now. But during the three hectic days between Kennedy's private talk with his newspaper friends about the Vice Presidency and his own nomination, Robert F. Kennedy's prophecy that Johnson would be passed over seemed more realistic than his brother's belief that Johnson could and should be nominated.

To Johnson's supporters for the Presidency, their cause was

no more quixotic than Kennedy's. Who said that a Southerner would be harder for a majority of the country to take than a Catholic? What major fault could the party as a whole find with Johnson's voting record except on civil rights? And who could compare Kennedy to Johnson for maturity and experience? In the final days before the convention, therefore, Johnson and his backers settled down to kicking and gouging attacks on Kennedy that were personal in the extreme. And through a clerical error they were given one last chance of demolishing Kennedy's candidacy.

The day before he won the nomination, John Kennedy confided to one caller that by his own calculations he might be as many as twenty votes short of enough to win on the first ballot, and wondered whether it was possible to pick up any of Johnson's first-ballot votes on the strength of his intention of making Johnson the Vice Presidential offer. Not unless Senator Smathers could be persuaded to swing some of Johnson's Florida delegates Kennedy's way, the candidate was told. "The trouble with that," Kennedy replied, "is that Smathers wants to be Vice President himself."

How else could Kennedy benefit from what he was about to do for Johnson? If Adlai E. Stevenson could be persuaded to place Kennedy's name in nomination, that would almost surely sweep Kennedy in on the first ballot. But Stevenson had the excellent excuse that before the primaries he had pledged not to take sides; then, too, his own unavowed campaign for the nomination was warming up. Perhaps if Johnson, recognizing the collapse of his candidacy, could be persuaded to release Stevenson from his pledge of neutrality, Stevenson would find it embarrassing not to go along with Kennedy. It was worth a try, and an emissary was dispatched to sound Johnson out along this line.

Awkwardly, that emissary arrived to make his pitch only a few moments after Johnson had received word of a gaffe at Kennedy headquarters. A form letter signed by Kennedy, asking permission to appear before state delegations to ask for their votes, had been sent to the Texas delegation, for which it was not intended, as well as to delegations having no favorite sons. Johnson was jubilant when he learned of the chance for a dramatic confrontation at which he would be in charge. What should he say and how should he say it? He was again full of zest for battle. It was surely no time to talk of surrender. The emissary never sounded Johnson out on helping Kennedy with Stevenson, and that chance to put Kennedy into Johnson's debt was gone.

Then came Kennedy's appearance before the Texas delegation. Word of it had spread, and the room was thick with television cameras and onlookers. Johnson introduced the Senator from Massachusetts with a fifteen-minute harangue in which he referred over and over again to inexperience and youth, and stressed his own wide knowledge of government. Bobby Kennedy sat next to his brother throughout, whispering to him much of the time. Then Kennedy rose. He spoke with the same dignity he had displayed before another group of Texans, the ministers of Houston. The contrast was marked. Johnson had misfired. Kennedy had every right to be personally aggrieved by Johnson's manner, but he did not choose to treat the matter personally.

Until after his own nomination, Kennedy kept his counsel about his inclination toward Johnson. His closest lieutenants believed that the choice for Vice President was between Senators Jackson and Symington. But when he woke up the morning after his nomination, Kennedy phoned Johnson and later visited him at his hotel suite. Their talk was general, but the offer of second place to Johnson was implicit, and the manner was persuasive. Indeed, Kennedy put the matter in such a way that it was hard for Johnson to refuse: he wanted to be President of the whole country; he had first to be the leader of the whole of his party, and to be that he needed Johnson with him.

When the two men parted, it was understood that Johnson was available.

NEGOTIATING THE NOMINATION

About 1:45 that same Thursday afternoon, July 14, only a few hours before the convention was to nominate a Vice President, one of the men who had pleaded the cause for Johnson with Kennedy the previous Monday dropped into Johnson's suite. Johnson excitedly confided that Bobby Kennedy was at that moment with Sam Rayburn in an adjoining room talking about the Vice Presidency. In a few moments Mrs. Johnson came in, and then the Speaker. Bobby, the Speaker reported, wanted to see Johnson. Both Rayburn and "Lady Bird" reportedly were somewhere between negative and neutral toward the idea of Johnson in second place on the ticket. After some discussion, it was decided that in any case Johnson should discuss the matter only with Senator Kennedy himself, and Bobby was so informed by Mr. Rayburn.

When a mutual friend called from Johnson's suite to give the candidate the same information directly, Kennedy kept him on the phone several minutes talking about the mess he was in since word had got out, during the morning, that Johnson was his choice. Pressure on him to take Senator Symington of Missouri instead was tremendous, Kennedy reported—clearly he was having second thoughts. Would he lose more than he would gain by taking Johnson? The big city leaders thought Johnson a good choice. But Walter Reuther and Arthur J. Goldberg were protesting. "And Alex Rose is threatening not to list me on the Liberal ticket [in New York] because of Johnson." Then, responding to the complaint that it was too late to change his mind, Kennedy told his friend to call back "in three minutes" for a final decision.

Giving him ten minutes instead, the friend phoned again at 2:45. "Tell Lyndon I want him," Kennedy said at once, "and will have Lawrence [Governor David L. Lawrence of Pennsylvania] nominate him. . . . Please call Adlai for me and tell him the decision and ask for his full support."

Presumably everything was set. But the opposition to Johnson had not given up.

About 3:00 P.M. Bobby Kennedy came back to see Rayburn. Johnson, he said, could shortly expect a call from John Kennedy. Time passed, but no call came. Johnson was on edge. With him in his room were Governor Price Daniel of Texas and Senator Robert S. Kerr of Oklahoma, and they were objecting loudly to his acceptance—"a betrayal of the South." (By that time Speaker Rayburn had come around to supporting Johnson's decision to accept and Kerr subsequently joined him, but not Daniel.)

About four o'clock—the call had not yet come—Johnson's appointment secretary hastily rounded up an emergency strategy meeting (a caucus of fifteen Hawaiian delegates was politely asked to move out of the Majority Leader's suite to make room). An extremely nervous Johnson faced Mr. Rayburn, John B. Connally, Jr. (later Secretary of the Navy), Mrs. Johnson, James Rowe (a longtime lawyer-adviser), the Washington publisher Philip Graham, and Robert G. Baker, Secretary to the Senate Policy Committee. Bobby Kennedy, Johnson almost shouted, had just come in and told Sam and him that there was a lot of opposition and that Johnson should withdraw for the sake of the party. With a sharp nod, Rayburn directed one of the group to "call Kennedy."

Kennedy was on the phone at once, saying that Bobby was "out of touch." "You'd better speak to Lyndon." "Okay." Johnson, sprawled on the bed, accepted the phone that was handed to him: "Yes, yes . . . yes . . . okay," he said, as Kennedy read him the statement announcing his choice of Johnson. Johnson handed the phone back to the man who had made the call, who then sug-

gested to Kennedy that he speak to Bobby. Someone fetched
Bobby from the next room. Looking solemn and dead-tired, he
listened to his brother for a few seconds. "Well, it's too late now,"
he said, after a pause, and half-slammed the phone down.

After a moment, with some urging and pushing from those in
the room, Lyndon and "Lady Bird" Johnson were propelled
through the door into the hallway, which was blazing with lights
for the TV cameras. They stood on chairs, as directed, and Johnson read his statement of acceptance. Their faces, as one witness
put it, "metamorphosized into enthusiasm and confidence."

JOHNSON'S CONTRIBUTION

By choosing as his running mate the man whom he considered,
after himself, the best man for President in 1960, Kennedy acquired a possible antidote to religious bias in the South; he removed a potential rival for power from the Congress with which
he would have to work as President; he took the first step toward
restoring the Vice Presidential office to its original importance;
and, consciously or not, he created a Democratic heir-apparent to
follow him in office.

As he had told friends, Kennedy expected that Johnson would
help the ticket "with important segments of the party all over the
country." But it is doubtful that Kennedy or even Johnson himself
foresaw the kind of campaign the Vice Presidential candidate
would wage or the part it would play in making Kennedy President. From the moment of his nomination Johnson the realist
ceased to be a Texas Senator, or even the leader of the loyal opposition in the Senate, and began rehearsing for his new role of
number-two man in the United States, understudy to the President.

Reporters who followed him on an early campaign trip through
the Midwest were the first to notice the change. "Those who know
Senator Lyndon B. Johnson in Washington as a subtle parliamentary strategist and an apostle of political compromise would hardly
recognize him as a campaigner for Vice President," wrote Anthony
Lewis in the New York *Times*. "On the stump this week he has
been partisan and aggressive and anything but subtle. He has
mixed folksy humor, biting sarcasm about the Republican party
and frontal attack in the Harry Truman style."

Again and again he derides Vice President Nixon's claims of "maturity
and experience." He reminds his audience that President Eisenhower

said it would take him a week to think of something that Mr. Nixon had recommended as a policy.

He remarks that "Mr. Nixon made a goodwill tour to Latin America. He built up so much good will that we had to call in the Marines to get him out."

As for Mr. Nixon's beliefs, he says the Vice President reminds him of the teacher who was told that half the school board thought the world was flat and half round and was asked what he taught.

"I can teach either," Senator Johnson has the teacher answer, to the laughter of the crowd.

Even President Eisenhower is not safe from the Johnson scalpel. He said last night that the President "was a little late in life in deciding a few things—like what party he belonged to and what church he belonged to."

But the Republican party bears the brunt of his assault. Senator Johnson attacks it as the friend of the "princes of privilege" and "economic royalists" and takes his audiences back through the days of McKinley to lay out all the horrors of the party.

He comes up with homely examples that seem to score. Yesterday he said the Republican bill to supply medical care for the aged would require any recipient to swear "a pauper's oath—you'd have some case worker out examining your mother to see if she'd hidden some pin money."

Senator Johnson has brief prepared texts at each stop but speaks mostly off the cuff. When he feels a response in the crowd he warms to his job and becomes increasingly emotional, telling his listeners about depression tragedies and mixing in old Texas stories with a political point.

Two themes he hits again and again are praise for the personal qualities of the Democratic Presidential candidate, Senator John F. Kennedy—"a man of courage, judicious, confident"—and the religious issue.

He tells the story of the Baptist co-pilot who was shot down during World War II with Senator Kennedy's brother, Joseph P. Kennedy, Jr. "Before they were allowed to die for their country," Senator Johnson says, "no one asked them where they worshiped God."

The one characteristic that Washington friends would surely recognize is Senator Johnson's energy.

After the Kennedy-Nixon television debate Monday night he spent most of the rest of the evening telephoning to politicians and friends, including Republicans, to check reactions to it. He had almost no sleep.

Johnson had indeed changed the style that Washington associated with him. He didn't really have to change his tune about any important planks in the party platform except those that cut across such Texas interests as oil and white supremacy. Johnson learned his political philosophy from Franklin D. Roosevelt. Through the years, he toned it down but only as much as he reckoned he must to stay alive in Texas politics. Now, running in the United States at large, he was no longer under any such necessity. Moreover, he seemed to relish his new freedom, and this was communicated to his campaign audiences.

To be sure, as the LBJ campaign moved East, incongruities appeared: the five-gallon hat, the unfamiliar accent, and the raspy voice ("It makes your throat hurt to hear him," a Brooklyn bystander remarked!); the homilies left over from stump speaking in the South. ("I'm converted," a cynic in a Queens audience said to his companion, "but I don't know what to.") When Johnson bore down, however, his Northern listeners got the message.

An example was the occasion, one October afternoon, when Johnson made a speech before the Trade Union Council of the New York Liberal Party. The meeting got off to a seemingly hopeless start. Johnson had not arrived—and the early edition of the New York *Post,* which most of the audience had brought along, carried the report that he had disdained the Council's invitation to appear. Alex Rose, President of the Liberal Party (the same Alex Rose who had threatened to keep Kennedy off the Liberal ticket if he ran with Johnson), opened the meeting. He explained the misunderstanding that had produced the report and then tried to warm up the audience for Johnson's arrival. Rose told them that Johnson was "the best man to unify the party. . . . We have no apologies [for having a Southerner on the ticket] . . . Roosevelt chose Garner. . . . I am one who believes the South is part of the United States. There are more reactionaries there, but we can't expel them from the Union."

The four hundred key union officials sat silent, waiting to be shown.

"When we used to visit Johnson down in Washington on legislation," Rose went on, "we didn't always get what we wanted from him, but we always got what he promised."

At this, the audience visibly warmed.

"We visited Johnson *and* Nixon on the minimum-wage bill. Johnson was not too easy, but he understood us and he led the fight for the $1.25 an hour and not Nixon. And we haven't heard a word from Lodge on that issue."

Rose was able to summon some clapping by the time Johnson and his entourage swept into the room. When Johnson finished speaking, he got an ovation.

"He didn't leave out anything," one labor politician said to me

admiringly after the meeting. "He came an unknown quantity,
but he left a hero." What the group wanted and what Johnson gave
was assurance of his support for a higher minimum wage, for
medical care for the aged under Social Security, for the civil-rights
plank in the Democratic platform, and for revision of parts of the
Landrum-Griffin Labor Act. And the way he gave it made them
believe him. "What I say here today about the civil-rights plank,"
he said, "I will say tomorrow and every day everywhere I speak in
the South."

And he did. In fact, that same evening the Vice Presidential
candidate gave a Richmond, Virginia, audience an even larger
helping of New Dealism than he had given the New York Liberal
Party. Speaking in the former capital of the Confederacy, he said,
"I did not come down here to promise Virginia exemptions from
the obligation to carry out the decision of the Supreme Court, but
an invitation" to join the nation in extending civil rights. "A hundred years of debate among ourselves is enough, I think. Don't
you?"

Wherever the LBJ Campaign Special paused in a whistlestop
tour of eight Southern states in early October, the people heard the
same liberal Democratic philosophy, with generous helpings of
"homefolks" stories mixed in. ("Lyndon ought to serve dish gravy
with this," a local reporter remarked after one typical performance.)

EYE ON THE FUTURE

From the moment of his choice by Kennedy, Johnson was careful of the record. He "didn't leave anything out" for Southern audiences that he put in for Northern ones. To be sure, Senator Smathers of Florida, John Kennedy's close friend and the co-ordinator
of the Presidential campaign for all the Southern states, was on
board the LBJ Special, and he took care to remind local leaders
that, regardless of campaign promises, if the Democrats were in
power, Southerners would run Congress. But Johnson stayed in
step with Kennedy and the platform on civil rights. And he permitted no slur or slight to the head of the ticket. When the Gov-
ernor-elect of Florida introduced him to an Orlando audience with
flattering praise but did not mention Kennedy's name, Johnson
remedied the omission before he made his remarks. No sources of
conflict with the White House were allowed to arise.

Johnson's eye was on the future. But he put first things first and his first job was to hold the South for the Democratic ticket in 1960. That meant minimizing the two strikes against Kennedy—his pro-civil-rights position and his Catholicism. The Johnson strategy was to preach tolerance in public and put pressure on party officials in private. It was a rare audience that did not hear the story of Joe Kennedy, Jr., and the Baptist pilot, who went down to sudden death together fighting for the United States—"Nobody asked what church they attended." Meanwhile, the local politicians who introduced him in towns throughout the South sweetened the bitter pill of civil rights for their audiences, as Johnson had already sweetened it for them, by pointing out that with Kennedy in the White House, Johnson, not Nixon, would be presiding over the Senate. As one forthright chairman in Greenville, South Carolina, inelegantly put it: "My observation as a lawyer is that if you can't get your choice for foreman of the jury, for God's sake try to get one of your men on so you won't get hurt too bad."

There was a continuous demonstration of the fine art of pressure politics in the lounge car of the LBJ Special. In five days of whistlestopping from Washington to Miami and across to New Orleans, more than 1,200 local Democratic VIP's got on and off at the 48 stops the train made; they conferred with Johnson individually or in groups while riding from one station to the next and had their photographs taken with him by the train photographer. Guests usually left with the feeling that after the election the White House would have a little list of those who had done their part to put the Democrats in, and of those who hadn't.

In South Carolina, Johnson was either unusually persuasive or his listeners were especially alert, for his train had barely cleared the state when local party leaders were on the phone to Washington asking for help. And whom did they call? The leaders of the national AFL-CIO! Johnson had given them to understand that South Carolina could not expect to get the time of day from the new Administration after the election if they did not carry the state in November, and as the local leaders explained to the labor leaders in Washington, "we can't do it without the nigras, and they won't even talk to us, much less cooperate, but they trust your labor people. Help!" Labor sent more men and money to organize the Negro vote. The Democratic ticket won South Carolina by 10,400 votes, and according to party estimates 40,000 votes were cast by Negroes.

Johnson scared the "Courthouse Crowd"—who still have formidable strength outside the big cities of the South—more than Catholicism or the Democratic platform scared them. "Forget about the platform and what you like and don't like," he told them in effect. "We're going to win and you had better be with us."

When it came to the other element that was to prove decisive for the Democrats in 1960—the Southern Negro vote—Johnson had a rare piece of personal good luck. Unknown to the candidate for Vice President, to this day I think, one of the few white Southerners trusted by the Negroes made the rounds of the entire South in his car, pledging his personal word to Negro leaders that "Lyndon will do right by you." He assured them that Johnson as a national candidate, no longer the prisoner of Texas, would keep his pledge to uphold the civil-rights plank. This was Aubrey Williams, who with Harry Hopkins pioneered the Roosevelt relief program during the depression. Williams, as head of the National Youth Administration, had chosen Lyndon Johnson to be the first state director of the NYA for Texas. They had not lost touch, although since 1943, when NYA died with the coming of wartime recovery, Williams had fought a lonely, unpopular battle for desegregation, first as a publisher in Montgomery, Alabama, then as president of the Southern Conference Education Fund, a frequent target of Senator James O. Eastland's Internal Security Committee. Williams' *bona fides* with Southern Negro leaders is fourteen-carat gold. They took his word for Johnson and passed it along to their followers; which made it that much easier for the Southern Negro vote to swing swiftly and overwhelmingly to the Democrats after Kennedy's dramatic phone call to Mrs. Martin Luther King, Jr., in Atlanta just before Election Day, expressing sympathy for her husband's imprisonment on a minor charge.

JOHNSON'S EFFECT ON THE ELECTION

In a postelection examination of "Why It Wasn't Nixon," *U.S. News & World Report* printed answers which it claimed "reflect Mr. Nixon's own analysis." To the question "What effect did Lyndon Johnson, as Kennedy's running mate, have in the South?" the answer was "Johnson can't be downgraded at all. He dealt very effectively with the courthouse politicians. . . . He was enormously effective in dealing with these people who can turn out a controlled vote." And to the further question "What states in the South would Nixon have carried if Johnson had not been on the Kennedy ticket?" the answer was "Obviously, Texas. And there's no question about the Carolinas. Something went on with both Johnson and former Governor Luther Hodges of North Carolina, now Secretary of Commerce, in dealing with the textile manufacturers of the Carolinas. There was a big switch in the last two weeks before the election. A lot of important people who had been leaning to Nixon suddenly went the other way. The rest of the South would have been pretty speculative."

Had Richard Nixon had the kind of help Johnson gave Kennedy in his Southern campaign, the GOP might now hold the White House. Both candidates rejected the idea of trying to win without the South; both decided to try hard for a maximum Southern vote. Nixon personally invested an enormous amount of time in that effort. By picking Johnson and assigning him responsibility for the region, Kennedy gained time that he could use in the crucial Northern and Eastern cities.

As it was, Nixon polled almost 49 per cent of the popular vote in 11 states of the South; he actually carried Virginia, Tennessee, and Florida and came very close to winning in South Carolina and Texas. Nixon was counting on anti-Catholicism to hold down the normal Democratic vote in rural areas and on the new Republican strength in urban areas to put him across. "He was playing," *U.S. News & World Report* authoritatively stated, "to what obviously was a more compatible economic and philosophic viewpoint, as opposed to the platform that Kennedy was running on." And theoretically his strategy was sound. While the Kennedy-Johnson ticket won a higher percentage of the total Southern vote and a larger electoral vote, Nixon outpolled the Democrats in metropolitan areas of more than 50,000 population. Had Kennedy and Johnson not performed their respective jobs better than was expected, Nixon might easily have been the over-all winner in the South simply by holding those states the Republicans captured from the Democrats in 1952 and 1956.

Johnson's job was to persuade the backwoods and the small towns that the Pope was not going to move into the White House if Kennedy was elected, and that he who did not help to prepare the feast would have no seat at the table when it was served. Kennedy's part was to attract enough Catholic and Negro votes in Southern cities to offset the recent urban trend toward the Republicans in Presidential elections. Neither of them alone could have prevented the electoral revolt that threatened in the South in 1960. As it turned out, the Democratic ticket carried two Southern states Stevenson had not carried in 1956—Texas and Louisiana—and held all those he had. In doing so, according to an as yet unpublished study of the Democratic showing in the South in 1960 by Professor Bernard Cosman of the University of Detroit, Kennedy polled a larger popular percentage than Stevenson in seven Southern states. His gain was largest in Louisiana, and both there and in Texas, Dr. Cosman's study shows, the Catholic population is large enough to have influenced the outcome.

"Catholic and Negro support probably helped Kennedy improve upon Stevenson in the cities," says Dr. Cosman. "While Kennedy did not carry the metropolitan South or the metropolitan sectors of any Southern state, he was stronger than Stevenson in two-thirds of the cities—41 out of 64. Most frequently, the President enjoyed the largest gains in cities where Catholic and Negro registrants were numerous.

"Kennedy did well among Negro voters. In Charleston, Columbia, and Dallas, Negro wards and precincts produced the largest Democratic percentage-point gains from 1956 to 1960. In the black belt, Democratic gains increased in size at each higher level of Negro registration. The two black-belt counties with a majority of Negro registrants switched from Eisenhower in 1956 to Kennedy in 1960." Even so, the President failed to match Nixon's showing in the cities, and the ticket was stronger in the countryside where anti-Catholic voting was expected to produce a possibly fatal fall-off in the regular Democratic vote.

Unquestionably, the religious issue cost the Democrats far more in the South than elsewhere. Concluding that "the religious issue was the strongest single factor" in the 1960 election, the Michigan Survey Research Center attributes to the religious issue a loss by Kennedy of 16 per cent of the two-party vote in 15 Southern and border states (where voting in 1960 was 25 per cent higher than in 1956). But a good many of Johnson's white Protestant kinfolk from the Piney Woods, the Piedmont, and the Black Belt must have joined the few Negroes who vote there, because the predicted Catholic rout in the rural South did not take place.

Together, Johnson and Kennedy brought the greater part of the South back into the Democratic column. The principal factors working in Johnson's favor were the fear he threw into the "Courthouse Crowd"; his sermons on tolerance; the spread of word among Negroes, courtesy of Aubrey Williams, that Johnson was through with filibustering; and the response of poor folks to his invocation of the name and spirit of Roosevelt. As for Kennedy, by good fortune he had an opportunity to express, in a dramatic way, sympathy for Dr. Martin Luther King, Jr., and hence for Southern

Negroes generally; his appeal to young people stood him in good
stead in the South as elsewhere; and he had the support of his
fellow Catholics.

Any organized group that produced as many as 100,000 votes
in the closest Presidential election in 76 years can claim to have
been the final force in electing John F. Kennedy, with his margin
of only 118,262 votes out of the 69 million tabulated. But the remarkable reversal of trend in what was due to be a bad year for
the Democrats in the South, where Lyndon Johnson carried the
main responsibility for the campaign, was evidence if needed of the
"Great Persuader's" political punch. It also bore out the wisdom
of Kennedy's judgment in choosing Johnson. And it seemed to
entitle the new Vice President to some special show of Presidential
favor.

L.B.J.'S NEW STATUS

In the days between January 3, when the 87th Congress convened, and January 20, when the new President and Vice President
were inaugurated, there was some confusion over the status of Lyndon Johnson—in the minds of the press, the public, and the Congress, if not in the mind of Johnson himself. Even after he resigned
his seat, it was still hard for the Senate and the press not to think
of him as the leading member of the club. And events in the opening days of the new session seemed to support the view of those
who insisted that Lyndon Johnson was going to try to have it both
ways—run the Senate from behind the scenes and use the power he
would derive from that position to bargain for a larger role than
Vice Presidents usually have.

Before Congress opened, the Vice President-elect was calling
conferences in his office in the Capitol, bringing together Executive
and Legislative leaders—Secretary of State-elect Dean Rusk, Senate Democratic Whip Mike Mansfield, Foreign Relations Chairman J. William Fulbright, and Armed Services Chairman Richard
B. Russell—to discuss the crises in Cuba and Laos. Johnson let
it be known that he would keep the lavish offices in the Capitol that
had been especially decorated for him as Senate Majority Leader,
in addition to the more modest space Vice President Richard
Nixon had occupied. And when Mike Mansfield, picked by Johnson to succeed him as Majority Leader, proposed to the first Democratic caucus that Johnson continue to preside over future caucuses after he became Vice President, the suspicious and skeptical

ok it as proof conclusive of a Johnson double design: to run the enate through Mansfield, carry tales from the Capitol to the White House and vice versa, and so establish himself as indispensable broker between the two.

As Mansfield proposed that the Vice President be given the special privilege of presiding over party caucuses, Johnson sat lent in the Chairman's chair, his head bowed. He did not raise his eyes when a succession of surprised Senators rose to object. Joseph S. Clark of Pennsylvania, Wayne Morse of Oregon, Albert Gore of Tennessee, Paul H. Douglas of Illinois, and A. S. Mike Monroney of Oklahoma questioned the propriety of a member of the Executive Branch presiding over legislative meetings. Seventeen Democrats went on record as opposed when Mansfield's motion came to a vote—a larger minority than had ever opposed Johnson, as Democratic leader, on an organization matter.

There are those who think that this uprising caused Johnson to change course. But Johnson and Mansfield plausibly claim that there was never any ground for the opposition's fears: Mansfield merely wanted to provide for a neutral substitute in the chair when he (Mansfield) wanted to take part in caucus debate. (It *is* awkward for a party leader to preside at caucuses when his own feelings run high.) Senate President Ernest W. McFarland sometimes sat in for Majority Leader Johnson during the Eisenhower Administration. Johnson's defenders further insist that he was too smart to think he could control a Senate in which he no longer had a vote.

If Johnson ever harbored the hope of playing a double role, he relinquished it quickly, for on February 27, at the first Democratic Senate caucus after he had been authorized to preside, the Vice President called the meeting to order, immediately handed the gavel to Mansfield, and did not resume the chair during the session. Within a few months the complaint among Democrats was that Johnson was giving not too much but too little time to Senate affairs; and the press had apparently forgotten all about Johnson's scheme to place himself in a control post between the two ends of Pennsylvania Avenue.

It turned out that those who thought that Johnson could not bring himself to let go of the Senate reins, or in fact make himself junior assistant to the young Senator who had served under him, misjudged their man. Rowland Evans of the New York *Herald Tribune* caught the truth so many were unwilling to see:

A close friend of Mr. Johnson watched him at the moment on Tuesday when, having just resigned from the Senate after eight years as

Democratic leader, he yielded his chair to Senator Mansfield and walked out of the chamber with a purposeful stride.

"A look of something like relief was on his face," the friend said "He has so completely mastered the job of being Senate leader that i was becoming a chore. Now he is no longer a Senator from a single state with a regional bias. He has been nationalized, a changed man with a new job."

Johnson, of course, was bitterly disappointed at his failure to win the nomination, and for the first few weeks he was demanding even of semistrangers who found themselves in his company why they had not supported him for the Presidency. Then he adjusted to reality. He made it clear to those closest to him that the competition with Kennedy was over: that he and the President were "wholly together in purposes and in human terms," as a confidante paraphrased his words; and that he was "genuinely grateful for an unbroken series of generous acts toward him by the President," who had been "magnanimous in large ways and small."

Kennedy, from the day he invited Johnson to join him on the ticket, behaved toward him with the sympathy of one proud and sensitive man for another. He realized the difficulty Johnson was experiencing in moving from a greater to a lesser position of power and did what he could to cushion the shock.

In "small ways" he saw to it that Johnson received all the deference to which he had become accustomed in the Senate and that the Johnson womenfolk had their share of attention, too. To make the Vice President comfortable in his new situation, the President gave him an office in the Executive Office Building, next door to the White House—a favor never extended to Nixon and an ingratiating gesture to one with Johnson's passion for perquisites. On the occasions, frequent at first, when White House insiders made slighting remarks about Johnson, the President barked reprimands that did not encourage repetition.

In "large ways" Kennedy set about upgrading the Vice President's job. In his first month as President, Kennedy wrote Johnson an unusual letter, not made public, setting forth the responsibilities the Vice President would bear in his Administration. He would have executive duties, power to carry them out, and a staff to assist him. This was a new departure. Even the expanded role Richard Nixon played in the Eisenhower Administration was nevertheless largely advisory.

Perhaps recalling the time when the shoe was on the other foot and Johnson had given him preference in Senate-committee appointments, the President assigned to Johnson work that could substantially help him in the future. In the public mind, the Senator from Texas, despite all his claims to being a forward-looking Westerner, was an insular Southerner. The jobs Kennedy gave him, properly performed, could change that "image." Johnson's special assignments were to enforce the prohibition of racial discrimination in hiring by the Government and its contractors; to co-ordinate the United States program for the exploration of space; to serve as chairman of the advisory committee to the Peace Corps; and to act as special representative of the President in diplomatic contacts with nations abroad. In short, Kennedy gave Johnson the opportunity to make a strong record in the fields in which he had been weakest as a Presidential candidate in 1960— the kind of opportunity for experience Eisenhower had in mind when he suggested to Nixon in 1956 that he switch from the Vice Presidency to a Cabinet post.

ELIMINATING JOB DISCRIMINATION

Strangely enough, Johnson was most at home in the first of his special assignments. To show how much at home, his press agents made much of a story that was recounted in the New York *Times* in connection with the announcement of the Vice President's appointment to the chairmanship of the President's Committee on Equal Employment Opportunities.

In the spring of 1937, a freshman Representative from Texas made an indignant protest to the Farm Security Administration. This government agency made loans of $200 to $300 to destitute farm families to enable them to buy seed, fertilizer and other necessities.

What irked the Texan was this: Although many white farmers in his district had been given loans, very few Negro farmers had been able to get them.

"And we have Negroes down there," he said, "who are every bit as responsible as the white farmers who got the loans."

Milo Perkins, the man in charge of the loan program, investigated, found the Representative was right, and ended the discrimination. As a one-time Texan himself, Mr. Perkins knew that Negroes did not vote heavily in the district and he wondered why the Representative had been so insistent in their behalf. Later, on further acquaintance, he concluded that the Representative had been animated by an outraged sense of justice.

Last week President Kennedy gave the outraged Texan, now Vice President Johnson, a chance to exercise his sense of justice on a national scale by making him chairman of a new committee to fight racial discrimination in hiring by the Government and its contractors.

To be sure, Johnson's sense of justice about this particular issue had not been in evidence for some time, but it seems to have blazed up again with the assignment to head the President's Committee. And so far the signs indicate that he will make more of the post than Richard Nixon did. For one thing, the President handed to Johnson with his new job a new directive containing enforcement powers Nixon never had as head of Eisenhower's Committee on Contract Compliance. Johnson's committee can revoke contracts and invoke numerous sanctions against employers who practice racial or religious discrimination. (Actual enforcement of the penalties is in the hands of Secretary of Labor Goldberg and Assistant Secretary Jerry R. Holleman, former head of the Texas AFL-CIO.) Johnson, unlike Nixon, also has substantial money and manpower, including, for the first time, a national investigating staff.

Since Johnson took over, his staff boasts, more jobs in firms engaged in Government business have come under nondiscrimination agreements, which are voluntary, than during the whole time Nixon was in charge. In the first six months, Johnson's committee persuaded nine of the largest companies in the United States, which together hire almost a million workers, to sign similar agreements. By early 1962, more than fifty major companies had followed suit. Johnson's future program calls for agreements to eliminate discrimination not merely in employment but also in recruiting and training programs and in advancement on the job.

There is also some thought of setting up special Government programs to retrain the unemployed among minorities. And here again the Vice President is at home, for twenty-five years ago, as Texas Director of the National Youth Administration, he was fighting the same hiring practices of employers and the same apprentice policies of unions that still bar the young Negro from many trades. Not only in Texas, but elsewhere, undertrained Negroes of all ages are a problem today, as they were in the 1930's.

As a young Congressman, Johnson came into the orbit of New Deal Southerners around Franklin D. Roosevelt, who believed with Hugo Black, then a leading liberal in the Senate, that the way to improve conditions for the Negro and the poor white man in the South was to give the Negro the vote and a fair chance for a better job. It was their contention that, given political and buying power, the Negro would grow strong enough to fight his own battle for equality in other spheres. Johnson, therefore, was one of the early converts to the cause of repealing the poll tax as a prerequisite for voting. His conversion, to be sure, did not extend to support of federal legislation to bring about repeal; a constitutional amendment, the long way around, seemed to him the less painful process.

Johnson does best the sort of job that calls into play his great gifts as a persuader. And it takes a lot of persuasion not only to get industry to sign nondiscrimination agreements but also to get the leaders of labor and of minorities to accept less than the employer's hide nailed to the barn door. It seems likely that Johnson does not find it disagreeable to argue the case for equal employment opportunity, which means so much to so many. It boosts his political stock nationally with minorities, and it puts him on the side of industrial expansion in the South and in the country generally. There are leaders of the National Association for the Advancement of Colored People who fume at the lack of militance in the cancellation of contracts, but Johnson's committee is more than within the letter of the Kennedy commandment to "maintain a sense of momentum" in its special field. Naturally, the Vice President has been getting letters from the South—angry letters— about the new role he is playing in civil rights, but letters from Texas don't bother him as much as they used to.

MAN IN SPACE

In his role as head of the drive for equal employment opportunity Johnson is an enforcement officer, carrying out policy decided by the President and his brother, the Attorney General, who is recognized as the man in charge of all matters of civil rights in the Kennedy Administration.

But in his role as co-ordinator of all space projects throughout the Government, Johnson has had a voice in policy. One of the choices awaiting the new President was whether or not to enlarge United States activities in space. The Vice President was influential in the decision to move ahead boldly, even at the risk of costly failure in a race with the Russians. His years of experience with the Armed Services in Congress earned him a voice in the National Security Council debate on the subject, and Johnson spoke out firmly and persuasively for greater speed.

But even though, in this area, he entered administration councils at a higher level, the Vice President has not shown as much zeal for the space assignment as for fighting job discrimination. In fact, he was so slow at staffing the Space Council and moving it into the stream of action (Eisenhower asked Congress to create the Aeronautics and Space Council but never put it into operation) that there were rumors of White House dissatisfaction.

Not until five months after he was given the space post did Johnson complete his team. As head of the civilian Space Agency he helped select James E. Webb, Budget Director under President Truman. Webb, lately a corporation executive, had no space expertise. He did have a reputation for efficient management, and enough Johnson patronage appointees were scattered through Webb's agency to give the Vice President inside knowledge of the rate of progress. As his own chief assistant in the Space Council, Johnson finally picked Edward C. Welsh, a former professor, known for his discreet and efficient staff work as assistant to Senator Stuart Symington, whom he served as specialist on military affairs. Welsh does the day-by-day co-ordinating that the council was established to do and directs the Johnson staff in developing policy recommendations on large questions as they arise—their first advisory opinion dealt with the operation of weather and communication satellites. Johnson meanwhile gets publicity as a "man of the future" as he tours space installations, tries out simulated guidance tests, and hobnobs with John Glenn and other astronauts.

Judging by the team he assembled and his work habits as a leader, Johnson will not try to become a space "czar." He will confine himself to making sure that when disagreements arise between the numerous departments and agencies involved in space work, the disputing parties will "sit down and reason together," a favorite Johnson formula. And with the man of his choice in charge of the civilian program and men he has known well for twenty years running space affairs in the services, the Vice President should have a somewhat better chance of success than those who, under various titles, have tried before to mediate space rivalries.

For one thing, the military men, always better prepared and organized than civilians when they compete in Government councils, do not look upon Johnson with the disdain they usually display toward civilian co-ordinators. After thousands of hours spent together in Congressional hearings and in the social contacts that go with membership on the Armed Services committees of House and Senate where Johnson has served, the Vice President and our top military men speak one another's language—or perhaps it is more accurate to say that Johnson has learned to speak in their terms and to understand their point of view.

In universal, as in global matters, military men, using the committees of Congress as their seminars, have taught the Vice President most of what he knows. This may ultimately be dangerous, but at this stage in the development of a program for space Johnson's intimacy with them is more a blessing than a liability since establishment of central civilian control over space exploration was ruled out long ago, and the major task now is to minimize time-wasting and costly rivalries within the services and between military and civilian projects. The Vice President's acceptance by the military therefore becomes an advantage.

THE WIDE, WIDE WORLD

In the other area in which his education also derives largely from his association with military matters and men—the field of international affairs—Johnson found himself singularly unprepared. As a legislator, the Vice President was not given to reflection or introspection. Affairs of the moment absorbed him fully, and in the Roosevelt and early Truman years these were more often domestic than foreign. Even when the balance changed after World War II, Johnson, the talented maneuverer, was more often called upon to do or die than to reason why. More than once as Senate Democratic Leader he saved the annual foreign-aid bill from defeat or mayhem, and the liberal internationalists could count him on their side. But this seemed more a matter of loyalty to his party and his early Rooseveltian training than of conviction based on knowledge and understanding.

By his own account, when Lyndon Johnson offered himself for President in 1960, he had not read a serious book all the way through since he graduated from Southwest State Teachers College. Except for a Pacific tour in World War II, his only trip abroad had been to attend an Interparliamentary Conference in London. Like Roosevelt, he took in most of his information through the ear, and with friends Johnson was likely to do more talking than listening. The same was true when he was in operation on the Senate floor—conversing and giving the word. The listening he did was mainly in committee sessions. The sessions at which international affairs came up were those of the Armed Services Committee, and the subject was foreign military aid.

Senator Johnson, apparently, did not consider his sketchy background in world affairs a political handicap for higher office. Certainly he registered deep shock when old and close friends frankly refused him their support in the campaign for the Presidential nomination in 1960 on the ground that he did not have the knowledge and experience to conduct United States foreign policy. (Some sophisticated men who did support him argued that United States foreign policy in the sixties required tactical skill far more than new ideas or broad experience.) But it did not take Johnson long as Vice President to realize how much he needed to know about the world beyond the United States Senate.

Fortunately, his first foreign-affairs chore was elementary. John R. Rooney, New York Democrat and Chairman of the House Subcommittee in charge of State Department Appropriations, had to be persuaded that diplomatic allowances should be increased to allow the new President to appoint men without private means to key ambassadorial posts abroad. Rooney, a passionate economizer, would surely block the proposal on principle unless the way was prepared. The "Johnson treatment" which had carried so many days for the Democrats in the Senate seemed in order. Less than two weeks after the election the names of Johnson and Rooney appeared together on the list of the President-elect's callers at Palm Beach, where presumably Kennedy personally asked Rooney for the favor. When Kennedy two weeks later designated Johnson to represent him at the ceremonies inaugurating the new nation of Sierra Leone, the Vice President invited Rooney to ride along in his plane. The celebrated "treatment" may have modified Rooney's repugnance for an increase in the budget. Something did, for he allowed the President part of what he had asked.

"Operation Rooney" was no effort. But soon afterward the Vice President found himself in deep diplomatic water with only an elementary knowledge of how or where to paddle. It was as though the President had decided that the quickest way for his Vice President to learn was the hard way. But perhaps it was only that the world was out of hand, and the new President needed help from the next man in line.

Truce negotiations to end the fighting in Laos had stalled. Viet Cong forces threatened to upset the uneasy balance in Vietnam. The Southeast Asia Treaty Organization allies were generally restive, fearful that United States involvement in the Congo, Cuba, and Berlin was dimming concern for Asia. Johnson had got on well in his first ceremonial appearance in Africa as the President's envoy. As a matter of principle, the new Secretary of State was trying

ot to emulate John Foster Dulles' perpetual tourism. So Johnson
was tapped to carry reassurance to the East.

Now all the pigeons from the Vice President's years of neglect of
oreign affairs began coming home to roost at the same time. Mr.
ohnson was not prepared for his mission to Asia. He privately
dmitted his anxiety about the trip—he didn't know much about
ie area, he explained, or about the political leaders there. But
ow that it was finally necessary, the Vice President began to ap-
ly himself to the new study with customary Johnson energy. He
ut in long hours reading the briefings that were prepared for him.
nd he listened respectfully to directions about protocol. Friends
ho understood the sketchiness of his preparation in international
ffairs were frank in telling the Vice President that he must carry
ut orders meticulously, never improvise.

He remembered his instructions. But on the 29,000-mile journey
at took him to the Philippines, to Formosa, to Japan, to Vietnam,
 India, and finally to Pakistan, he also used the tactics he had
ound so useful in the South during the election campaign. In his
ublic appearances, he waved the American standard and gave
sians the reassurances of unswerving United States support they
ere waiting to hear; in his private conversations with the leaders
 the nations he visited, he undoubtedly bore down on *their*
bligation to make co-operation a two-way street.

MISSION TO ASIA

How well Johnson performed his mission to Asia is a matter
disagreement. Press accounts back home made much of the fact
at the Vice President of the United States let out a Texas cowboy
ll in the Taj Mahal to test the acoustics. And the second day in
etnam, Johnson shattered the rules protocol had laid down for
m.

As Johnson drove into Saigon the first day [Carroll Kilpatrick reported
the Washington *Post*] the police and soldiers held back the crowds
veral hundred feet from intersections. The next day, when he began
 tour of about fifty miles outside the city, the crowds were allowed
ittle nearer to Johnson's car, which was surrounded by motor cycle
lice. . . . . He got out of his car and went into the crowds with his
xan-style handshaking and speechmaking. The crowds were en-
isiastically friendly.

Several hours later, as the Vice President headed back toward the

city, the crowds were five or six times bigger than earlier and mor
demonstrative.

Perhaps the visit will soon be forgotten, but Johnson demonstrate
to Vietnamese officials and American officials in Vietnam that people
to-people diplomacy has merit. As he said, at the end of his 29,00
mile journey, he never saw a hostile face or heard a hostile voice.

To the chiding of his State Department advisers who had in
structed Johnson in the taboos against shaking hands or touchin
heads in Asia, the Vice President reportedly responded: "Dam
it, I haven't patted anyone on the head."

One reporter, assessing the total effect of Johnson's trip to th
Far East, asserted that "those who went with him gave him hig
marks." And when United States Ambassador to India Joh
Kenneth Galbraith flew back to Washington for consultations a fe
weeks later, he too praised the Vice President's performance. On
columnist reported that when Galbraith asked Nehru, followin
Johnson's departure, "How did you like our Vice President?
Nehru replied, "Oh, he is the kind of political leader I can under
stand!"

There was fault-finding in the Senate, however. The day ac
counts of Johnson's behavior in Vietnam were widely carried in th
American press, one of Johnson's former Senate colleagues, a mem
ber of the Foreign Relations Committee who has traveled widel
complained to me irately, "You can't conduct diplomacy like
Texas barbecue. I have been around Southeast Asia enough to kno
what dignity those people expect of national leaders. In most o
those countries, the heads of State are closely identified with th
heads of the Church, if they are not one and the same. Informalit
is out of place. Johnson needed some one along to pull his coat
tails."

Whatever its effect on Asia, the Vice President's tour converte
him into a passionate partisan for foreign aid. For the first time i
the experience of his friends and associates, Lyndon Johnson'
heart was now in the battle he had formerly fought so often fo
strategic reasons. It was with the pride of a new belief that he an
nounced to the National Press Club in Washington on his return
"I have become a zealot in the conviction that the tide of histor
can be turned in our cause of freedom." And the new zealot wen
to work in the practical L.B.J. way. He carried his message to th
Senate and House committees on foreign affairs in off-the-recor
speeches described by members as "thrilling, brilliant, heartening
and wonderful."

After listening to the Vice President for three hours and forty

five minutes behind closed doors, members of the House Foreign
Affairs Committee came out to tell the press that the Vice President was "the wonder-boy of the age," that "everybody is for him,"
and that "if we do what he says, we will be all right." Representative Frances P. Bolton, Republican of Ohio, said Mr. Johnson's
presentation was "marvelous, and I hope he gives it to the country."

FOLLOWING THROUGH

The enthusiasm would not last until the votes were taken on the
Kennedy foreign-aid bill for 1962, but Johnson did his part to stir
up the opinion makers who influence Congress. The week President
Kennedy returned from his talks with Khrushchev in Vienna with
an aching back, United Press International editors from all over
the country were assembled in Washington for their annual meeting, and the National Conference of Mayors was gathered in the
capital to discuss plans for civil defense. The President was scheduled to address both groups. Kennedy made his speech to the editors, and the announcement the following day of the seriousness of
his back ailment explained why it had been pallid. Johnson appeared before the editors on the following day, as scheduled, and
subsequently he substituted for the ailing President before the Conference of Mayors. At both appearances, he stirred his audience
with unaccustomed eloquence. His journey, he said, had convinced
him that "never has it been more important that the Congress and
the American public support the efforts of free Asians to banish
the curse of poverty, illness, and illiteracy. I know that, given
something for which to fight, the people of Asia will man the ram-
parts of freedom with valor. But you know, as they know, that people do not fight in the steaming jungles to preserve hunger, squalor,
and oppression." He told that most provincial group of men, the
mayors of the United States, that America must lead the world or
"shrivel up." And when he had delivered a ringing call for bipartisan support for foreign aid, citing as a model his own backing
of Eisenhower's foreign policy in the eight preceding years, "The
mayors and their wives," a Scripps-Howard correspondent reported, "gave him a ringing, standing ovation, almost as fervently
as if he had come out solidly for turning all Income Tax revenue
over to the cities."

Mrs. Johnson helped bring the story to the editors' wives. Instead of entertaining them at an ordinary tea, she enlisted fifty of the best known and most glamorous women in Washington, including embassy ladies and the wives of Cabinet members, and introduced them to the women whose husbands had been meeting every major male celebrity in town during the week, and rounded out the party with a little speech about where she and the Vice President had gone in Asia and what they had learned.

The Johnsons had turned their Asian trip into good public relations for the Kennedy foreign policy. Dick and Pat Nixon had done the same for Eisenhower; but in the new Kennedy scheme, Johnson had, as Nixon did not, authority to move from advice to action. The Vice President had naturally paid special attention to his relations with the new civilian chiefs in the Pentagon. He and the new Secretary of Defense liked each other from the start; Secretary of the Navy John Connally had been Johnson's manager in his Senatorial campaigns; and after his years of specializing in military affairs the Vice President found the labyrinthine Pentagon no mystery. When he returned from Asia, therefore, the Vice President, without announcement, sat down in Secretary Robert S. McNamara's office with the Secretaries of the Army, Navy, and the Air Force, and the Joint Chiefs of Staff, to talk about improvements that could be made in our military missions and in their relations with ambassadorial staffs.

The Pentagon bought some of Johnson's ideas. The President listened to his recommendation that budget watchdogs be sent into the field to keep track of the actual expenditure of foreign-aid funds from the point of appropriation to the point of actual spending. The United States Information Agency and the International Cooperation Administration also had the benefit of his not very new advice: Better people are needed overseas.

Ambassador Galbraith, reckoning on the Vice President's desire for effectiveness, managed to squeeze another dividend from Johnson's Asian visit. Tramping through an Indian village with Galbraith, Johnson had been reminded of his first memory of electric lights in Johnson City, Texas. The electricity had been produced by a kerosene generator. Talking to the Vice President in Washington several weeks later, the Ambassador asked Johnson if he could remember who made that generator. If it was still in production, perhaps the United States could help light some villages in India without waiting for large-scale electrical development.

Let Russell Baker, reporter for the New York *Times,* tell the rest of the story:

The Vice President, off to New York to attend a dinner for Premier Amintore Fanfani of Italy, spent a few hours trying to remember the company nameplate on the old Johnson City generator.

He recalled it as "Fairbanks." Next day, he telephoned Thomas G. Lanphier, Jr., an old friend, recently made President of Fairbanks-Morse and Company. Mr. Johnson outlined the problem and asked if Fairbanks-Morse had ever made kerosene generators and whether it could produce something to Mr. Galbraith's specifications.

Mr. Lanphier went to work. He reported back that the company produced such generators forty years ago, and had never discontinued the line, although production was down to a trickle. He worked up cost estimates for a possible pilot project in India.

Early this month, Mr. Lanphier sent two company executives to India to see Mr. Galbraith. . . .

As a result of their survey, minor changes in the generator were ordered, including an adaptation for deep well pumping.

The machine, which Fairbanks-Morse calls "Electrical Generator Set Z," is a rugged, simple engine capable of pumping well water and generating enough electricity to light a small village. . . . In the words of a company spokesman, it is "so simple that it can be maintained and repaired by anyone who can handle a wrench."

All of this was pleasant and satisfying to Johnson's ego. But where the President really needed help was at the Capitol. Here Johnson wanted to be careful to avoid any accusation that he was interfering in the affairs of the Senate. He sized up the situation and the individuals concerned—as he had always done as Democratic leader. But then, instead of taking direct action, he went to the President or to members of his staff with advice and counsel on how to proceed to get the votes. In some cases, to be sure, the suasion was direct, but for the most part Johnson's role in the drive for a new kind of long-term aid to nations overseas was strategic rather than operational. He was there to be consulted when the Majority Leader wanted to consult him, but he was, so to speak, no longer the oil driller but the prospector who points out where to drill. And the reality of his shift from legislative manipulator number one to number-two man in the Executive Branch was made clear when, in the midst of the Congressional battle over foreign aid, the President dispatched the Vice President to Berlin.

Khrushchev had confounded United States policy makers by making a move for which they had planned no countering action. We had concentrated on how to deal with another Berlin blockade if the Communists sought to cut off West Berlin again, as they had in 1948. But when, instead, the Communists sealed the border be-

tween East and West Berlin early on Sunday morning, August 13,
Washington, as Walter Lippmann wryly observed, "had no policy
to deal with what actually happened—unless sending the Vice
President and General Clay to West Berlin can be called a policy."

ASSIGNMENT: BACK UP BERLIN

After three days of silence from the Western allies on the Soviet
action, Mayor Willy Brandt sent an urgent note to President
Kennedy reporting that morale in Berlin was sinking and that mass
flights from the city might take place unless counteraction came
soon. To buck up Berlin, the President dispatched the Vice President on a weekend mission that had an electric if not a lasting
effect. Accompanied by General Lucius D. Clay, former American
Commander in Chief in Germany, and Charles Bohlen, State Department specialist on Soviet affairs, Johnson talked first with
Chancellor Konrad Adenauer (who later claimed Johnson cost
him his re-election by leaving him out of the Berlin mission).
Then, with the help of a personal letter from the President pointing
out some facts of life, he persuaded Mayor Brandt that the time
was not propitious for the drastic moves Berliners yearned for—
taking charges of Soviet crimes against humanity before the United
Nations Assembly, for instance, when the UN was trying to settle
the French-Tunisian dispute over Bizerte. Johnson and his entire
party went down to the Autobahn to greet 1,500 American troop
reinforcements when their trucks rolled in, and he mingled with
more than a million Berliners in the streets.

It might have been Dallas or Brooklyn or Los Angeles—or by
now Saigon or Karachi—for Johnson, newsmen reported, "frequently left his automobile and plunged into dense crowds to chat
with people, passed out ball point pens bearing his name and, to
the special delight of the West Berliners, distributed dozens of
gold-edged cards of admission to the Vice President's Gallery in
the Senate at Washington."

Maybe it was One World, after all. You could reassure Germans
—for a little while—just as you reassured voters in Texas.

The Berlin correspondent for NBC-TV reported the next day
that Johnson's visit had been "deeply reassuring to a people who
put great stock in words." Apparently the Germans liked handshaking too, for when his plane put down briefly in Ireland the next
morning and Mayor Dan O'Malley of Limerick walked out to greet

him, the Vice President put out a swollen right hand with the request, "Go easy on it, Boy. It's a little sore."

President Kennedy welcomed the Vice President back from "his remarkably successful and important trip" with "thanks for this most important service . . . to our country." And the press, generally, concurred in the view that "the German visit now boosts even higher the Vice President's reputation as a successful special Ambassador."

Of course, since even a "successful special Ambassador" is hardly a substitute for a policy, the effect was ephemeral, and morale in Berlin soon sagged again. But nobody blamed Johnson for that.

THE HOMEY TOUCH

When the occasion demanded, as in Stockholm, the Vice President could put on a top hat and walk with the King of Sweden to the funeral ceremony for Dag Hammarskjold and not appear out of place. But it was the homey touch he brought to diplomacy that gave the press something new to write about.

It probably would not have occurred to John Foster Dulles to put on a cook-out for Konrad Adenauer when that elderly statesman visited the United States. But it seemed natural enough in Texas—where German-descended citizens of New Braunfels, Texas, serenaded the erect old chancellor on his way to an ox roast at the LBJ ranch. President Mohammed Ayub Khan of Pakistan, a rider and hunter, seemed to find his visit to Texas almost cozy. And if a later foreign visitor, Bashir Ahmed, the camel driver from Karachi, seemed a little less at ease in Johnson City than his President had, perhaps it was because he was not so much at home with horses.

When the Vice President arranged a door prize of a new green pickup truck for Bashir Ahmed on their visit to the Texas State Fair, and dropped him off in Kansas City on the way to Washington to eat prize beefsteaks for breakfast and shake hands with Mr. Truman, the White House was said not to be amused at the questionable press agentry. Johnson certainly had not expected the camel driver to accept his invitation to "come see me in Texas" when they exchanged greetings on a street corner in Karachi. And he certainly had not expected to score his largest diplomatic triumph through the little man of Pakistan. The courtliest and most

poetic guest the capital could remember, Bashir charmed everyone
he met—lady reporters in particular. When they speak, he said,
"petals drop from their lips." Mrs. Johnson's Southern sweet talk
couldn't match his felicitous phrases about the beauties and won-
ders of Washington. "What's the use," one young potential rival
of the Vice President remarked, as he watched the captivating
Pakistani on television. "When Johnson rides right by millions of
Pakistanis and picks out Omar the Tentmaker blindfold, what's
the use?"

At the White House, there was some concern about what would
happen when the camel driver went home to his modest hut. But
even if Bashir's visit should backfire later, the Vice President's
average of performance as a beginning diplomat was high enough
to permit one error. And, by that time, relations between the President and the Vice President had advanced to the point where only
differences on large matters of principle were likely to cause discord.

The mutual respect that had originally brought them together
increased as Kennedy and Johnson discovered how easily and well
they worked together. Slowly, some doubting members of the
Kennedy staff also developed a reluctant respect for their enforced
new comrade-in-arms. "I have to hand it to him—once he takes
on something, he's terrific," one of the Kennedy hierarchy said
with grudging admiration after the successful 1961 campaign at
the Alamo. Johnson, it appeared, had to be nudged into openly
supporting Henry Gonzalez of San Antonio for Congress against
a right-wing Republican. Republican John G. Tower, in his surprising capture of Johnson's former Senate seat, had carried Bexar
County, and Johnson had reported to Washington that his people
had looked over the Congressional district for which there was a
special election and saw no chance for the Democrat. But when
the decision was taken to go to the rescue of Gonzalez anyway,
Johnson led the charge. On the final day of the campaign, he
stumped the district without letup; he flew in Mexican film star
Cantinflas to talk to the thirty per cent of San Antonians who are
of Mexican origin; and he said over and over again, "Let's prove
a man can be elected in Texas regardless of his race." On election
night, when Gonzalez won by 10,000 votes, the political "pros"
reported back to Washington that "L.B.J. made the difference."

The mutual respect has deepened, but it has not ripened into
intimacy. Although the Kennedys and the Johnsons spend many
hours at the same social functions, the Johnsons are not often included in the Kennedys' small personal circle. A friend who has

watched the two men working together likens their relationship to that of members of a fine string quartet—perfect harmony between first-class professionals. (Fine musicians, it seems, also confine their personal contacts to the concert hall. Even the brothers Schneider of the Budapest Quartet go separate ways at dinner.)

After his first year in office, the President could look back on his first big decision and reflect that it had served its purpose. Johnson had been a major help in winning the election, had let go of the reins of the Senate gracefully, and had pulled his full share of the Executive load. The Vice President, in turn, could look ahead to the advantage of a running start for the Democratic Presidential nomination in 1968, after Kennedy's second term, if he continued to play straight with the President and grew and developed with his job.

II

Kennedy's Commandos

The evening after his election, the President-elect and Mrs. Kennedy were alone at Hyannis Port with three close friends. In the happy, relaxed conversation after dinner, one of the men remarked, "There is just one thing I want you to do—fire J. Edgar Hoover!"

"No," the second interrupted, "much more important than that, get Allen Dulles out of the CIA *immediately*." He had sat at the dinner table of a national columnist the night after the U-2 incident, he said, and heard Dulles declare that flight "a triumph of American foreign policy." "Dulles," Kennedy's guest warned, "would be trying to carry on his dead brother's policies in your Administration."

The next morning the two friends, looking over the papers together, read that as his first appointive acts, the President-elect had requested the directors of the Federal Bureau of Investigation and the Central Intelligence Agency to remain in their posts.

The new President was obviously in a hurry to identify himself with the Establishment in government. That was essential to his first purpose—to win national acceptance of his leadership. To have gained the White House by a majority of only 112,881 in the closest race in American Presidential history was not a heartening beginning for one determined to go down as a great President, a President of all the people.

How to become that was in John F. Kennedy's thoughts as he lay in the sun at Palm Beach later in November, doing what the political science books recommend that a Presidential candidate do after he has been elected—rest his body and reorient his mind.

He had parceled out some immediate parts of the job ahead.

Clark M. Clifford, former counsel to President Truman and a skilled Washington negotiator, was acting as Kennedy's liaison with the Eisenhower staff to arrange for the transfer of power.

David E. Bell, a Harvard professor with practical experience as a Budget aide in the Truman Administration, had been selected for the key spot of Director of the Budget. With so promising an appointee for that central lookout position in the Government, and with the streamlined personal staff Kennedy planned to organize, the new man in the White House might, in time, have a chance to dominate the vast bureaucracy.

At Kennedy's request, Adlai Stevenson had agreed in July to prepare a detailed study of foreign-policy problems the new President would face, with recommendations on how to handle them. Stevenson aide John Sharon had flown down from Washington a week after election to deliver the document.

Prospective appointees and special advisers also flew in and out —as did Kennedy. No sooner was one side of him warmed by the Palm Beach sun than he was off making contact with some symbolic figure who could lend him added strength. With graceful deference, Kennedy in turn sought out Herbert Hoover, Harry Truman, Eleanor Roosevelt, Dag Hammarskjold, and Cabinet members from previous Administrations, Republican and Democratic. He conferred with President Eisenhower, and even called on Richard Nixon to repair relations tattered by the campaign.

THINGS TO COME

Kennedy's desire to be in the White House had not blurred his vision of what he would find waiting on the oval-room desk when he got there. In July 1959, before the campaign was really warm, Kennedy relaxed in a deck chair on the porch of his Hyannis Port home and talked with his biographer, James MacGregor Burns, about what the next President would face:

"The 1960's will be a terribly difficult time. I think Eisenhower is going to get home relatively free—at the end of his term there will probably be full employment, a level price index, the drop in food prices may equal any increase in industrial costs, there will probably be a deal on Berlin for 18 months or so, and the now-independent countries will have survived."

"But," Kennedy continued, "it will be like Calvin Coolidge giving way to Herbert Hoover—all the pigeons coming home to roost will be circling over the man coming in. . . . It is going to be a hell of a revolutionary time—the increase of population here and abroad, changes in the underdeveloped world, changes in weapons strategy, and all the rest. . . .

"The job of the next President will be the hardest since Roosevelt," Kennedy said, "and I think Roosevelt had the hardest of all except Lincoln and perhaps Washington. The job will be tremendous, and a great responsibility will center on the President. The real dilemma we face," he said, voicing a thought that was to recur in his Inaugural Address, "is whether a free society, in which each of us follows our own self-interest, can compete over a long period of time with a totalitarian society, in which the carrot and the stick are used to force all human and material resources into the service of the State.

"There are many short-term advantages which a totalitarian possesses in that kind of competition. The struggle between Sparta and Athens furnishes a classic case. The responsibility of the President, therefore, is especially great. He must serve as a catalyst, an energizer, the defender of the public good and the public interest against all the narrow private interests which operate in our society. Only the President can do this," Kennedy concluded, "and only a President who understands the true nature of this hard challenge can fulfill this historic function."

Both the "hard challenge" and fulfilling "this historic function" would seem even harder once Kennedy was in the White House with full access to secret information and accurate knowledge of how many circling pigeons were coming home to roost. But beforehand, how had Kennedy intended to take hold of his responsibilities as Chief Executive of the United States? The thoughts the Senator expressed to Mr. Burns on that subject grew out of his years in Congress: "The best the President can do is to track down the best talent he can get—people with ideas which are actionable, because the problems are quite sophisticated now—and then try, by his political management, by his mobilization of public opinion, by his hard work, almost day by day in Congress, to bring along that more conservative and localized body." An important rule to remember, the Senator had remarked earlier in the year, is that in politics one must keep moving, must try for the breaks, must look for the openings, must not stand still. If you move ahead, he believed, you might have some luck that would otherwise be denied.

THE RULES AT THE BEGINNING

A year and a Presidential campaign later, as he planned his first days in the White House, these were the principles Kennedy was preparing to practice. And well before Inauguration Day, the President-elect had decided on two rules to follow at least in the beginning stage of his Administration. He would conduct himself so as to create a strong initial impression and to convey a steady sense of momentum and progress. That seemed a reasonable way for a pragmatic President to begin. It took into account the need for time in which to build more conclusive public demand for his program than most Congressmen read into the election returns. It allowed for the need to make co-operation comfortable for Southern and Republican moderates. And, to commend it further, the course called for qualities Kennedy had perfected during a career advanced by commando tactics: style and timing.

Careful preparation, plus fierce fighting by a precision team—this was the formula that had won the election. In the first days, he would run things from the White House with a group of his own men. That would be the way to get his Administration into action in a hurry. The inner circle would be small—Kennedys and honorary Kennedys—trusted friends whom Jack had collected from college, the war, and politics.

By ingrained habit the Kennedy team had not looked up from the task of getting elected until the voters had started to the polls on November 8. There were no checked-out lists of possible appointees for key jobs in Government or drafts of Executive Orders and legislation to "reverse the deterioration" and "start moving" in all the directions that his campaign speeches had urged.

During the summer, Chester Bowles, among others, had suggested assigning a squad to begin casting important jobs in Government. But that was a sensitive assignment calling for trusted men, and it would have been daft by Kennedy standards to take generals off the battlefield to work on postwar planning.

So the talent hunt to fill 600 Presidentially appointed jobs in Government and recruit for 1,200 strategic second-line positions started from scratch after the election. (Men deeply involved in the 1952 and 1956 Democratic Presidential campaigns as well as in the Kennedy campaign of 1960 say that Adlai Stevenson would have been readier with Cabinet appointments and priority programs to announce—to which Kennedy men reply that possibly this is one reason Stevenson never got to announce them.)

It was easy to name the White House staff. Kennedy simply gave his personal team new titles. Theodore C. Sorensen would become Special Counsel to the President. Lawrence F. O'Brien and P. Kenneth O'Donnell, who had been assistant campaign managers, were to become, respectively, Congressional Liaison and Appointments Secretary. Lesser lights would be Special Assistants. All of them would still be working directly for the President; their assignments, as always, were subject to change. Trusted intellectuals —Arthur M. Schlesinger, Jr., McGeorge Bundy, and Walt Whitman Rostow—were enlisted. And the Kennedy commandos were in business at a new address.

Beyond the White House the task became harder. How, in the two months between election and the beginning of the new Administration, could people of the required caliber be found for all the key jobs to be filled? Kennedy had been serious when he pledged repeatedly during the campaign that "should I be elected President, it would be my intention to ask the ablest men in the country to make whatever sacrifice is required to bring to the Government the ministry of the best available talent. . . . For no Government is better than the men who compose it—and I want the best." And he was serious, too, when he declared that "all appointments, both high and low, will be made on the basis of ability—without regard to race, creed, national origin, sex, section, or occupation."

That called for other than the usual ways of staffing new Administrations. In 1912, Woodrow Wilson's friend Colonel Edward House simply "moved in party circles making notes about possible Cabinet members." James A. Farley was one of many who made notes on Cabinet for F.D.R., and he supervised staffing of New Deal agencies below the top in the old patronage way. Eisenhower's friends retained a management consulting firm, McKinsey and Company, to help the General select men for his government —and the resulting horde of short-term visitors from the business community scarcely learned the way to their offices before it was time to go home again.

THE TALENT HUNT

Since neither IBM machines nor the processes of patronage could carry out Kennedy's intent, everyone went back to work, with the President in constant command. "We all had been thinking that once the election was over, we could relax a while and congratulate ourselves and reminisce about it and trade stories about people in the campaign and who did what," Larry O'Brien recalled later. "Then, suddenly, it was no time to relax. There was this great big new job of selections to do. All of us had some suggestions, naturally. Jack began studying various names for some of the key appointments, and after a while he said, 'I thought that *this* part would be a pleasure, but it isn't.' " The President's brother-in-law, Robert Sargent Shriver, Jr., and Larry O'Brien were told to pick a few helpers and fan out in all directions, talk to everyone they knew who might have suggestions of good men to join the Government, get names, lots of them, check them out, present the President, or, in all but the most important cases, his brother Bobby, with a limited number of good alternatives for each post. Once Cabinet and sub-Cabinet officers were appointed by the President, the talent hunters were instructed to assist them to fill the lesser posts, using the same standards as for the higher posts.

Within a week after the election the talent hunt was on. Shriver was probably picked for this job because he was the Kennedy family man most open and outgoing in his personal relationships and the one with the widest nonpolitical contacts as a result of his work with the Kennedy family foundation, the Chicago Board of Education, and the Merchandise Mart. To assist him, he chose two young lawyer-intellectuals with equally wide nonpolitical acquaintance—Harris L. Wofford, Jr., now Special Assistant to the President specializing in civil-rights matters, and Adam Yarmolinsky, now Assistant to the Secretary of Defense. A second team supplied political contacts. Larry O'Brien chose as his two assistants Ralph A. Dungan, a Kennedy Senate aide, and Richard K. Donahue, a Massachusetts lawyer—both politicians and both now Special Assistants to the President. Among them, O'Brien, Dungan, and Donahue knew all the people who had crossed the Kennedy political trail, and to what effect. In a short time the two teams dredged up between 6,000 and 7,000 names for the 600 to 700 Cabinet, sub-Cabinet, and other Presidentially appointed positions that Kennedy had to fill.

Working from nine in the morning until midnight every day, the talent hunters made hundreds of telephone calls. What the President was looking for, they told their contacts, were able men and women prepared to serve a full four years. (Judging from the results, able women are in seriously short supply.) What they learned over the wire and through follow-up correspondence was entered on a special form devised for this new kind of casting. Printed sheets, which volunteer typists filled out far into every night, provided space in which to grade each prospect for "judgment, toughness, integrity, ability to work with others, devotion to the principles of the President-elect."

When the talent hunters encountered a problem of casting for a department or agency in which none of them were expert, they sent for someone who knew more than they did—frequently a member of the Washington law firm of Covington and Burling, whose business with the Government requires them to maintain a kind of little cabinet of specialists in public affairs.

The Shriver-O'Brien operation had branch offices at Harvard, Yale, and Columbia. In Cambridge, Professors Kenneth Galbraith, Arthur Schlesinger, Jr., and McGeorge Bundy, members of an unofficial research committee for Kennedy before and during the campaign, suggested and checked out possible New Frontiersmen from Harvard or other faculties. Dean Eugene V. Rostow at Yale and Professor Richard Neustadt at Columbia performed the same service.

With only sixty days in which to perform miracles, the recruiting teams, now combined into one, kept setting up impossible deadlines—"all suggestions for Treasury appointments must be in Friday afternoon . . . Interior, Tuesday . . . Justice, Wednesday . . . Commerce, Thursday morning." But the mission was somehow accomplished.

While they were culling prospects, the FBI was investigating them. (Unlike past Administrations, the Kennedy regime checked on appointees before they were chosen, to eliminate "rotten eggs" and to avoid months of delay on confirmations of top officials.) When the recruiting team had a number of good possibilities for a post—cleared by the FBI—the list went to the President or his brother.

The result was the most homogeneous administration in history below Cabinet level, and the most intellectual. Even presumably political appointees were intellectuals. Robert Kennedy chose as his Deputy Attorney General a scholarly Colorado lawyer, Byron R. White, who was well qualified, quite apart from the fact that he had served as co-chairman of Citizens for Kennedy during the campaign. Many of those recruited from the academic world were men to whom the route from the university to Washington was now a familiar two-way street. They had worked at both ends and expected to continue going back and forth between teaching and Government, as the political tides changed. Most of them knew each other as part of the intellectual-operator establishment that had burgeoned as Government increased in size and influence.

"The expansion of Government under the New Deal and in the years since has more or less required a steady increase in the use of experts of the kind that are nowadays found mainly in the universities," as Richard Rovere pointed out in *The New Yorker* after the Inauguration.

Kennedy was the first President to *staff* a Government with men whose primary qualifications are their knowledge of problems, their understanding of theory, and their capacity for logical analysis. There was a danger here, Rovere warned: "The great majority of them are new to power, and their education has included little in the way of training in the uses of power. It is a most radical experiment—a gamble that has never been tried even in the European democracies, which, over the years have made far greater use of the intellectuals than we have."

Kennedy was intent on installing, even in the second and third ranks, competent, effective men, capable of understanding his policies and carrying them out. If those qualities were not always accompanied by "proved power of decision," he would settle for proved ability. The number of men in these echelons who would be making big decisions was not very great, and they would be working closely enough with the President to permit him and his staff to judge their performances personally. For Mr. Kennedy meant to operate from a very tight center of power. The associate closest to his thinking on this matter, Ted Sorensen, summed up the Kennedy theory of administration to a questioner this way: "If you mean that the President intends to run the Executive branch of the Government with the help of his White House staff, you are right."

KENNEDY'S CABINET

That fact dictated a variety of decisions in the selection of the Kennedy Cabinet, a task that was complicated by what the President-elect wanted his top men to do. Service in Eisenhower's Cabinet would not have been good experience for service in Kennedy's. Kennedy was more interested in the effectiveness with which Cabinet members would function as individuals in their own fields than in what they might contribute as parties to group decisions. He intended to dispense with the weekly Cabinet meetings that had been an Eisenhower ritual, and in fact held only ten formal meetings in his first eight months as President.

He was determined to maintain closer contact with his Cabinet by direct consultation and to abolish many of the co-ordinating committees and interdepartmental boards that had grown up under Eisenhower and had turned much of the communication between the President and his Cabinet into calls for conferences. Since the relationship would be close, Kennedy put much emphasis on finding men "on the same wave length" as himself, in order to make communication with them short and sweet.

There was another prime consideration in the major appointments—the need to win larger acceptance of his leadership than he had registered in the election. The inclusion of real or nominal Republicans in the Cabinet might lessen Republican doubts of his "fiscal responsibility" and encourage a return to bipartisanship of foreign policy. These considerations added to the attractiveness of C. Douglas Dillon and Robert McNamara—and reduced the chances that Adlai E. Stevenson, Chester Bowles, or G. Mennen Williams would land in the first rank.

Also in his mind was gratitude for past favors and the possible need for future ones. Abraham A. Ribicoff, the first Governor to endorse Kennedy for President and the organizer of the New England bloc that gave substance to his candidacy; Representative Stuart L. Udall, who, commando-style, stole the Arizona delegation out of Lyndon Johnson's bag; Governor Luther H. Hodges, whose early backing helped stem the threatened Southern revolt against the Kennedy ticket—all deserved well of their party leader and got their rewards.

There was a personal consideration in the appointment of Robert F. Kennedy as Attorney General. It was not the desire to reward a qualified brother with a Cabinet post, but the need to have by his side his closest, most trusted friend—the one whose advice he valued most, the one he could be absolutely sure would speak his mind at all times, the brother to whom the President could talk as though to himself.

Finding good Cabinet candidates was easier than persuading such people to leave their present posts and adopt a life of economic austerity and twelve- to fourteen-hour days, seven days a week. Kennedy personally pursued the difficult prospects with telephone calls and private talks in which he appealed to their sense of duty.

Shriver came into talent-scout headquarters one morning with Robert McNamara's name written on one of his innumerable slips of paper. "What do you know about him?" Shriver asked.

Shriver's assistant, Adam Yarmolinsky, had dined with McNamara once and was enthusiastic. A check of many sources yielded recommendations that, in Kennedy family *patois,* were "terrific." Shriver took a plane to Detroit, agreed with the checked-out verdict on the Ford Company president, and brought McNamara back to Washington secretly to meet J.F.K. The job for which they were casting then was Secretary of the Treasury. Somewhere along the line someone suggested that McNamara be cast instead for the harder job of Secretary of Defense. Kennedy's concern was to find a man strong and forceful enough to establish civilian supremacy over the military. Former Defense Secretary Robert A. Lovett, in whose judgment Kennedy had great confidence, recommended McNamara highly—as he did Dean Rusk for Secretary of State.

Dean Rusk's name kept coming up whenever knowledgeable people discussed the best man to assist the President in conducting United States foreign policy. The range of recommendations for Rusk was impressive. Dag Hammarskjold made a point of praising Rusk when Kennedy called on him at the United Nations after the election. Dean Acheson and the Soviet expert Charles Bohlen were enthusiastic. Senator Fulbright liked him. And so did Kennedy when he finally met Rusk toward the end of the long search for his Secretary of State.

Kennedy had special requirements for a Secretary of State. The President was seeking an experienced practitioner of international relations to carry out, not decide, foreign policy. Mr. Kennedy would make the decisions, in accordance with the powers vested in him by the Constitution. In addition, Mr. Kennedy wanted a man whose past actions and utterances would not foreclose bipartisan support for his foreign policies in Congress and in the country—one whose stated position on issues was not so firm and well known as to lead people to think that the Administration's foreign policies were a foregone conclusion.

On balance, Rusk seemed to suit Kennedy's specific needs best.

Adlai Stevenson, with his world-wide prestige, was the ideal Ambassador to the United Nations. And Chester Bowles, with his special standing in the new underdeveloped nations, was the man to advise the President on those areas.

Senator Fulbright, perhaps the President's first choice for Secretary of State, who was ruled out of the running by the fact that he had been a signer of the Southern Manifesto, was to remain as the Administration's chief supporter and friendly constructive critic on foreign affairs in Congress.

THE FUNCTION OF KENNEDY'S CABINET

When the job of picking the Cabinet was done, Kennedy, by general admission, had chosen a group of superior men who fitted into his conception of the function of the Cabinet. Writing at the end of 1958, Richard F. Fenno, Jr., in his study, *The President's Cabinet,* stated that "Woodrow Wilson was the only President to develop a coherent theory about the role of the Cabinet in our political system." Writing at the end of 1961, I can believe that Dr. Fenno may come to change his adjective from "only" to "first" and add John F. Kennedy's name as second. Kennedy's theory is a variant of Wilson's latter-day view of the President's Cabinet. Like Wilson, Kennedy came to office practically free of advance commitments. And like Wilson, who saw the President "as both party leader and people's tribune, standing a bit apart from the party and using his popular support as leverage to influence or control it," Kennedy concluded, as had Wilson, that "such a President might not need to assemble a Cabinet of already recognized party leaders."

Professor Wilson wrote in 1907 that "self-reliant men will regard their Cabinets as Executive Councils; men less self-reliant or more prudent will regard them also as political councils, and will wish to call into them men who have earned the confidence of their party. The character of the Cabinet may be made a nice index of the President's theory of party Government; but the one view is, as far as I can see, as constitutional as the other." As a candidate in 1912, Wilson made clear how he would operate if he were President of the United States, rather than president of Princeton: "The idea of the Presidents we have recently had has been that they were Presidents of a National Board of Trustees. That is not my idea. I have been President of one Board of Trustees and I do not care to have another on my hands. I want to be President of the people of the United States." As President, Wilson followed the council concept, describing his Cabinet as "an Executive not a political body."

Department heads in Kennedy's Government would function neither as a "Board of Directors" nor even as an "Executive Council" in the full Wilsonian sense but rather as an *ad hoc* group of administrators meeting irregularly on matters of mutual concern.

As Kennedy has worked it out, his Cabinet meets only to consider specific matters of sufficient current significance to require the attention of the group as a whole. As one of those usually involved in Cabinet matters summed it up, "Sessions are not held out of any faith that togetherness, regularly scheduled, will be productive enough to take the time of the President and his principal officers."

One result was to overcome, partially at least, an old problem. Jesse Jones once explained why he had so little to say at F.D.R.'s Cabinet meetings: "There was no one at the table who could be of help to me except the President, and when I needed to consult him, I did not choose a Cabinet meeting to do so."

Kennedy believed he would accomplish more by an open-door policy that encouraged Cabinet members to bring him problems in their early stages instead of waiting to discuss them at lengthy meetings at a later stage. That course fitted in with his own natural preference for doing business with smaller, more expert groups. And when, after the first few months of his Administration, crises abroad forced him to give close to ninety per cent of his time to national-security matters, a system of individual conversations, individual meetings, and individual phone calls enabled him to keep abreast of major domestic problems with the greatest economy of time.

This was fine for the President. Cabinet members, however, apparently felt a little cheated, for when one of them suggested informally that they get together occasionally without the President, the response was enthusiastic. Since midsummer 1961, the Kennedy Cabinet, *sans* Kennedy, has been gathering for at least monthly sessions to exchange information and experience bearing on administrative and housekeeping matters.

When the whole Cabinet and the President do meet every three weeks or so, the session is usually long and carefully organized. The Cabinet Secretary, Kennedy's long-time political aide, Timothy Reardon, circulates an agenda, and Cabinet members are expected to do their homework in advance.

The meetings stick close to the agenda. Usually the President makes a few opening remarks. Then comes an opening presentation, sometimes made by a Cabinet member but more often by a specialist on the subject scheduled for discussion that day. The Director of the Budget Bureau has spoken on fiscal issues, the Chairman of the Council of Economic Advisers on the recession and on general economic questions, the Chairman of the Civil Service Commission on personnel problems, and various Presidential assistants on legislative, scientific, and other matters. These opening statements go beyond the advance written materials everyone is supposed to have studied. After that, there is "Quaker meeting" discussion. Whoever is moved to speak does so, in no particular order of protocol. The President usually asks questions, but Cabinet members are not called on one by one to express their views. Kennedy's questions, according to a participant, often seem designed to get Cabinet members to reveal attitudes, interests, or biases of their department that might cause collisions with other agencies of the Government.

Under the Eisenhower Administration a Cabinet secretariat of half a dozen people worked up detailed agenda, conducted timed rehearsals of the meetings themselves, and prepared visual aids to be presented. Kennedy ordered his one Cabinet secretary to strip away the extras and limit the meetings strictly to discussion.

ORGANIZING THE WHITE HOUSE

More than any President since Wilson, Kennedy had studied the office and the problems of executive organization, and he took pleasure in considering the theory of government. As Chairman of the Reorganization Subcommittee in the Senate, he had learned a lot about the organization of the White House. In effect, his job as Committee Chairman was to wind up the Hoover Commission's voluminous investigation of the Executive Branch. One strong opinion he formed was that the President should be closely involved at every stage in the making of a decision.

After holding hearings on a Hoover proposal to create a White House post of Executive Vice President for administration, Kennedy told the Senate he was against it. "The American Presidency," he declared, "was not intended by its creators as primarily a ceremonial or coordinating job, with its most essential responsibility delegated to non-elected officials." He lost no time as President in disassociating himself from an Eisenhower request to Congress to institutionalize the role that Sherman Adams had played. Eisenhower had asked for the creation of two Presidential deputies—a First Secretary of the Government for foreign affairs and an Executive Assistant to the President for domestic matters. Kennedy would be his own deputy in both departments.

The new President looked with little more favor on other Eisenhower innovations—the much-enlarged White House staff (from 250 under Truman to 400), the paraphernalia of enlarged Cabinet authority, the enlarged role of the National Security Council, and the complex of interdepartmental committees and boards that had proliferated in the eight Eisenhower years.

Kennedy intended to change much of the Eisenhower way of doing business. And he did not intend to be a long time in beginning. When Kennedy's predecessor had succeeded President Truman, Laurin L. Henry of the Brookings Institution records in his analysis of *Presidential Transitions,* "It took approximately a year for the Eisenhower Administration to complete its reviews and adjustments of basic policies and take significant action on most of the major items on its agenda. Meanwhile the upper bureaucracy was demoralized and ineffective, and the Administration leaders felt frustrated by the slowness with which they were achieving control and moving toward their policy objectives."

Mr. Kennedy was determined not to lose a year hacking his way out of the jungle of government by committee. Ten days after inauguration, he concluded his first State of the Union Message with "a few remarks about the state of the Executive Branch."

"We have found it full of honest and useful public servants—but their capacity to act decisively at the exact time action is needed has too often been muffled in the morass of committees, timidities and fictitious theories which have created a growing gap between decision and execution, between planning and reality, in a time of rapidly deteriorating situations at home and abroad; this is bad for the public service and particularly bad for the country; and we mean to make a change."

In place of large standing committees, with secretariats and elaborate paper work, there would be small, temporary "task forces" to deal, commando-style, with specific problems as they arose and to be disbanded when the work was done.

If there were doubts about overhauling the Eisenhower machinery of government, the reappearance of a classic interdepartmental committee story, dating from Truman's time, may have helped to dispel them. The story, as the New York *Times* recalled it, had to do with one such group that had as its purpose "to plan for the contingency of Stalin's death." The premise was that when the dictator died, there would be uncertainty and division in the Soviet Union and that this situation could be exploited by aggressive propaganda and acts of policy.

"But when the committee met, the State Department man disagreed with the officers from the Joint Chiefs of Staff, the Defense Department disagreed with the Central Intelligence Agency, and the propaganda expert thought all of them were wrong.

"So the committee, in utter frustration, finally agreed on one monumental recommendation: When Stalin died, the Voice of

America should arouse the world's imagination by going off the air."

Surely there was no excuse for such a system. The new President responded by tearing it out, root and branch. The National Security Council, established by statute as a Presidential advisory body, would of course continue, but like the Cabinet it would meet less frequently, only when a problem had reached the point where discussion was profitable. The Planning Board of the NSC and the forty-five committees under the Operations Coordinating Board and virtually all the rest of the interdepartmental-committee structure through which the Eisenhower Administration governed were junked within weeks after Kennedy took charge.

There was general agreement that planning and co-ordinating would revert to the regular departments of Government, with increased White House participation in all decisions. And slowly that began to happen. But as Budget Director Bell admitted to a Senate Subcommittee six months after the old boards were abolished, "In the early period, everyone had tied all his procedures to this machinery that was suddenly abandoned and nobody knew where to look next."

What evolved was extension into Government of the "task force" idea Kennedy had used between his election and the Inauguration to get special jobs done with a minimum of folderol. "When the President took office, there were certain things that had to be done straight away, and with some urgency," Secretary Rusk later explained to the Senate. "For example, we had to meet a deadline on negotiations on nuclear test bans. We had to get a program up to the Congress fast on problems arising out of the Act of Bogota—on the $500,000,000 Social Development Plan. We had to get our foreign aid program whipped into shape.

"These matters were handled by special task forces, specifically drawn in to get a job done at a pace at which the normal machinery could not be expected to operate."

THE PERIOD OF SETTLING IN

The first three months for Mr. Kennedy were halcyon days. While a fascinated nation exulted in the glamor and vigor radiated by the new occupants of the White House, the President gloried in the range his new office permitted an energetic young man.

The public reaction to this attractive display of activity was an outpouring of sympathetic good will.

Typical and pertinent is a letter I received a month after the inauguration from a well-known lady who lives abroad but who was on a visit to the United States when the change of administration took place and not long afterward dined privately with the first Family.

"I am unable to write in any sensible way about young Mr. President because I am in love with him," began my friend, who is more famous for her acerbity than for her charity.

It is my hope [she continued] that this condition will spread and become universal in the US and then he will be in the strong position of Mr. Roosevelt—so popular with the people that he can fight the Establishment of the Congress and all other backward elements. . . .

In life I found him so cozy that I behaved as if I had known him for thirty years. Shocking, but an indication of how easily and unpretentiously he handles his role. . . . Naturally, I talked my head off, and maybe he was charming me like birds off a tree (which he did), but he gave me the impression that we saw eye to eye, so of course I also think he is morally splendid.

He strikes me as a man ready and eager to learn, anything from anyone; and fast as fast in how he takes in; and I'd say he never forgets. I'd also say he sorts out what he hears, for himself; and thinks steadily every single minute. His most frequent word was "Why?"; he looks for meaning. One does not feel one has impressed him or put anything over; one feels he'd give a fair hearing, and ask more, and get his information as fully and honestly as possible. First class mind, was my feeling. But then, I was swept off my feet; I had no idea I'd be mad for him. In general, I am un-mad for politicians and dislike holders of power. Contrary with him. Maybe because I felt that he holds the power for a purpose, not for vanity, not for himself. I do not think he is vain, which is an enormous thing to say.

News and opinion writers, in that month after Inauguration, were saying many of the same things, less well. The picture of the new captain and team in the White House that television projected was one of perpetual motion. And the flood of speeches, statements, special messages, and legislative requests to Congress—close to 50 in the first 100 days—began to convey the sense of momentum and constant progress that Kennedy desired.

President Kennedy's period of settling in at the White House was remarkably smooth and rapid. He and his inner circle had no difficulty establishing authority and command in those areas of policy where they had an accumulation of knowledge—they lit into the immediate matter of budget revisions with a confidence born of preparation. Mr. Kennedy had picked the kind of men he wanted for the particular kind of Presidency he intended to create.

And the new organization with which he was replacing Eisen
hower's committee system of government was developing muscle
when Kennedy was confronted with the need for judgment in a
area to which his experience did not extend.

THE QUESTION OF CUBA

The new President found among his legacies from the Eisen
hower Administration a bear trap—secret detailed plans for a
attack to be launched against the Castro Government by Cuban
refugees. Cuban refugees who were being trained by the United
States, supplied by the United States, and, according to the plan
would be escorted by United States forces on the day of the in
vasion.

To countermand the plan or allow the invasion to proceed or
schedule? This was the question before the new President. And he
could not postpone the decision, Mr. Kennedy was told.

To scrap the blueprint would be to challenge General Eisen
hower and the Intelligence and Defense establishments of the
Government before Kennedy had had time to make his own de
terminations.

Accompanying the top-secret report on his desk were the recom
mendations of all the top brass of the Pentagon and the CIA
without exception, that a Cuban invasion be launched by early
spring. President Eisenhower had given orders a year before to
begin the training at secret camps in the United States and in
Guatemala of what was now a force of almost three thousand
Cubans. They were overready. Guatemala would no longer co
operate in concealing them, and the troop situation was explosive
What was more important, President Kennedy was told, Cuban
airmen and technicians in training behind the Iron Curtain would
soon be returning home to fly and service MIG fighters of which
the component parts, in crates, were being smuggled to Havana in
shipments of Communist arms. Given six months more in which
to prepare, so top Intelligence and Defense officials told the President, Castro would be too strong to oust by any means other than
direct military intervention.

What was in the best interest of the United States?

The new President was well aware that Article 15 of the Charter
of the Organization of American States specifies that "No state or
group of states has the right to intervene, directly or indirectly, for
any reason whatever, in the internal or external affairs of any

other state." But suppose the President did bend the law a little to achieve a great gain? Might not much time and money be saved for the main job of getting on with the Latin American Development Plan if there were no Castro to cope with? Weren't there safeguards or limitations the President could place on the Eisenhower plan that would make our part more defensible and less detectable—and still enable us to take the big step forward that the experts told him was practically a sure thing if he would give the word?

During the Presidential campaign Senator Kennedy had yielded to the temptation to make as much as a responsible candidate could of public fear of Castro. Were his campaign words with him as he weighed the decision? He had dwelt on "the transformation of Cuba into a Communist base of operations a few minutes from our coast . . . an incredibly dangerous development to have been permitted by our Republican policy makers." He had taunted Richard Nixon for talking about standing up to Khrushchev but never mentioning "standing firm in Cuba." "If you can't stand up to Castro, how can you be expected to stand up to Khrushchev?"

Some thought that the Democratic candidate had gone too far in fanning sentiment for United States military intervention in Cuba, even though toward the end of the campaign he was always careful to specify that the United States must pursue legal means in breaking the Castro regime.

On October 15, 1960, Kennedy assured a Johnstown, Pennsylvania, audience that, as President, he would end harassment of anti-Castro forces by our Government. *"While we cannot violate international law,"* he said, "we must recognize that these rebels represent the real voice of Cuba (italics mine)." And when Nixon struck back by charging Kennedy with intentions of illegal attack on Castro, the Democratic candidate could reply by telegram: "I have never advocated and I do not now advocate intervention in Cuba in violation of our treaty obligations and in fact stated in Johnstown, Pennsylvania, that whatever we did with regard to Cuba should be within the confines of international law."

Kennedy delivered a major speech on what to do about Castro in Cincinnati, Ohio, on October 6: "What can a new Administration do to reverse these trends?" he asked. "For the present," he answered himself, "Cuba is gone. Our policies of neglect and indifference have let it slip behind the Iron Curtain—and for the present no magic formula will bring it back. I have no basic disagreement with the President's policies of recent months—for the time to save Cuba was some time ago." (The Democratic candidate could not know that the Eisenhower Administration was working on what it hoped would be a magic formula.)

Kennedy concluded with a Stevensonian line.

Whatever we do in Cuba itself, ultimately the road to freedom in Havana runs through Rio and Buenos Aires and Mexico City. For if we are to halt the advance of Latin Communism we must create a Latin America where freedom can flourish—where long-enduring people know, at last, that they are moving toward a better life for themselves and their children—where steady economic advance is a framework for stable, democratic government—and where tyranny, isolated and despised, eventually withers on the vine. . . . Only if we extend the hand of American friendship in a common effort to wipe out the poverty and discontent and hopelessness on which Communism feeds —only then will we drive back tyranny until it ultimately perishes in the streets of Havana.

Thus Kennedy, the candidate, had committed himself to strengthen the "non-Batista democratic anti-Castro forces in exile and in Cuba itself who offer eventual hope of overthrowing Castro." He had also repeatedly endorsed the Stevenson-Bowles position that the surest way to bring freedom to Cuba was through a gradual, legal, "common effort" to wipe out the conditions breeding Communism in all Latin America.

Did the two pledges have to be contradictory? Wasn't it possible to carry out the plan for the anti-Castro invasion without injury to future United States relations with other American states?

REMODELING PLANS FOR THE INVASION

The President and his men consulted the architects of the Eisenhower invasion plan about remodeling it to suit their requirements. First, the President specified, no American military forces could be used. Some substitute would have to be found for United States air cover of the actual landing in Cuba provided by the first plan. Then, the warring factions among the refugees must unite. And, third, the CIA must double check its findings of strong anti-Castro sentiment in Cuba, and make certain that there would be no rout— that, at the worst, the invaders could escape into the hills.

Some of those who were in on the discussions did not share the President's concern with details. All they wanted, one participant in the planning recalls, was a crack at Castro. Richard M. Bissell, Deputy Director of the CIA, speaking with the authority of one

who had played a successful part in the overthrow of Jacobo
Arbenz Guzmán in Guatemala and in other covert ventures,
vouched totally for the CIA's political information that Cuba was
ready to revolt against Castro. The CIA began to bring pressure
on the refugee factions to merge. Military chiefs approved the
substitution for United States air cover of the invasion proper of
an advance air strike by counterfeit deserters from Castro.

The President's practical questions were answered one by one—
by the sponsors of the plan. The sponsors were also the experts on
whom the new President was totally dependent for intelligence
and military advice. Neither he nor anyone in his immediate circle
was professionally trained in those fields. The interdepartmental
planning boards of top bureaucrats that, during the Eisenhower
regime, might have second-guessed the CIA and the Joint Chiefs
had been abolished by Kennedy. The return to their former authority of invigorated regular departments of Government—specifically, in this case, of the Department of State—was not yet a
reality. Determined to get the best man for his purpose, Kennedy
had delayed so long in choosing his Secretary of State that Dean
Rusk was still not in firm command in his department. There had
been so much ceremonial visiting to do abroad, and so much
housekeeping to attend to in a department that had been run out
of Secretary Dulles' briefcase for eight years, that Rusk had not yet
made himself *the* adviser to the President on foreign affairs.

In short, coming when it did, the question of carrying out the
Eisenhower plan for invading Cuba was one with which the Kennedy Administration was not equipped to deal. The President had
no military or intelligence experts of his own choosing to question
the sponsors of the plan. His Department of State and its Secretary were far from self-confident enough to express a contrary view
of a technical matter that had not originated with them. And those
of Kennedy's personal advisers who had reservations about the
proposal were less direct with him than they would become, while
his own questioning was far less sharp. That being the case, when
the President, at a final conference, went around the room asking
for opinions, the fact that both Dulles and Bissell, speaking for
Intelligence, said "Yes, Sir, I am for it," seemed to him, as one
close adviser recalls, reason enough to go ahead.

THE RATIONALIZATION

From then on it was every man to his own rationalization. One
sophisticated insider recalls how he reasoned at the time. Support

of the invasion of April 17 could be distinguished from "uninvited
intervention" in the legal sense, he felt, because it was intended to
test the will of the Cuban people, not to topple their government.
The size of the invading force, he contended—and was still con-
tending months later—was evidence of that purpose: it was obviously insufficient in number to accomplish anything the public
did not back, but sufficient to catalyze revolt against Castro if the
desire for it existed. As evidence that the proposed invasion was
considered an Intelligence not a military operation, he offers the
fact that the CIA, not the Pentagon, was in charge of the planning.

Those who persuaded themselves our action was defensible on
this ground explain that they were only doing what Walter Lippmann, the Administration's severest critic after the failure, agreed
was justifiable. Acknowledging that "secret efforts to influence
each other are the ancient and universal practice of great states,"
Mr. Lippmann pointed out that "There is in international relations
a public world and there is also an underworld. The relationship
between the public world and the underworld—between the government in office and the spies—has never been codified."

"But there have developed certain rules—a kind of common
law—and one of these rules is that the secret operation must remain secret in the sense that it remains invisible, that it is never
acknowledged, its failures are never explained and its successes
are never celebrated. . . . It is feasible, and in the practice of
States it is not prohibited, to give clandestine help . . . to Castro's
opponents. . . ."

Those who quote Mr. Lippmann to this effect ruefully recognize
that he added, "so long as it remains clandestine."

"This is a limiting rule for a wide open democracy like our own.
It means that while clandestine help can be given to the Cuban
underground, an operation of the size and character of the Cuban
invasion cannot be undertaken. As affecting the United States
there is no great difference between what is feasible in practice
and what is permissible in law. *It was not feasible to overthrow
Castro with fourteen hundred refugees, and it was unlawful to
attempt it* (italics mine)."

ADVERSE VOICES

President Kennedy did not have to wait for the post-mortems to
hear adverse voices, however. Some aides in the White House and
on the political staff of State who learned of the plan (the CIA

insisted on a strict "knowledge-by-necessity" policy during preparations) spoke up against it. They argued that the plan probably would not succeed; that if it did it would be hard to convince the Latin Americans the United States had not directed the intervention; that the stability of the Cuban revolutionary council we would be backing was unpredictable at best; that the immediate threat of Castroism elsewhere was not overwhelming if we acted positively in strategic places like Colombia, Uruguay, and Brazil. (To one who had argued in this vein, the President, when it was all over, is said to have remarked: "I wish I had listened to you.")

At least one man for whom the President has the highest respect pleaded with him not to give the word. Senator Fulbright, on whose committee Senator Kennedy had served and who reportedly was his first choice for Secretary of State, spoke out before a meeting of a dozen insiders on April 4, the day before the President made his decision to go ahead. The wise course, Fulbright passionately insisted, was not to try to overthrow Castro but to work constructively elsewhere in Latin America. He repeated, in effect, what Kennedy had said during the campaign, echoing Stevenson: "The road to freedom runs through Rio and Buenos Aires and Mexico City." But by then it was too late.

Evidence is persuasive that during the long, secret debate before he made his decision to go ahead, President Kennedy never discussed the proposed Cuban invasion with either Adlai Stevenson or Chester Bowles, who had been his chief advisers on foreign affairs during his campaign. This was especially strange in the case of Stevenson. He was the man in the Administration most admired in Latin America and best informed about its attitudes. And Kennedy, after the election, had sent Stevenson on a ten-nation tour of Latin America to keep his knowledge up-to-date. A short time before the invasion was to occur the President did send a representative to New York to inform his United Nations Ambassador in part of what was contemplated. But Stevenson learned the truth about the April 15 attempt to wipe out Castro's planes on the ground preliminary to the invasion only after he had assured the United Nations Assembly that the attacking planes were not ours. The President never asked Stevenson to take part in the conferences leading up to the decision nor to express his opinion of the project, and obviously therefore Mr. Stevenson had no share in the last-minute decisions he was widely reported to have influenced decisively. Undersecretary Bowles, in turn, learned of the invasion plans only because he was Acting Secretary of State on a day when documents about it came across Rusk's desk.

If, as it now appears, the President was satisfied with the rationalization that illegal intervention was not involved, it is possible
to understand, to some degree at least, why he did not draw Stevenson or Bowles into the discussions. He could be sure that both
men would object to the plan for invasion—Stevenson, after all,
had reported after his latest tour that, in Latin America, the "principle of non-intervention is a religion."

The day after Senator Fulbright's final protest against going
ahead with the invasion plan, the President gave the word for it.

Had Fulbright's advice been sought earlier, had Stevenson and
Bowles had a chance to argue the other side of the case, would the
President have decided differently?

Most of the post-mortem arguments and discussions about the
failure of the Cuban affair centered on the invasion plan and its
execution. Had the President been wise in refusing to approve air
cover for the attack? Was there proper co-ordination between the
underground in Cuba and the refugee attackers? When it was clear
that the invasion would fail without it, should the President have
ordered aloft planes from the USS *Boxer,* anchored offshore in
international waters?

All this was to assume that a successful invasion would have
been in the best interest of the United States. Walter Lippmann,
who called Senator Fulbright "the only wise man in the lot" for
advising the President against the invasion, had some wise words
of his own to say after the fact:

> Bad as have been the consequences of the failure, they are probably
> less bad than would have been the indecisive partial success which was
> the best that could conceivably have been achieved. For in order to
> support the rebellion in Cuba we would have had to continue to vio-
> late not only our treaties with the other American states but also our
> own laws which prohibit preparation of foreign military expeditions in
> the United States.
>
> In abandoning the rule of law, which is at the very heart of Western
> freedom, we would have cast away our power to oppose revolutionary
> Communism with anything except physical force.

"THERE ARE LESSONS FOR US ALL . . ."

In the cold climate that followed the Cuban failure, Mr. Kennedy not only stood by his vow to be the kind of President "who
is willing to take the responsibility for getting things done and
take the blame if they are not done right," but also admitted pub-

icly that "there are from this episode useful lessons for us all to learn," and set about learning them.

Time would tell whether Cuba had heightened Mr. Kennedy's devotion to the rule of law. The careful course the United States pursued seven months later when a political explosion threatened in the Dominican Republic suggested that experience had been a good teacher. Yet, in that very period, one of the President's chief advisers stated firmly, though not for attribution, that he would today again be for undertaking a "well-organized undercover penetration designed to permit an expression of Cuban opinion."

But it was immediately clear that the President now saw where he had been misled and by whom. And it did not appear likely that he would again be so uncritical of a proposed enterprise. In late April and May the President repeatedly, almost compulsively, told callers that he had been wrong in thinking that he could rely unquestioningly, or semiunquestioningly, on the advice of the men in command of the CIA and the Joint Chiefs of Staff. Bobby Kennedy, after serving with a group the President appointed to investigate the Cuban affair, could conclude that "obviously, it would have been better if it hadn't happened, but it would have been disastrous if he [the President] had not learned the lesson of Cuba." The lesson was to double check the judgment of even the most experienced advisers.

One White House principal in the Cuban decision is more inclined to self-criticism. All of those involved, he feels, misjudged public opinion, failed to realize how much opposition there would be to the United States taking the initiative in the invasion, or how many would fail to see the technical distinction between illegal intervention in the affairs of another nation and what the White House thought it was sanctioning. The lessons this official saw, for all of them, in this experience, were: Don't substitute hope for intelligence, and remember to weigh the public interpretation as well as the "real" meaning that will attach to a given action.

Several visitors reported that the President had criticized the part played by the Joint Chiefs in the decision to launch the invasion. The President would have to remedy an obvious weakness —his lack of an intimate adviser in the White House who could do for him in military and intelligence matters what Sorensen did in matters of domestic policy or what he was coming to trust Bundy to do in foreign affairs.

At the end of June, General Maxwell D. Taylor was added to the President's staff. Bobby Kennedy had worked with General Taylor, sifting the CIA ashes after the Cuban disaster, and had

recommended him to his brother as a "tough, incisive, well-or
ganized, articulate, taciturn, self-confident expert."

But while the Cuban affair was still under investigation, an
before General Taylor had been added to the team, the President'
task was to do better with what he had. He set up a lookout of "hi
own men" to watch the conduct of United States psychologica
warfare. Bobby Kennedy, General Taylor, Labor Secretary Gold
berg, U. Alexis Johnson, a career man in the State Department
and USIA Director Edward R. Murrow were assigned to advise o
better ways to tell the United States' story to the world and t
keep an eye on intelligence and propaganda efforts as a whole.

In addition to setting up these new backstops, the President, im
mediately after Cuba, assigned himself to some graduate refreshe
courses in foreign affairs. From now on, he would master th
political background of possible crises before and as they arose
And soon, as I have said, as much as ninety per cent of his tim
was going into national-security matters. Sorensen and Bobby wer
separately instructed to add foreign affairs to their portfolios an
to be prepared to back up the President in this field when he felt th
need for someone who was informed and in whom he could plac
absolute trust. They were not to concern themselves with foreig
policy in general, but only with policy in specific areas. Durin
November, for example, Sorensen's docket included Berlin an
Arms Control, but not Laos. Their job was to supplement th
President's personal judgment of expert advice—not to interfer
with the regular machinery of the State Department and the CIA

AFTER THE SHAKEDOWN

A little tidying up improved operations around the White House
The area of national security that had been assigned to Bundy wa
divided—General Taylor was given major responsibility for con
tacts with the Pentagon and Bundy for contacts with the State
Department. Each man had under him a small group assigned t
problems by specific areas.

The senior White House staff that emerged after the shakedow
consisted of Sorensen for domestic and general-utility matters
O'Donnell for politics and appointments, O'Brien for dealing with
Congress, Bundy for foreign policy, and General Taylor for mili
tary affairs.

On matters of domestic policy, Cabinet officers usually ap

proached the President through Sorensen. But the Secretary of State had, and used, a direct channel to Mr. Kennedy.

A central aim, and effect, of these structural changes was to restore the Department of State to a position of greater importance than it had had in years. Senator Henry Jackson of Washington and members of his Subcommittee on National Policy Machinery questioned Budget Director Bell closely on the new system three months later.

SENATOR JACKSON: Mr. Bell, we (on the committee) believe very strongly in the primacy of the Secretary of State in advising the President on the full range of national security problems.
In other words, he is sort of an orchestra leader.
I just wondered what your approach or philosophy is in that regard.
MR. BELL: The same as yours, Sir, the same as that of the committee, and I think that is the same way the President feels, the same way I know Mr. Bundy feels.
We all look to the Secretary of State, just as you say, as the leader in the development of national security policies in its broad sense.
I think this President has given evidence, by . . . changing the reliance on interdepartmental committees, that he wants to give to the Secretary of State this responsibility.

Budget Director Bell was explicit about how the role of the White House had been redefined. "The staff of the Special Assistant to the President for National Security Affairs, Mr. Bundy, performs a secretariat function in that it keeps up with actions taken under the President's decisions.

"They are not responsible for seeing that the action takes place. They are responsible for knowing whether it has taken place and for reporting it to the President. They keep a score sheet, but they are not the responsible action organization."

The President, Mr. Bell went on to explain to the Senators, "is using a system under which he places responsibility on a Cabinet officer or a top subordinate in a Cabinet department, for preparing an analysis or coming up with recommendations on a given issue or subject.

This Cabinet officer or top subordinate is expected, himself, to arrange for whatever coordination is needed in order to obtain the views of other departments concerned and to make sure the matter which is to come before the President and the National Security Council has been considered by others in the government who ought to consider it. . . .
Those officers and the staffs that work with them are expected to be in a real sense the significant centers, both for policy making and

for following through on Presidential action, for making sure that the different parts of a Presidential decision that affect a given area or country are appropriately pursued, that the things that are supposed to happen in fact do happen, and happen in correct relationship to each other.

The office of the Assistant Secretary of State for a geographic area has really been up-graded very substantially in the minds of every one in this administration. They are frequently the key people on whom responsibility is placed for pushing ahead with a given set of decisions.

It had been those people, in the case of Cuba, who had disagreed most vigorously with the decision taken by the President but had never been fully heard. Presumably, under the new system, they would be among the first to be heard.

After three months, the Senate Policy Machinery Subcommittee wanted to know how the new system was working. "In some cases, exactly as it should," reported Director of the Budget Bell, the man with the broadest view of the whole process.

Namely, there has come to the President a very clear and definite analysis of the problem and an outline of a proposed policy which is specific, costed out, with all the elements included in a very nice presentation of a proposed position and a proposed series of actions.

This has been available to everybody concerned sufficiently in advance so that those who might differ with it have had a chance to think about it and formulate their points of view and the matter was in a position to come to the President and be debated crisply on real issues.

That was the way the system ought to work, he said, and there was no reason it couldn't work that way nearly every time. But he was quick to concede that "there have been cases in which the system hasn't worked perfectly."

Perhaps the fellow who was task force chairman did not quite know what was expected of him [the Budget Director charitably explained]. He may have come up with a bit of a least common denominator report, or it may have been a matter in which the time table was very short and the people concerned did not really have a chance to get all the issues staffed out.

The outlook was bright administratively, he thought. "We have had a very brief experience. I think it is clear that the understanding of what the President wants, and how he wants the system to work, is becoming much more widespread."

REORGANIZING THE DEPARTMENT OF STATE

Letting the departments know what he wanted and getting it were two very different things, the President found. Quietly Kennedy and his inner circle began reclassifying the men they had brought into the government as "talkers" or "doers" and planning future shifts.

The State Department was the major source of frustration for the President because he spent by far the greatest part of his working hours on matters in which State was involved. Having cleared the way for the department to take back authority that the Defense Department and the CIA had gathered unto themselves over the years, Mr. Kennedy was said to be annoyed when nothing much happened. The Department of State seemed more drag than help to him in the conduct of foreign affairs. "Sending a memo to the State Department," one Presidential aide remarked, "is like putting it into a bottle, throwing it into the sea, and hoping it will wash up on shore someday." And though the facts were surely not so dramatic, feeling at the White House was.

Questions addressed to career men on the delays and confusion in the State Department elicited the answer that it was the Undersecretary's fault. Traditionally the "housekeeper" for the department, the Undersecretary of Kennedy's choice was not popular with Foreign Service officers he had repeatedly passed over in recommending men for ambassadorial and ministerial posts. The President was told that installing a new Undersecretary who would devote himself to daily operations in the Department of State while the Secretary dealt with global matters was the first step toward improving matters.

An effort to do this in mid-July had to be postponed when news of the plan leaked to the press and supporters of Bowles (including Adlai Stevenson, who urged the President by cable from Rome to reconsider) created an uproar too loud to ignore.

In April the Kennedy circle had been unprepared for the reaction against their intervention in Cuba. In July they were again surprised that so many were shocked to hear that Bowles, a principal opponent of the Cuban action, was about to be the first man fired out of the Kennedy government. But by this time the new Administration had become more sensitive to public opinion. It quickly reversed its field, and Bowles stayed put.

Four months went by, in which most of Bowles's administrative duties were quietly handed over to George Ball, Undersecretary for Economic Affairs, and Bowles was kept busy on assignments overseas. During that time, Sorensen and Bundy surveyed the whole State Department-White House situation. The President and Secretary Rusk discussed problems and people, and in early November they agreed on the first drastic shift of personnel in the new Administration.

Bowles would become a roving specialist in underdeveloped areas. Ball would become Undersecretary in Bowles's place. Ball, an original Stevenson man, had steadily risen in Kennedy's esteem; he was bright, quick, well organized—and on Kennedy's wave length. George G. McGhee, the man Rusk had insisted on having as his Policy Planning Chief but who was more of a "doer" than a "thinker," was shifted to the third-ranking position of Undersecretary for Political Affairs, and Bundy's former White House Deputy, Walt Rostow, more "thinker" than "doer," was given the policy position Mr. Kennedy had wanted Rusk to give him in the beginning. In line with the basic decision to consolidate authority in the operating divisions of the regular departments, Richard H. Goodwin, who had handled Latin American matters for the White House, moved a few blocks west as the new Deputy Assistant Secretary for Latin American affairs in the State Department. Another White House aide, Frederick G. Dutton, left the post of Secretary to the Cabinet to replace former Representative Brooks Hays of Arkansas as State Department Liaison with Congress. The kindly Mr. Hays, a casualty of Little Rock, obviously would not be able to coax out of Congress what Kennedy wanted in 1962 on tariffs and trade in particular. In a final shift, W. Averell Harriman, the roving ambassador, agreed to come back to Washington as Assistant Secretary for Far Eastern Affairs and settle down to the monumental task of overhauling United States policies in that area.

Now the President had "his own men" in the State Department with whom he could communicate swiftly when he wanted to know something or wanted them to do something. And in making himself more comfortable with the department that claimed so much of his attention, Kennedy was also responding to a major criticism that Senator Henry Jackson leveled at the national security machinery just at that time. After a two-year study of how well our Government was staffed and organized "to meet the challenge of world Communism," Jackson had concluded that "no task is more urgent than improving the effectiveness of the Department of State." Specifically, he said, "the Department as a whole attaches too little importance to looking ahead in foreign policy, and is too wedded to a philosophy of reacting to problems as they arise. The Policy Planning Council is not now in the main stream of policy making." In Rostow, the President and the Secretary of State now had a man noted for "looking ahead."

State needs more officials . . . who are broadly experienced in dealing with the full range of national security problems which now engage the Department. The administration of foreign policy has become "big business." This places a high premium on the ability to manage large scale enterprises—to make decisions promptly and decisively, to delegate, and to monitor.

The President well understood that, under the new system, the need for "take charge" men of broad experience and high caliber at the Assistant Secretary level was urgent. The appointment of Averell Harriman as Assistant Secretary for Far Eastern Affairs had the effect of upgrading that rank. As a former Secretary of Commerce, Ambassador to the Soviet Union, and Governor of New York, Harriman filled the requirements for broad experience. He had held more positions of public trust, the President remarked, than probably any other American except John Quincy Adams.

On the face of it, there was now at State "a more effective matching of people with responsibilities," which was the President's stated aim. But there were two other vaster organizations concerned with national-security affairs—the Department of Defense and the CIA. Secretaries McNamara and Rusk were making notable efforts to keep their departments in close step. McNamara was directing a thorough shake-up of his own. But it was not yet clear whether the man who took over from Allen Dulles in mid-November would feel any need for change in the organization he inherited.

Apparently the same desire that had led him to ask Mr. Dulles to remain in his Administration in the first place—the desire to demonstrate that this sensitive part of the Government was outside of politics—prompted Mr. Kennedy to choose as successor to Dulles a Nixon Republican, John A. McCone, California industrialist and Chairman of the Atomic Energy Commission under Eisenhower. McCone is known for his enthusiasm as a cold warrior and his energy and initiative as an operator, but it remains to be seen how willing he will be to keep CIA in step with foreign policy as laid down by the White House.

ADDING UP THE SCORE

How well had the President picked his men? Significantly, in the first staff reorganization, in the Department of State, it was positions that changed, not players—only a few minor members of the original team were benched in the first year. Mr. Kennedy had initially given an unusual amount of thought to choosing the men around him. He should therefore have less reason than many of his predecessors to bring in masses of substitutions.

Customarily, it takes less time to discern the basic personality of an Administration than to identify the men of lasting power in it. As late as 1938, Franklin Roosevelt was still disposing of less than purposeful men in high places in his Administration. It was only after the setback of the 1938 election that Harry L. Hopkins replaced the genial Daniel C. Roper of South Carolina as Secretary of Commerce and Frank Murphy took over as Attorney General from Homer S. Cummings. Some of the Kennedy "early bloomers" would fade, too.

Various of the talented men around the President were already becoming restive at the length of time it was taking to advance to higher positions. The President's pragmatic methods of administration almost guaranteed that proved ability to get things done would be rewarded with ever more responsibility and authority. Ambitious men could be sure that the effort to match the right man to the right job was not over.

As Kennedy's first year in power came to a close, it was possible to identify the men that stood closest to the President. And in most cases, the reasons for their special relationship go deep enough to be lasting.

To the outside observer, the most "in" of the inner circle surely seems to be the President's brother, Robert. As the President had predicted, the Attorney General's performance had silenced much of the criticism that "youth and inexperience" disqualified him for his post. Bobby struck some mighty blows for civil liberties and forced the gambling world to look for safer havens from the law. But he displayed, also, a shakiness in his concern for individual civil rights that called forth "I-told-you-so's." The President, however, showed every sign of satisfaction that his basic estimate of his brother's ability had been proved sound. When he assigned the Attorney General to the new role of Presidential scout in international affairs, and the cries went up again that Presidents should keep brothers in their places, the President was unmoved;

he Attorney General was undismayed. What Kennedy could resist the challenge of assignment to the unfamiliar? After all, the
mountain was there.

Ted Sorensen, by a loyalty and devotion beyond most men's
ability to give another, had fended off challengers to the place at
Kennedy's right hand that he had occupied in the Senate. By
working harder and starting out smarter than most of those who
coveted his role, Sorensen not only survived but also grew in importance. As the lieutenant through whom all domestic matters
passed before they reached the President, and as one of two intimates (the other was brother Bobby) whom Kennedy ordered to
immerse themselves in foreign affairs for his protection after Cuba,
Sorensen rose to the highest status in the White House to which
a non-Kennedy could aspire.

McGeorge Bundy came up fast in the first year, as he had come
up fast in every phase of his career. In the opening months of the
new Administration, a writer could accurately describe Bundy and
his Cambridge colleagues, Walt Rostow and Jerome B. Wiesner,
as the White House's three "scholars of the nuclear age." And
Rostow could tell their joint biographer that in the White House
circle, the three were "almost substitutable for each other. We are
interchangeable parts." But with his special talent for getting
ahead, Bundy soon left the other two behind. His style suited the
President—a self-confidence that can only be described as total,
an unconcealed contempt for the irrelevant or imprecise, a taste for
aggressive positions arrived at through step-by-step logic, and a dislike of defeat or failure as strong as that of any Kennedy. Because
of the President's preoccupation with the national-security matters
that were Bundy's preserve, the young ex-Harvard Dean was in
and out of the President's office half a dozen times a day, and
proximity did not change the good first impression. After Sorensen
was assigned some foreign-policy responsibilities, he and Bundy
worked together almost daily—beautifully, they separately agree.
In his own field, Bundy is now approaching Sorensen's status.
And according to Kennedy intimates, he is also approaching the
status of personal friend so seldom conferred on professional
associates of the President.

Kenneth O'Donnell and Larry O'Brien, the head men of the
"Irish Mafia"—as Washington calls the inner group—landed on
their feet and from the first functioned as though they had always been in the White House. O'Donnell guards the gate to the
Kennedy presence and uses his x-ray eye to separate the worthy
from the unworthy among those with whom the President must

deal as leader of his party. O'Brien is trusted with one of the most difficult and vital tasks any man could perform for this President— negotiating Congressional approval of his plans.

George Ball, Undersecretary of State for Economic Affairs, made the President's "doer" list early. He performed well in reversing the adverse United States balance-of-payments position abroad, got on well with his counterparts among European financial officials (all of whom he knew well), was at ease with the complex facts, figures, and personalities involved, and showed leadership in helping smooth the way for Britain to join the European Common Market and imagination about what response, in trade policy, that vibrant new institution would require from the United States. Ball, who is plain-spoken, wrote crisp, well-documented memos that were to the point. He went to the head of the junior class and was the natural choice when it was decided to move Chester Bowles out of the job of Undersecretary.

Arthur Goldberg, associated with both Kennedys during the Senate Labor Rackets investigation, proved to be more than a Secretary of Labor. The President was delighted by his intrepidity in taking on rough assignments, and his willingness, in spite of his background as a lawyer for labor, to approach problems from the consumer's view; labor was less delighted. Kennedy consults Goldberg on all manner of things and is said to consider him one of his most successful choices for the Cabinet.

Robert McNamara lived up to the advance billing given him by the talent scouts. In a very short time there was no doubt in anyone's mind who was boss in the Pentagon. And in spite of some early errors in handling the press, McNamara came through to the public as a man who was a match for the military and not to be intimidated by Birch Society generals. No one's stock rose faster with the man in the White House, and at the end of the year, it continued high.

After an uncertain start, Dean Rusk started up the ladder to become, by the time of the Berlin crisis, First Adviser to the President on Foreign Affairs. Although he had to function through an amorphous mass of a department, Rusk managed in the first year to achieve a fair performance in the role President Kennedy had in mind for him. It was not the role the Secretary of State had played under Truman or Eisenhower, when the Secretary made policy as well as carrying it out. Rusk caught on to what was expected and set about doing it in an intelligent, energetic way. The Berlin crisis gave him his chance to recoup the Secretary's rightful status, and at the end of 1961 he was rising on the White House scale.

Douglas Dillon does not exercise the virtual power of veto that George Humphrey and Robert Anderson held over many of President Eisenhower's decisions. But Dillon apparently has attained a position of great individual influence with President Kennedy. Those who find the attractive Republican banker's views too conservative blame Dillon for reinforcing Kennedy's natural caution in matters monetary.

Lyndon Johnson grew in grace. The volume and variety of work Kennedy gave him attested to that.

The Vice President served as a cheer leader in gloomy West Berlin, as a broker with business to break down discrimination in employment, as a mediator between competing groups in the field of space, as a balloon-floater for the President on controversial issues, as the keeper, in the President's absence abroad, of the code controlling the ultimate weapons.

As he settled down to a routine of dealing swiftly with an unending stream of matters, Mr. Kennedy's personal style underwent a few visible changes. By autumn, White House correspondents observed that the President was more reserved, had organized his time to permit more reflection and less hurry, and was much less likely to be seen bouncing in and out of the offices of his aides. Perhaps he was favoring his back. Perhaps he was adjusting his pace to the anticipation that his term of office would be "one crisis after another," as he predicted to a group of newspaper publishers in September. One can hope he had learned that "When in doubt, do something" is a fallible formula—especially for Presidents.

III

Getting Along with Congress

"There is just one rule for politicians all over the world: don't say in power what you say in opposition; for if you do, you only have to carry out what the other fellows have found impossible."—John Galsworthy

I was leaving a Democratic Senator's office one winter afternoon shortly before the inauguration of President Kennedy when an aide smilingly handed me a copy of this quotation. The Senate had recently fought its biennial battle over reforming its rules. Liberal Senators had waged the fight against filibusters without benefit of Kennedy's help—and lost for lack of two votes they believed he could have swung.

The mood in the office of the Senator, a rules-reform leader, was one of rueful understanding, not rancor. But one did not have to walk far on Capitol Hill to find Northern and Western Democrats who felt let down. It had been one thing for General Eisenhower, who knew little of the workings of Congress, to leave it to its own devices; it was quite another for a former member of both House and Senate to deny support to those who were trying to change rules that would surely stop part of the new President's program in its tracks. Why hadn't Kennedy helped?

Only a few at that time—before the Inauguration—knew that Kennedy's inaction was the result of a deliberate decision. This decision was based on experience—fourteen years of it in Congress—and on the election returns in the Congressional contests, which Kennedy knew how to read. He purposely set his sights low and adopted tactics that would not deplete his political arsenal on the first round.

The arithmetic was simple. The Democrats had lost 22 seats in the House—most of them held by moderates or liberals—and one in the Senate. The Senate would probably go along with most of the Kennedy program; as a body it has been growing more liberal in recent years just as the House has grown more conservative. The task in the upper house was to build up the largest possible reservoir of good will, for use in international emergencies when Senate help might be required. The real problem lay in the House, where the line-up would be 174 Republicans and 263 Democrats, with 99 of the Democrats from the 11 states of the old Confederacy. That meant a substantial increase in power for the coalition of Southern Democrats and conservative Republicans.

Kennedy had made 220 specific policy pledges between nomination and his election. How many of them could he realistically ask his particular Congress to approve? In fact, how much of the most basic legislation to "reverse the deterioration" of the past eight years could he maneuver through?

Analyzing the votes of the preceding Congress and projecting that analysis to the 87th Congress indicated that three of the measures which Kennedy had promised would get top priority— for development of depressed areas, for an increased minimum wage, and for school aid—would die in the House.

Further analysis showed that, at root, the problem was the same one that had plagued every President since F.D.R. lost the 1938 Congressional elections. A study issued by the authoritative reference service, *Congressional Quarterly,* two weeks after Kennedy's election dissected the problem. In 1960, the study showed, the majority of Southern Democrats voted against the position taken by a majority of Northern Democrats in forty per cent of all roll calls in the House. The differences occurred on such issues as civil rights, foreign aid, tax reforms, minimum wages, aid to education, housing, farm price supports, and medical care for the aged—and most of these would come before the new Congress. On roll-call votes in which the Republican-Southern Democratic coalition operated, Republican Leader Charles A. Halleck, in 1960, had found an average of 73 Southern votes on the conservative side. The conservative Southerners, however, could not prevail without massive Republican support and won only three roll calls when less than a majority of the Republicans voted with them.

THE KENNEDY STRATEGY

To the new President the answer was obvious. To gain a working majority in this particular Congress, he must expand the

Democratic center and win over Republican liberals who had felt obliged to support Eisenhower. Expanding the Democratic center really meant persuading a substantial number of Southerners to follow the President instead of their regional leaders when they differed—and neutralizing or winning over at least some of those leaders. That meant accentuating the positive as much as he could where the South was concerned.

One way was to omit any requests for new civil-rights legislation during the first session of Congress. That the President had already decided to do. Why not, then, build up further credit with the Southerners and avoid a party-splitting fight at the very start by taking no part in the effort that was sure to be made to tighten Senate rules, including Rule 22, which protect filibusters? None of Kennedy's proposals other than those pertaining to civil rights were really susceptible to filibustering; liberal economic proposals usually escape that form of attack because Senator Barry M. Goldwater does not have the staying power to employ it, and Southern conservatives are careful not to wear out their ultimate weapon. True, the 1960 Democratic platform, like the Republican, had bowed in the direction of the disruptive filibuster that preceded passage of the 1960 Civil Rights Act. The Democratic plank urged that "action be taken at the beginning of the 87th Congress to improve Congressional procedures so that majority rule prevails and decisions can be made after reasonable debate without being blocked by a minority in either House." But this action would just have to be classified as "temporarily impossible."

The plan Kennedy intended to follow with Congress barred direct combat with the Southerners except when there was no other way to achieve an essential goal. Whenever possible he would employ the diplomacy of compromise and, when forced to fight, he would limit his side to the use of conventional political weapons. But Kennedy knew that, in order to make any record at all, there was one fight he would have to provoke at the start—and it was a fight that would take every ounce of Presidential charm and muscle. Senator Joseph S. Clark of Pennsylvania explained it at some length in the Senate a few days before Congress adjourned for the Democratic Convention.

The great difficulty which the Congress is having in passing needed legislation before adjournment calls attention once again to the archaic and undemocratic rules and procedures under which we on Capitol Hill attempt to legislate.

The rules of the Senate and of the House are stacked against the people of the United States . . . actually we have organized ourselve

so sloppily that we may well be unable to meet the critical challenge
to pass effective legislation in the national interest which will confront
us next January. It is bad enough to dilly dally through the eight years
of the Eisenhower Administration. We will be playing Russian roulette
with our national survival if we do not set our house in order before
the next President presents his State of the Union Message.

Senator Clark went on to be uncommonly candid about what
the Congress must do to be saved. The House, he acknowledged,
was the sole judge of its own rules and procedures. "Nevertheless,"
Senator Clark stated, "I believe the general public is entitled to
know the effects of the House rules on the legislative process in the
Senate." Then he went on:

It seems clear to me that the program of the next President of the
United States will founder on the rocks of House Rules Committee
opposition unless the other body takes steps to change its rules and
procedures before the 87th Congress gets down to business.

We, in the Senate, have legislated throughout the present session
in the shadow, not only of the House Rules Committee, but of the
House Ways and Means Committee. [Clark went on, ignoring in his
frustration the convention that members of one body do not criticize
the other.] We are continually being told by our leadership, by our
committee chairmen, and by our Senate conferees, that we should
neither pass nor insist on the liberal legislation we believe necessary
to the country's well being, because the House Rules Committee will
not permit the bill to go to conference or, if taxes are involved, the
House Ways and Means Committee will permit needed taxes and a
temporary increase ceiling on the national debt to expire rather than
to yield to Senate efforts to close notorious and discreditable tax loopholes.

HOW HOUSE RULES OBSTRUCT THE SENATE

Clark cited chapter and verse for his complaints:

The House Rules Committee pickled the Senate-passed Depressed
Areas Bill for over a year; and when the House liberals finally, with
the assistance of the Speaker, got their own less adequate bill on the
floor and through the House, we were told that we dared not change
as much as a syllable of the House Bill,—for if we did the Rules
Committee would never permit the proposed legislation to go to conference.

So we were forced to forego our independent legislative judgment
and swallow the House bill.

Then came the Education bill. Again we were told we dare not include teachers' salaries in the coverage, for the House would not agree and the Rules Committee would block a conference. This time we rejected the advice and voted our convictions. It now appears our leaders were right—the House Rules Committee has so far refused to permit a conference.

Next came Civil Rights. For day after day, and night after night, we were told in the Senate we dare not pass an effective Civil Rights bill, for, if we did, the House Rules Committee would pickle the legislation for the rest of the session. This threat was, in my judgment, a real influence in persuading the Senate to table the effective parts of proposed Civil Rights legislation: Part 3, a really effective voting-registrar procedure, FEPC legislation, and legislative assistance to school integration. . . .

Next came the Housing bill. I was told that if I pressed the Public Housing Amendment, as I had pressed the Teachers' Salary Amendment to the Education bill, the House Rules Committee would find a way to kill the whole Housing bill. As these words are spoken, the Rules Committee has refused to permit even the House's own bill to go to the floor. . . .

All these bills would come up again in the new Congress; which suggested to Senator Clark that "the program of the next President will also be wrecked unless we make major changes in our own rules and procedures."

What happened in the August rump session of Congress after the conventions gave dramatic point to the rules changes both platforms had called for. For four weeks the House Rules Committee, led by Chairman Howard W. Smith of Virginia and controlled by the Southern Democratic–Republican coalition, refused to allow any of the legislation for which the session had been called to reach the floor. Senate leaders showed so little indignation at the House blockade that Senator Clark was moved to take the floor again shortly before adjournment "to speak briefly on how the Senate should be organized next year to enact the Democratic platform, in the event our party's candidates are successful in the November election."

First [he said] the leadership should be committed to enact the Democratic platform into law.

Second, the leadership should represent the majority view of the Democrats in the Senate. This majority view will support the Democratic platform.

Third, the best way to achieve these results, in my judgment, is first to provide for the appointment of three Whips, in addition to the Majority leader [so that] we would have in the leadership both geographical and ideological representation on a fair basis.

Fourth, we should reconstitute the Policy and Steering Committees of our party so that they will fairly represent both the major geographical areas and the differing ideological views of Senators.

Fifth, a majority of the Democratic members of the committees, including, in some cases, the Chairmen, should have signified their support of the platform in the legislative area dealt with by their respective committees.

Sixth, and finally, I believe we should provide for periodical and frequent meetings of the Democratic conference at times and places convenient to the members, perhaps at lunch, in order that the leadership may report to the other Democratic members of the Senate, the recommendations which they make with respect to policy.

Clark's remarks were by way of comment on the fact that if the Democrats won in November, key Senate bodies such as the Committees on the Judiciary and Finance in the new Congress would be chaired respectively by James O. Eastland of Mississippi and Harry Flood Byrd of Virginia—neither of whom supported the Democratic ticket or platform in 1960; and that the Democratic Majority Conference Steering Committee, which fills Democratic vacancies on standing committees of the Senate, was regionally lopsided, with seven Southerners in its thirteen-man membership during the 86th Congress. The nine-man Majority Policy Committee, which schedules legislation for floor consideration, was out of balance, too, with five members from the South or Southwest.

PREPARING THE WAY TO CHANGE THE RULES

During the two months of campaigning that followed adjournment, Senator Clark and two Representatives—Richard Bolling of Missouri, a member of the House Rules Committee, and Frank Thompson, Jr., of New Jersey—bore down on the lesson of the rump session at every opportunity. Bolling, wherever he campaigned, urged local Democrats to pledge their candidates to support rules changes in the new Congress, and he personally saw to it that the candidate's brother and adviser, Bobby Kennedy, fully understood the problem. Thompson, a good friend from Kennedy's days in the House, worked on the candidate himself.

Clark concentrated on Kennedy too during the last two weeks of the campaign, most of which the candidate spent in Clark's home state of Pennsylvania. After Clark had talked to him several times about the importance of revising the rules, Senator Kennedy, who had only to be reminded, not educated, said in effect: "Joe, do your damnedest to drum up support and if you are in shooting distance of having enough votes to put the changes through in January, I will give you some help." Clark then went to work in earnest. On November 18 he announced that he had written to every Senator appealing for bipartisan support for ten changes, fundamental ones, that did not include Rule 22: "Tinkering with this rule will get us nowhere," he wrote.

Instead, to deal with filibusters, he urged adoption of a new rule permitting a majority of the Senate after fifteen hours of debate to "move the previous question," after which further debate on pending business would be limited. In addition, he proposed a new bill of rights which would permit a majority of the members of any standing committee to convene meetings to take up legislation and to end debate regardless of the wishes of the chairman, plus a new rule prohibiting irrelevant discussion in Senate debate and another providing that a majority of the Senators named to any conference committee with the House must be sympathetic to the bill as passed by the Senate. Clark further urged repeal of the rule which permitted a single Senator to prevent committees from meeting while the Senate was in session.

In December, a group of labor and liberal organizations met in Washington to add steam to the rules-reform drive. Prospects appeared good for at least reducing the number of votes of those present required to limit debate from two-thirds to three-fifths. The "guess sheet" presented at the strategy meeting showed that the liberals would be licked on the proposal to end filibusters by a simple majority: 48 Senators were listed as definitely opposed, 40 in favor, and 11 in between. On the question of a three-fifths or sixty-per-cent rule, however, the "guess sheet" showed 51 Senators definitely for, 40 definitely against, and 9 in between, a far from hopeless situation from the sponsors' view.

The Kennedy staff, especially his aides Richard Goodwin and Myer Feldman, were privy to all this. And Senator Clark met privately with Kennedy on December 13 to discuss the subject. To make sure no one assumed he had committed himself to support of Clark, however, the President-elect told his December 20 press conference that it would be up to the House and Senate to make their own rules. He did comment that they should "permit a majority of the members to bring a matter to a vote after a reasonable period of time."

But while those who favored new rules were grouping their forces, Senate Democratic leaders began a series of "cold water" statements. The "Kennedy program would be jeopardized" by a party-splitting fight, they said, and the issue should therefore be deferred to a more "propitious" time. Senator Mike Mansfield of Montana, scheduled to succeed to the Majority Leadership in place of Lyndon Johnson, led off with a television speech on December 12. Senator Clinton P. Anderson of New Mexico, who had led the fight to liberalize Rule 22 in 1959, joined Mansfield in opposition, as did Hubert Humphrey of Minnesota, who said he saw "no reason to rush this thing." The word obviously had gone out from the President-elect.

NO ASSAULT IN THE SENATE

Kennedy had decided to fight on one front at a time, and the front the first year would be in the House. The Administration would not undertake, as its first action, an assault on the Senate rules. The risk of failure, and of a loss in world prestige, was too great. And, if in the Senate the South's cherished symbol of the filibuster was left intact a while longer, perhaps a few Southerners in the House would go along when the rules issue came up there.

Whatever the liberals could do to modify Senate rules would be all to the good, Kennedy had decided; but they would have to go it alone. They *would* go it alone, he knew. For, unlike the President, a Senator from Pennsylvania, New York, or Illinois was risking his prestige only if he did *not* oppose the continuance of rules protecting filibusters. And Senators favoring rules changes felt obliged, on principle, to try their strength when the 87th Congress opened because they believed delay would have the practical effect of preventing any modification of Rule 22 for another two or perhaps even four years. Vice President Nixon delivered an "advisory opinion" in 1957, and again in 1959, that a simple majority of the Senate has the constitutional right to adopt new rules at the beginning of a new Congress, uninhibited by the two-thirds requirement of Rule 22 respecting cloture. But, come January 20, Nixon would be succeeded as Vice President by Lyndon B. Johnson, whose position on this issue had yet to be established.

Then, too, there was always the hope that Kennedy would change his mind and intervene. Kennedy had continued to show interest to the extent of phoning Senator Clark from Palm Beach several times in early January to inquire how he was getting along with the rules crusade. And when Clark responded by asking the President-elect to call several of the nine "doubtful" Senators on the "guess sheet," there was silence, but no word to dissuade.

The seven-day Senate debate on the rules began on January 3 in circumstances much happier for the rules changers than on previous occasions. Formerly, they had faced the combined opposition of Majority Leader Johnson and Minority Leader Everett M. Dirksen; now Senator Mansfield, making his debut as Majority Leader, was maintaining a studiedly neutral role. He personally believed the rules should be tightened, although not as the first order of business when his aim was to unify, not divide. But he allowed the Senate to discuss the matter fully and freely for seven days. He did not encourage either President-elect Kennedy or Vice President-elect Johnson to make their views known. And Mansfield's leisurely style of leadership produced ten days that shook Capitol Hill.

THE "LYNDON GAP"

Some called the period from January 2, 1961, the day before the new Congress convened, to the afternoon of January 11, 1961, when Senate Resolution 4 was referred to the Rules Committee, the "Lyndon Gap," others the "New Freedom." As the Washington *Post*'s experienced Capitol Hill reporter Robert C. Albright observed, "Democratic Liberals, who for six to eight years have strained and fretted under Johnson's strong driving leadership of the party in the Senate, suddenly found themselves a practically unvoiced majority."

"Some of the participants, who can calmly reminisce about it now, compare it whimsically to the explosion of independence in the Congo and the other erupting new African Republics." "Democracy," one participant remarked at the time, "has finally raised its ugly head in the Senate."

In the heady atmosphere of those ten days, the liberal bloc demanded, and got, caucus after caucus of the full Senate Democratic majority—something Johnson, as leader, had avoided. Clark's ten-point program for revising rules and procedures, plus a multitude of other ideas for broader participation in party decisions, were aired *in extenso* and with some success. Clark himself, Senator Harrison A. Williams, Jr., of New Jersey, and Senator Thomas J. Dodd of Connecticut were added to the strategic Steering Committee; a Southern majority of seven out of thirteen was changed to a minority of seven out of sixteen.

But in the end Senator Mansfield, with some semblance of com-

and, achieved his and President-elect Kennedy's purpose—the
voidance of a party split over the rules as the first order of busi-
ess.

On the day before the final vote the President-elect came to
ohnson's office in the Capitol to confer with Mansfield and John-
on. That afternoon, the Majority Leader announced he would
nove to refer the pending bill to the Rules Committee. The next
ay he did.

Mansfield told the Senate that, in his personal opinion, a three-
fths cloture rule was "desirable," but that it should be considered
n committee before coming to a vote. He promised that he would
leave no stone unturned" to report the measure and bring it to a
ote "at a later date." (He did, and it was killed in the September
djournment rush.) Forcing a fight on the rules at that time, the
Majority Leader explained, would interfere with passage of the
President's program, and he pleaded with those Senators who were
n doubt about how to vote not to embarrass him in his new posi-
ion as Leader. That plea almost certainly carried his motion for
eferral. It was approved 50–46. A shift of two votes would have
defeated it, and there were three surprises on the final tally. Dem-
cratic Senators E. L. Bartlett of Alaska and Oren E. Long of
Iawaii, and Republican Senator Leverett Saltonstall of Massa-
husetts had all pledged their votes to the rules-change side, but
oted with Mansfield in the showdown.

Did the new President, not yet officially in office, the Senate
Leader, in his first performance, the new legislative liaison team
or the White House, new to Capitol Hill, throw away an easy
gain? Would closer counting of noses and closer communication
vith the rules-change leaders have indicated a revision of strategy?
f Mansfield, at the end, had pressed less hard for pigeonholing it,
vould the cloture change have carried? If so, the President could
ave enjoyed the luxury of a free choice of whether or not to press
or strong civil-rights legislation before the 1962 Congressional
lections. Under the present rules, which as a practical matter
annot be changed before 1963 and perhaps not until 1965, he can
oress, but probably not prevail on more than minimum measures.

SHOWDOWN IN THE HOUSE

The House was a very different kettle of fish. Here there was
no escaping a collision with the Southern leaders. The President
ad to challenge the system of minority rule by which Southerners

with long seniority dominated affairs in the House, and he had to do it now. The day could not be postponed as Kennedy reckoned it could in the Senate, for most of his program would not even come to a vote until the President had challenged and defeated the coalition that ruled the House and frustrated the more liberal Senate through its control of the House Rules Committee.

The situation he faced had prevailed for all but a brief period since 1938, and indeed the conservative coalition had begun to operate in Congress the year before that. Southerners were upset by repeal of the two-thirds nominating rule Roosevelt had pushed through the 1936 Democratic Convention because it deprived them of veto power over Presidential candidates; and conservative Republicans in Congress shared their shock at F.D.R.'s "court packing" proposals and the sit-down strikes of 1937. When Congress passed, and the Supreme Court upheld, the Wagner Labor Act in April 1937, conservatives North and South decided it was time to combine to stop the New Deal.

Wise in the ways of Congress, the coalition's first move was to take over the House Rules Committee—which they promptly changed from traffic cop to policy maker. Instead of simply directing the flow of bills from committees to the floor, which had been its role since the reforms following the rule of "Boss Cannon," the Rules Committee, under the coalition, undertook to decide the merits of given measures, and held back, as it pleased, bills favorably reported by the standing committees of the House.

The present Rules Chairman, Howard Smith of Virginia, was one of five anti-New Deal Democrats who negotiated the original coalition with conservative Republican colleagues on the ten-man Rules Committee in 1937. And in all the years between, Smith and his predecessors in the chairmanship, John J. O'Connor of New York and Eugene Cox of Georgia, had used their position to harass the New Deal, the Fair Deal, and the Eisenhower Crusade. For a brief period under Truman the 81st Congress limited the power of the Rules Committee by means of the "21-day rule"—this rule permitted a chairman to bring directly to the floor any bill which his committee had approved but which the Rules Committee had not acted on within 21 days. But on the opening day of the 82nd Congress, when the memory of Truman's 1948 miracle victory had begun to dim, the coalition was able to repeal the "21-day rule" and the Rules Committee resumed its hold over the House.

Liberals have never run out of complaints since the coalition moved in. Joseph F. Guffey of Pennsylvania gloried in denouncing the "Unholy Alliance" during all his years in the Senate. And in became as traditional for New Dealers and Fair Dealers, at the beginning of each new Congress, to try to limit Rules Committee power in the House as to attack Rule 22 in the Senate. But with the overwhelming Democratic victory in the 1958 Congressional elections, the prospect for change seemed in sight. The Democratic Study Group, established by the House liberal bloc the previous year, requested a formal conference with the Speaker to discuss the matter.

Always before, when they had gone to ask Mr. Rayburn's support in the attempt to change the rules, he had dismissed them with a terse: "You don't have the votes." This time the liberal delegation, headed by Representative Chet Holifield of California, believed they were within good shooting distance of having the votes and were determined to make Mr. Rayburn acknowledge it. The Speaker still didn't think they were strong enough to make the try, and in the Study Group itself such experienced nose counters as Representative Bolling agreed. But the Holifield delegation came away from the Speaker's office jubilant. He had promised not to permit Smith's Rules group to bottle up any bill cleared by a standing commitee on which the House was eager to vote.

As the session moved on and the bills they wanted did not, the Study Group wondered about Mr. Rayburn's pledge. Without informing the Study Group or the Advisory Council of the Democratic National Committee, which was also nervous at the lack of action, Rayburn and his lieutenants had met with labor representatives and agreed to give Senator Kennedy's pending labor bill absolute priority. When, after mighty maneuvering, that bill had been pushed through, Rayburn called in the liberals and told them what he was now prepared to do for them.

What time remained of the session before adjournment for the 1960 national conventions should be spent, he said—and they agreed—in making a Democratic record, for campaign purposes, in legislation on education, civil rights, minimum wages, and aid to depressed areas. (Medical care for the aged and housing were left off the list because, in the first case, the Ways and Means Committee was against medical care under Social Security, and in the second there was no great public demand at the moment.) In the process of making a record on these four issues, Mr. Sam pointed out, the liberals could dramatize the case against the Rules Committee. Rayburn would see to it that the measures reached the committee in rapid succession. Then, when the conservative majority refused to report out the bills, the leadership would make the

Rules Committee look bad by blasting the bills out by emergency means.

To those who were watching, the Rules Committee did undoubtedly look bad during the remainder of the session. When it blocked an aid-to-depressed-areas bill by a 6 to 6 vote, House leaders resorted to the first use, since 1950, of the Calendar Wednesday procedure. (On Wednesday of each week, the Speaker can recognize, in alphabetical order, the chairmen of standing committees who can then call up for a vote any bill previously reported by his committee.) The House passed the bill only to see it vetoed by President Eisenhower. An education bill was let out of committee under threat of using Calendar Wednesday again, then killed when the Rules Committee refused to send the House-passed bill to conference with the Senate because an antisegregation rider was added.

Under threat of Calendar Wednesday, the Rules Committee permitted the minimum-wage bill to go to the floor but refused to permit a Senate-House conference until there was a guarantee that House conferees would insist on the House version. The bill died in conference. The Rules Committee deepened the impression of recalcitrance by volunteering its disapproval of several measures not on the priority list—a subsidy for educational television, Foreign Service improvements, and public housing.

The flat refusal of the Rules Committee coalition to allow a single piece of Democratic priority legislation to reach the floor in the rump session made it crystal-clear to many Democrats in the House as well as to the man headed for the White House where the trouble lay in Congress.

Two weeks after the election, coalition leaders met at the summit. House Republican Leader Charles Halleck and Democrats Smith and William M. Colmer sat down in Washington to discuss strategy. When they had finished, Halleck spoke for the group: "We've seen eye to eye in the past and I expect we'll see eye to eye in the future."

In mid-December, Rayburn, Johnson, and Senate Leader-to-be Mike Mansfield went to Palm Beach to discuss their strategy for the coming Congress with the President-elect. They agreed, Mr. Kennedy announced, on matters which would be of "particular importance" in the 87th Congress, and discussed others that were of "concern." He did not announce that he and the Congressional leaders had also agreed that the time had come to break the Rules Committee hold which had blocked those measures before, and

at Rayburn had privately assured him that he (Rayburn) would
andle the matter.

In all their lobbying during the campaign for an assault on the
ules, Representatives Bolling and Thompson emphasized the
ecessity for making this the Speaker's cause. Otherwise, they
arned, it would fail. The election won, Bolling went home to
.ansas City to continue his campaign on the telephone, alerting
nd alarming everyone he could reach. In December he shifted
perations to Washington. On the last day of the month Rayburn
eturned to the Capitol, and serious talk began. How to proceed?

The Speaker, Majority Leader John W. McCormack, Demo-
ratic Whip Carl Albert, Bolling, and two Texas Representatives
·hom Rayburn included in the conferences were all for breaking
1e Rules Committee hold by decreasing its membership by one—
pecifically by removing Representative William Colmer of Mis-
issippi who had bolted the Kennedy-Johnson ticket and thus was
able to discipline by the Democratic Committee on Committees
·hen it came to choose Rules Committee members for the new
Congress. A word from Rayburn, and Colmer would be passed
·ver and a man amenable to Administration policy put in his place.

Having asked his confreres for their views and received a unani-
nous opinion, the Speaker overrode it—he would add three new
nembers to the committee instead of removing one. It was always
·etter politics to give than to take away, and this move would not
ile the South so much. He was afraid of upsetting the seniority
ystem, Rayburn explained to his strategy board, and perhaps
oading the purgees to retaliate, to say nothing of losing a number
·f good moderate Southerners, basically loyal to the party but ter-
ified by the purge idea. How could they explain a vote to purge a
vhite Southerner when they had not voted to purge a tan New
·orker (namely, Adam Clayton Powell, Jr.) who had similarly
leserted his party in the preceding Presidential election?

Rayburn said he would go to Howard Smith and try to work out
he expansion of the committee peaceably. Smith's reception of
he Speaker left no doubt but that a peaceable change was out of
he question. The most the Rules Chairman was willing to offer
vas a guarantee of the committee's approval of Kennedy's five
·must" bills in exchange for a sort of gentlemen's agreement to
·reserve the status quo. Rayburn assured his lieutenants that he
ntended to go ahead with his expansion plan, but, by this time,
he press was printing rumors of deals between Rayburn and
·mith, and House liberals who had not been in on the maneuver-
ngs were in an uproar.

At Bolling's request, the Speaker met with them and tried to calm them down while he worked out another approach to the problem. The best way now, Rayburn decided, was to call a party caucus and take a binding vote on the question of expanding the Rules Committee. But first Smith would have to agree to allow the bill for expansion to be reported out of his Rules Committee. Some suggested leaving Colmer off the Rules Committee until Smith agreed to release the expansion bill; but at this point Speaker Rayburn decided to live dangerously. In return for a simple agreement by Smith to report out the expansion bill, he would refrain from calling a binding caucus or from holding back Colmer's reappointment to the Rules Committee—and thus save face for the Southerners. Smith accepted the offer.

On January 18 the Democratic caucus approved a Rayburn resolution to enlarge the Rules Committee from twelve members (eight Democrats, four Republicans) to fifteen members (ten Democrats, five Republicans). On January 24, the Rules Committee reported out the expansion resolution by a vote of 6 to 2, with only the Democratic members present and voting. Smith and Colmer voted no; presumably Smith had arranged with the Republican members of his coalition to absent themselves and so permit him to live up to his promise.

The moment the Rayburn strategy was finally fixed, even before Smith fulfilled his part of the bargain, the bugle sounded the charge for the first battle on the New Frontier.

The eight days between the Democratic caucus of January 18 and the final vote on the bill were nerve-shattering for even cool customers like Mr. Rayburn. The day after the caucus, the Speaker still was not convinced he could win, and his mood produced the rumor that he might yet back away from the fight. Those close to him watched him weigh and balance for a doubtful twenty-four hours, and then come down again on the side of going ahead. In the end, he realized, the choice lay between antagonizing about 75 Southern Democrats who would bleed with Howard Smith, and betraying his own troops on whom he would have to rely for the rest of the session—and who, this time, were determined to overthrow Rules Committee control.

Rayburn publicly dismissed his doubts at a press conference on Saturday, January 21. Then Administration generals and their lieutenants got down to counting available men and weapons and planning how to use them fully.

Smith still had not fulfilled his part of the bargain. But when on January 23, the House approved the reappointment of all ten holdover members of his Rules Committee, Smith capitulated. He released the Rayburn bill on the 24th.

With Rayburn's Saturday assurance that there was going to be a fight, the Democratic tempo approached furioso. Over the week-end word had gone to Palm Beach where the President was taking the sun that to keep his pledge to "handle" the Rules problem, Mr. Sam needed help. And now both of the Kennedys, the President and the Attorney General, were on the telephone calling everyone who had a vote or could influence one. Cabinet members new to Washington had had their political indoctrination at the second Cabinet meeting when "Congressional Relations" was the featured topic. Old Washington hands, like Secretary of Interior Udall and Secretary of Labor Goldberg, and former Governors Freeman (Agriculture) and Hodges (Commerce) knew how to use the telephone and what local issues interested the man at the other end of the line.

The chief White House lobbyist, Larry O'Brien, a new man as yet untried on Capitol Hill, was at his battle station with his "wish book" for patronage seekers at the ready. O'Brien, Representative Bolling acting for Rayburn, and Andrew Biemiller, Legislative Director of the AFL-CIO, were put in on-the-spot charge of deciding who should work on whom and of getting the work done.

Labor's lobby moved in in full strength in support of the Rayburn measure; lobbyists for the National Association of Manufacturers and other employer organizations moved in against it. A White House spokesman informed reporters that Smith had allegedly been in contact with the NAM, the American Farm Bureau Federation, the Southern States Industrial Council, and the United States Chamber of Commerce, and that, as a result, letters from local Chambers of Commerce and business organizations were flooding the Hill. House members were also receiving mail from groups opposed to reducing Rules Committee authority because of their opposition to this or that special feature of the Administration program. The American Medical Association was against Administration recommendations for health care for the aged; the National Association of Real Estate Boards was on record against an expanded urban renewal program; and the National Lumber Manufacturers Association was a probable opponent of minimum-wage legislation.

Governor Ross R. Barnett of Mississippi wired all his fellow Governors in the South to "use every power . . . to influence Southern Congressmen to vote against stacking the Rules Committee."

The Democratic Study Group that had waited so long to join the battle distributed literature explaining the fine points of House procedure to new members and providing arguments for the Rayburn position.

The O'Brien-Bolling-Biemiller strategy board figured that their side started with from 190 to 200 of the 219 votes needed to win. The objective (which exactly paralleled Kennedy's objective when he had analyzed his over-all problem with Congress) was to hold Southern defections to less than 60 and win at least 16 Republicans away from their leaders. (The House GOP Policy Committee had unanimously disapproved Rayburn's plan.)

The vote, scheduled for January 26, was moved up to January 31. Democratic shepherds wanted more time to make certain the necessary number of sheep were headed toward the fold. Now the test would come the day after President Kennedy's first State of the Union Message when, it was hoped, Democratic hearts—even Southern ones—would be high. And everyone went to it all over again.

A fellow general reports that O'Brien, working from the Democratic Whip's office in the Capitol, "pushed straight through"— phoning state party chairmen to put the heat on doubtfuls, holding out hopes here, promises there. O'Brien's assistant, Henry Hall Wilson, Jr., of North Carolina, concentrated on Southern Democrats. When an official nose count showed Southern votes slipping away under pressure from business, Secretary Hodges, the former Governor of North Carolina, appealed to his state's delegation to show their gratitude for the unusual number of high positions Kennedy had given North Carolinians. Bobby Kennedy and the President helped start counterpressures in Georgia, Alabama, and the Carolinas. Rayburn and Lyndon Johnson rode tight herd on their Texas colleagues, and Rayburn did more than indicate that the way new members of the House voted on the Rules bill would be considered when committee assignments were handed out the following week. (Representatives John J. Flynt, Jr., and G. Elliott Hagan of Georgia and Horace R. Kornegay of North Carolina, who voted against Rayburn, wound up on committees they did not prefer; Representatives Joseph P. Addabbo of New York, Richard Ichord of Missouri, Ralph R. Harding of Idaho and Julia B. Hansen of Washington, who voted with the Speaker, received their first choices.)

Labor used its last ounce of leverage, too. Even men whom labor's political organization, Committee on Political Education, had not supported, were persuaded not to fight the President and the Speaker. COPE had not backed Representative Frank Thompson of Louisiana, but Bill Dougherty, President of the International Letter Carriers Union, had—and Dougherty carried the message. Rayburn had already lined up two members of the Louisiana delegation, and when Thompson came over to his side, so did two more Louisianans.

When the House was called to order at 12:30 on January 31, little was left undone that Administration Democrats had thought to do. Chairman Smith and Representative Colmer sat together on the committee bench. Mr. Rayburn relaxed in the Speaker's chair. Packed galleries radiated excitement; members of the House chattered away in private gossip as usual. There was applause from the Smith partisans when the Rules Chairman walked toward the microphone; and loud laughter when he remarked, "If there is any quarrel between the Speaker and myself it is all on his side."

"I don't know whose fight this is," Smith went on. "I hear it was the President's—he never said anything to me about it. . . ."

At 1:30 the Speaker walked down into the well of the House. Democrats and Republicans rose and cheered; Representative Smith sat still.

"Whether you vote with me today or not, I appreciate your uniform kindness and courtesy to me. . . .

"We have elected a new President who wants to do something to improve our situation in the United States of America and in the world. . . . I think the House should be allowed on great measures to work its will."

The Speaker asked his "beloved colleagues" to vote for his resolution, and climbed back onto the podium.

The long roll call began. O'Brien's final check showed that Administration strength had climbed from the approximately 190 votes they had counted on thirteen days before to 216 or 217. He hit it almost on the nose. The final vote: 217–212. Kennedy and Rayburn had won by five votes. Democratic defections exceeded the limit of 60 that Administration strategists had set for themselves—64 Southern and border-state Democrats voted "no." Even though the Second Senior Southerner, the venerable Carl Vinson of Georgia, stood loyally by Rayburn, only one other of Georgia's ten Representatives voted with him. But Administration odds had improved. Instead of the twenty or so Southern votes the Democratic leadership had averaged the year before, the Rayburn resolution drew 36 of the 99 sons of the South. And 22 Republicans defected from the Halleck side—most of them from urban areas, 17 of them from states Kennedy carried in 1960.

Rayburn refused to gloat before the TV cameras when he came off the floor, beaming. Smith remarked that he had done his "damnedest" and it was "all baloney."

AFTER THE SHOWDOWN

"We won the battle by five votes," Larry O'Brien remarked to an interviewer some time after the Rules victory in the House. "I often wonder what would have happened if we had lost by one vote."

Surely the President could have delivered on even fewer Democratic pledges than he did in the first session of his first Congress. For after Rayburn named three supposedly "reliable" new Democrats, Representatives Carl Elliott of Alabama, Thomas P. O'Neill, Jr., of Massachusetts, and B. F. Sisk of California, to the Rules Committee, it took on a new docility. Of four major Democratic measures it had delayed or blocked in the 86th Congress, the Rules Committee held up only one—the school bill—in 1961. That need not have occurred if Mr. Rayburn had had the heart to insist on the full measure of his victory. At the crucial point, after winning control of the expanded Rules Committee, House leaders did not insist on adopting new rules of procedure that would have limited the power of the Chairman to run the Rules Committee. The result was that Mr. Smith used the old rules to help the Catholics in his committee hold up the aid-to-education bill while they dickered to include parochial schools in it, thus insuring the measure's final defeat. The other Kennedy priority bills went through the Rules Committee without delay and were passed, constituting a major part of the Administration's claim to a successful first session.

There had been more than bravura to Representative Bolling's response to questions about the Democratic loss in the Congressional elections: "I'll swap 21 votes any day for the powers of the Presidency." The Rules Committee incident showed the difference White House support can make in the fortunes of the party in power in Congress. And out of the rumble over rules a real political combat team began to emerge.

Larry O'Brien had been remarkably effective in his first performance on Capitol Hill. A public-relations man, steeped in Massachusetts politics from boyhood but new to national politics and newer still to Congress and the Federal Government, O'Brien quickly mastered the fundamentals of his new job as lobbyist-in-chief.

The President, it appeared, could be counted on for active duty on the Hill. On a single day, at the climax of the Rules fight, Kennedy personally telephoned floor leaders three times to check on the effect of the phone calls he and others in the Administration were making.

When the smoke cleared, it became apparent that there was unusual solidarity among House Democrats. "The best coordinated fight ever," said a lobbyist on Rayburn's side. Rayburn aides like Albert and Bolling, who could reach into both liberal and conservative camps, the Southern moderates, and the liberal Democratic Study Group were still on friendly terms after the unique experience of working smoothly together on the Rules issue.

With so august a Southerner as Carl Vinson deserting the Howard Smith team to support the President on the Rayburn resolution, was it too much to hope that the gain in Southern votes registered on that test might become permanent? "When we landed Uncle Carl, half the battle was won," a liberal Democrat was to say later in summarizing accomplishments in the first session. Clearly, venerable Mr. Vinson enjoyed the role of independent loyalist in that first encounter; the special praise he received from Atlanta newspapers for his part did not hurt. A Vinson aide explains that Kennedy's office, when he was a Representative from Massachusetts, was down the hall from Mr. Vinson's. "They used to walk over to the House chamber together, and Uncle Carl became quite fond of Jack. Now he feels he should do all he can to help this young man succeed." If Vinson continued to support the President, other, less secure, Southerners might consider it safe to do so, too.

The victory spirit was still high when O'Brien invited Bolling down to the White House for another arithmetic session with his legislative staff. Together they began to count the votes they thought they had or could get for the five other pieces of legislation the President classed as of "special importance." Some fast figuring proved that the Administration team had played over their heads in this first test match. They had held nothing in reserve and could not hope to repeat that bare win for every item on the President's list. In fact, as things stood, housing seemed to be the only one of his priority measures that could command a natural majority. Beyond that, it would be a matter of creating a new coalition every time. Depressed-areas legislation, according to the figures, would be easier to pass than a minimum-wage bill, and a higher minimum wage would be easier to push through than medical care for the aged or school aid. The White House had cause for concern about the outlook for the Kennedy program.

February advanced into March, and Congress did little. The First Family had captivated the country's imagination during the Inauguration and held it in the weeks that followed, but Republicans in Congress made it clear that they were not bewitched. The Republican leaders, Senator Dirksen and Representative Halleck, were in no hurry to be about the new President's business. Republican assignments to committees were not completed until mid-February, six weeks after Congress convened, and committee hearings and reports were therefore far behind schedule. To Administration supporters, Congress was a general source of despair as the new government went into its third month.

James Reston of the New York *Times* journeyed to the Midwest to see how things looked from that area. Writing from Chicago in early March, he reported:

The most interesting paradox in America today is that while President Kennedy's personal popularity is rising, the opposition to his legislative program is rising too.

The mail on Capitol Hill is running heavily against the Kennedy program. The unorganized voters who sense the need for change are not writing, but the organized mail is pouring in. . . . As things are now going, Kennedy may very well win the popularity contest and lose his program. . . .

At this rate, the transformation of our society he has been talking about isn't going to take place—not, that is, unless he can personally mobilize the spirit of change that obviously exists here by carrying the battle beyond the Congress to the country.

Was Reston right? Must the President, at the very beginning of his term, prove the power of moral leadership by going over the heads of Congress? True, Kennedy had said during his campaign that what the country needed was "a President willing and able to summon his national constituency to its finest hour—to alert the people to our dangers and opportunities." But suppose "moral leadership" failed to work for John F. Kennedy at his particular moment in history? Suppose he called and the people didn't come, and he suffered from overexposure trying to rally them? Certainly Congress would not take kindly to being pressured. What he now knew about the Congo, Cuba, Laos, and Berlin strongly suggested to the new President that he would need all the friendly understanding he could build up in Congress. And, finally, if one began with last-resort exhortations, would not the future seem a constant anticlimax? Suppose a greater crisis came?

President Kennedy had heard a story Franklin D. Roosevelt, Jr., told about his father:

I remember when I was in Charlottesville before the war and my father refused to submit a Civil Rights bill to Congress and I went up to see him and I argued with him. This was a point of principle. And what he told me then was that he was President, not of a section of a country, but of the whole United States. And, whatever he did, he had to look not only at the now of the situation, but at the country, two, four, six years from then.

Well, he said he had the feeling that somehow we might be involved in a war, and it was his main job to get the country ready and properly prepared for it. To do that he would need the support of the South. And the civil rights issue would just cut them off from him at this time. And you remember what happened, the draft bill squeaked in by one vote.

Before he carried the battle beyond Congress to the country, President Kennedy decided, he would give the country more time to carry the word to Congress. The members would go home for the Easter recess soon. Wait and see if what they heard and saw quickened any pulses. Surely it was only practical first to find out how far he could advance his program by conventional political warfare and the traditional techniques of blarney, bludgeon, and boodle.

THE NEXT PRIORITIES

That decided, the Administration's strategists got back to work on plans for passing the first five priorities in the President's program. The first of the five scheduled to come before the House was the bill to raise minimum wages from $1.00 to $1.25 per hour and increase the number of workers to whom the law applied. The Democrats had long supported the proposal in principle and now urged it as one counteraction to the current recession.

The number of votes the Administration could count on in this case, the "guess book" indicated, would be about the same as it had been at the start on the Rules fight—30 votes too few. The principal source of opposition was the same, too. When the House had voted on a minimum-wage bill similar to the President's the year before, 80 of the 99 Southern Democrats had voted against it, as well as ten border and Midwestern Democrats. The House delegations from Mississippi, South Carolina, and Virginia were a hundred per cent opposed, and those from Tennessee, Florida, and Texas, only slightly less so. Only 27 Republicans were in favor.

The arithmetic seemed the same as before; and O'Brien had

proved that he could count noses and round up strays with the
best. But the problem this time was different—how to design a bill
as close to the President's recommendations as possible that would
be acceptable to a sufficient number of members to get it past the
Labor Committee and then through the House.

To experienced legislators, this is a classic and familiar problem,
but most of the members of the House in the 87th Congress had
never served with a Democratic President, and most of the White
House staff lacked experience on the Hill. Consequently, the bill
that was allowed to come out of committee did not take into account enough of the objections to the Administration's original
proposal to win over a majority of the House.

Three powerful groups were combined in opposition—laundry
owners, restaurant owners, and retail merchants. All three cat-
egories were exempt from the Fair Labor Standards Act. If Administration changes were approved, workers in these industries
would be among the 4.3 million additional Americans whose jobs
would come under minimum-wage protection. Well-financed and
well-organized lobbies representing these and other interested
parties were bearing down on Capitol Hill, and individual laundry
men, café owners, and storekeepers were writing and phoning
their individual Congressmen to insist that they save them from
increased wage costs.

To the experienced legislative eye, it was clear from the first that
at some point the Administration's original proposal would have to
be scaled down if any of it was to be saved. But the Congressional
liaison team from the White House was expert on votes, not on
legislative drafting, and Secretary of Labor Goldberg, who had
known Capitol Hill intimately as counsel for international unions
interested in legislation, was still adjusting himself to his new relationship with the Hill, while Representative James Roosevelt of
California was handicapped as floor manager of the bill by the un-
fortunate and undeserved lack of standing he enjoyed in the
House—the House hierarchy, with whom a deal would have to be
struck, did not recognize Roosevelt as an equal with whom they
were willing to bargain.

Meanwhile, labor's lobby—together with Secretary Goldberg
and the Executive organization, O'Brien's team and the liberal
bloc—were pushing as hard for the Administration's bill as they
had for the Rayburn resolution on rules. The preliminary check
had shown a deficit of 25 to 30 votes. Combined pressure for
Kennedy's side had switched an estimated 15 to 16 votes. But the
last hard count still showed the Administration bill losing, 208 to

224. What was the wise thing to do now? Take a licking on the House vote and take a chance on going to conference with the Senate and coming back to the House with an improved bill that could be passed the second time? Or make a last effort to avoid the first licking?

Operating on the general instruction that his job is to get as close to what the President wants from Congress as he can, O'Brien favored retreat. Rumors circulated that the White House was willing to take a drastically different bill that Mr. Vinson had introduced as an alternative. It accepted the Administration's first-stage rise of 15¢ per hour in the $1.00 minimum wage, but brought in only 1.6 million of the 4.3 million additional workers the Administration sought to include. Actually, the Administration was not ready to concede that much; but it wouldn't hurt to negotiate. Secretary Goldberg, already running up a high score as a Presidential trouble shooter, asked Mr. Vinson for an appointment. Adam Clayton Powell, Jr., Chairman of the Labor Committee, Representative Roosevelt, Larry O'Brien, and Assistant Labor Secretary Jerry Holleman went along.

Word spread around the Capitol that Powell and Roosevelt had accepted the Vinson version. Liberal members, who considered Powell and Roosevelt their leaders, were again in an uproar. The Administration hastily drafted Representative Albert to sponsor an alternative bill that moved in Vinson's direction, but not very far. Vinson held out until the Administration gave in. The minimum-wage bill really should have a "laundry amendment," everyone now agreed. Another nose count was taken on the assumption that exemption of 180,000 home laundry workers would be added to the concessions the Administration had already made.

That final step backward, the count showed, would win back Democrats from Florida, North Carolina, and Tennessee, and about half the Texas delegation. (More than one hundred Texas trade unionists were in Washington at that moment for a building-trades legislative meeting, largely devoted to lobbying for the minimum-wage bill. When the vote came, 11 of Texas' 21 votes went for the bill; 18 had gone against substantially the same proposal in 1960.)

Theoretically, the compromise bill was finally set to go sailing through. "From then on," as one of the pragmatists who put together this package of practical idealism explains, "things went as planned—except that we lost." By a single vote.

In their concern to corral the Southerners, floor managers for the bill had failed to keep their eyes out for other straying sheep.

As the President was to say on a later, blacker day, "There are from this episode useful lessons for us all to learn." At least eight avid supporters of the bill were straying around the Capitol—signing mail, drinking beer, or, in the case of two Northern Democrats, just chatting together in a downstairs corridor—when the fatal teller vote was being taken on the floor.

"Liberals are lousy legislators," one House veteran remarked sadly. "When the House is meeting in Committee of the Whole, a member has to be on the floor or no farther away than the Speaker's lobby in case the opposition tries to slip through voice votes or quick amendments. The conservatives all seem to know that, but many of the liberals are so happy 'ivory-towering' it in their offices that they lose count of time and pay no attention to the Whips when they are called."

Labor learned that there is a limit to its influence with friends among the city Republicans. About twenty of those who had promised to support the Administration bill ducked when the test came on a teller vote, with no recorded roll call. Only three Republicans were to be seen on the Democratic side when the two lines formed in the center aisle of the House to march past the tellers—Chester E. Merrow of New Hampshire, and Paul A. Fino and Seymour Halpern of New York.

But, coming when it did, early in the session, this loss may have done more for Kennedy's program than a gain would have done. "It scared everybody stiff," one Democratic leader said a week later. The common excuse among Democrats was "Our Whips just didn't whip hard enough," and there was talk of changing the whole system. But a member who makes a point of knowing about such things reported privately at the time that "The big flap the defeat caused about the Whip system was totally undeserved. The fact is that we not only had the regular Whips doing more than ever, but a special Democratic Study Group Whip system going as well, and labor at the same time working a man-to-man operation of its own to be sure that everybody was there.

"What it comes down to is the need for self-discipline and responsibility. There is no Whip system on earth that can make certain everybody is there unless everybody is, in part, his own Whip."

All in all, the net loss was small. The coalition substitute the House passed after defeating the patched-together Administration measure was changed again in the direction of Kennedy's original proposal by the Senate. And in May, after a few compromises in Conference Committee, the House concurred in the Senate version —which gives wage-hour protection to four million more workers, and is the first extension of the Fair Labor Standards Act since 1938.

In the days immediately after the minimum-wage debacle, one could sense, from talking with members and watching them together on the floor, a new resolve in the House to "straighten up and fly right." When the next of Kennedy's "important" bills came to the floor, the difference was almost comic. "I never saw so many Democrats running around trying to make sure that everybody else was there too," one veteran said. The antics of the Illinois Democrats, some of whose members had been among the missing on the day of the minimum-wage showdown, did not stand out in a House ahum with activity. With veteran Representative Thomas J. O'Brien in the lead, they marched as a body into the House and took seats together until time for the vote. When the tellers took their places at the head of the aisle, O'Brien signaled his men to rise and follow him through the "yea" side of the line. Beside the tellers stood the Illinois Whips with their lists, checking off every name until all Illinois Democrats were present and accounted for. Then the checkers checked their own names and marched solemnly past the tellers.

The result of this new self-discipline, and sterling work by O'Brien and Henry Hall Wilson, Jr., of the White House, was 25 to 30 more votes than the Democrats had been able to roll up in two previous efforts to pass the same bill.

By early May, when the compromise on minimum wages had gone through and when Congress had approved the full $600,000,-000 appropriation the Administration had asked to launch the Alliance for Progress, columnists were speculating on why the President was doing so well and warning the Administration against overconfidence. Castro and Laos had helped. Before Cuba crashed the headlines, it was not thought at all likely that Congress would feel so warmly toward aid to Latin America or so sympathetic toward a beleaguered President's request for support domestically. Here Congress was catching the rhythm of the Gallup Poll.

In that atmosphere, using basically the same methods and the strong backing of Mr. Rayburn, the Administration maneuvered programs for depressed-areas development and housing through both the House and the Senate. One of the founding fathers of the conservative coalition, Senator Karl E. Mundt of South Dakota, did not hesitate to call a spade a bulldozer. "It is obvious this coalition is not effective in the current Congress," he wrote in his regular letter to constituents. "Why? The blunt answer appears to be that the Southern wing of this coalition has been shot at and badly hit by a White House double-barreled gun, with one barrel labeled 'Political Patronage' and the other 'Political Pressure.'

"The combined votes of Southern conservatives and Northern non-urban Republicans, which from 1940 to 1960 won victory after victory . . . no longer functions effectively."

THE KENNEDY TREATMENT

Mundt's surrender was premature, but at the time his side did have cause for concern. Kennedy's conventional weapons seemed adequate to the limited war for limited objectives that he had chosen to fight with Congress in his first year. He had made his gains by accommodating his program to the coalition—shaving down requests until a sufficient number of the opposition were willing to settle for the compromise. It is a technique that requires time and patience. Fortunately, President Kennedy likes politics and all the little things that go with practicing the art of the possible.

First of all, Mr. Kennedy charmed the senior members of Congress, as he had charmed three elderly ex-Presidents before them. Mr. Rayburn told a TV interviewer after the election that he remembered Representative Kennedy as a skinny, sallow-faced youngster who didn't show any particular promise. After a few White House meetings, he waxed enthusiastic in private praise of the young President's intelligence and good sense. The good opinion Mr. Truman passed around on the Hill after he had the honor of being the new President's first White House caller helped. But it was the sincere deference with which Mr. Kennedy asked their advice that won over many venerable House committee chairmen (eleven of the twenty-one were from the South).

Of course, some good feeling had been generated in the South by an early increase in price supports for Southern cotton and by award of a number of defense contracts to Southern plants such as the $1,000,000 order that went to the Georgia plant of Lockheed Aircraft. "Uncle Carl" Vinson made many suggestions in various compromise negotiations. One of them, to double the amount of rural aid provided for in the depressed-areas bill, produced the necessary votes for passage. (A map demonstrating that gravy would definitely go to Dixie was freely circulated on the floor during debate.)

One Saturday afternoon in blossomtime the President found time to go over by helicopter to Harry Byrd's Virginia apple orchard and eat fried chicken with 150 of the Senator's neighbors. During the six weeks before that, he had invited groups of Congressmen to the White House almost every Thursday at 5:30 for coffee and a little socializing with the First Family. And back in mid-March, Mr. Kennedy had begun having what were described as "long confidential talks" with the most powerful members of Congress. His tactic, as one of Kennedy's newspaper friends expressed it, was to "use the carrot more than the stick"; but if that didn't work, to be prepared to "show his teeth a little."

The first "confidential talks" were with the chairmen of committees, including the flamboyant minister of Harlem's Grace Church, Representative Adam Clayton Powell. As Chairman of the House Committee on Education and Labor, Mr. Powell could play an important part in Kennedy's plans. Mr. Powell emerged from their meeting with new fire. Up to now, he admitted, he had had a "do nothing" record as a member of Congress. He had not even been a conscientious Tuesday-to-Thursday Congressman, as are so many Representatives from states within weekend commuting distance of Washington. But that had been because there was no incentive when the Chairman of the Labor Committee was Graham A. Barden of North Carolina who scarcely acknowledged the existence of a New York Negro.

The President had pushed the right button. Mr. Powell was propelled, temporarily at least, into action on the New Frontier. He swiftly reorganized the Labor Committee to outflank the power of Representative Phil M. Landrum of Georgia—as deadly a peril to the Administration as Howard Smith.

There were 4,000 non-Civil Service jobs to distribute and a hundred Federal Judgeships, 73 of them newly created. The rate at which the jobs were filled was slow until the big five of Kennedy's priority bills for the first session were law.

And then there was the "blandishing" of Everett M. Dirksen. John F. Kennedy's old friend from their days together on the Senate Labor Committee was now the Republican Leader. He was also the senior star of the long-running Ev and Charlie Show, on camera weekly from the Capitol; and he got off to a rousing start in his commentary on the new Administration by asserting that President Kennedy's first State of the Union Message had all the impact "of a snowflake on the bosom of the Potomac." Toward midnight of the longest day of the longest session of Congress in ten years, just before adjournment, Minority Leader Dirksen rose. He thanked Majority Leader Mansfield for thanking *him* for coming to the rescue of the Democratic President's foreign-aid program. Then he revealed that his main purpose in rising was to disclaim that he had "gone soft on Kennedyism."

"It has been said," Dirksen began, "that the President of the United States has undertaken to exercise some blandishments on the Minority Leader. Well, it intrigues me somewhat, because blandishments, after a sustained and almost continuous period of twenty-eight years in the national legislature, have no particular impact on me." Nevertheless, Senator Dirksen could hardly plead Not Guilty to helping the President. On September 9, after Congress closed, Majority Leader Mansfield told a national television audience that Minority Leader Dirksen had been a "tower of strength" on foreign policy, "tolerant and cooperative."

As Democratic leader, Senator Mansfield was soon running a happy ship. There was little clamor for the good old days under L.B.J. There was time for things that formerly the Senate never dreamed of. "In the gentlemanly hours between noon and tea time," one daily chronicler of Senate doings reported in July, "the Senate processes the President's programs so effortlessly that the papers find it hardly worth reporting."

Mansfield's method was what he called a "dispersal of responsibility." The men who ran the committees knew more about the bills they had handled than he did, the Leader declared, and he made a policy of putting them in charge when the measures they had processed reached the floor. In Johnson's time there had been but one leader, and his name was Lyndon. Now, though Mansfield shared the work and the limelight, it was a group matter. And his way proved popular. A loyal Johnson follower explained why: "Under Mike, I guess all of us feel a little bigger."

There was never much love lost between Johnson and strong-minded individualists like Senators Wayne Morse and Paul Douglas. And when they gained the floor for an extended presentation in Johnson's day, the Senate could usually be sure of some kind of fireworks. Mansfield designated Morse as Floor Manager for the Aid to Education Bill and assigned Douglas to maneuver the Depressed Areas Bill through the Senate. All was peace, poise, and calm.

A New York *Times* man in the Press Gallery caught the change in mood: "The slashing personal attacks from the floor, the rollicking eruptions of late-night scenes, the open horse-trading and personal vendettas that made the Senate a cockpit of drama have almost disappeared.

"In its place is the bland, new throw-away style of the corporation board room heavy with understatement, dully efficient, disdaining debate and bombast and even the surgical stroke of wit."

Life wasn't really all that dull for President Kennedy's troops in the Senate. After all, around any corner one might bump into Hubert Humphrey, who moves fast and is always popping another vitamin pill into his mouth to make him move a little faster. As the new Majority Whip, succeeding Mansfield, Humphrey quickly won a partnership status with the Majority Leader that Mansfield had never had with Johnson. As a liberal Democrat put it after four months of the new regime in the Senate, "Mike Mansfield is a fine, sweet, lovable guy. But when you want to get something done in the Senate nowadays, you go to Hubert." Another remarked, "The way Hubert wheels and deals, he reminds you of Lyndon." The *Wall Street Journal* observed that Senator Mansfield appeared to have split his Majority Leader duties with Humphrey. And the *Journal* reporter, Robert Novak, illustrated the Johnson-like part Humphrey was playing by telling the story of how the opposing tides within the Democratic party over depressed-areas legislation were persuaded to stand still.

Business spokesmen wanted the administration of the proposed redevelopment program placed under the Commerce Department where the business point of view traditionally has had considerable influence; liberal and labor spokesmen wanted it placed anywhere but in Commerce. Liberals wanted to make operations flexible by authorizing financing of the program directly through the Treasury; traditionalists insisted that there must be annual appropriations by Congress. Senator Paul Douglas, Floor Manager for the Administration bill, took the liberal side of the argument. The respected Senior Senator from Arkansas, William Fulbright, differed and could, it appeared, carry sufficient weight to sink the bill unless there was a meeting of minds. Here was a situation obviously made for Johnson, the great persuader. But apparently it was made for Humphrey, too. Why not, he suggested to Douglas, give in to Fulbright on Commerce Department control in return for his support of Treasury financing? By the *Wall Street Journal's* account, "When Senator Douglas demurred at conducting such horse trading, the Whip assured him: 'I'll bargain for you. I'm not so pure.' Bargain he did, and successfully; the Senate accepted the compromise with a minimum of fuss."

Unquestionably, Humphrey's talents were in the grand Senatorial tradition, and Mansfield and he together stood to make a strong record in putting through the President's program. But their greatest advantage was that they had their party leader in the

White House and his powerful backing for their efforts on his behalf. As someone put it, Mansfield and Humphrey had all the problems of a man sitting in the driver's seat of a big new limousine, headed down a straight superhighway with no other traffic in sight.

That open road, Mansfield's soothing ways with the Democrats, Humphrey's wheeling and dealing, the new Democratic group leadership, the President's blandishing of Senator Dirksen and his determination to be friendly with influential Democratic committee chairmen—Senator Robert Kerr who dominates three Senate committees, Finance, Space, and Public Works, rated a personal visit from the President to his Oklahoma ranch—all combined to produce a remarkable batting average for the administration in the Senate.

The Senate approved most of the President's requests without much delay or change, including the authorization of direct Treasury borrowing to finance development loans for foreign assistance and an acceptable public-school finance bill.

THE CHURCH AND THE SCHOOLS

The House was another matter. It was the end of August before the House had a chance to express itself on aid to education. By that time, the unaccustomed unity and drive that had produced Democratic successes in the early months of the first Kennedy session had all but disappeared. Speaker Rayburn, weakened by what was then diagnosed as lumbago, had manfully declared for Kennedy's bill providing funds for school construction and teachers' salaries, but one of Rayburn's followers was not speaking for himself alone when he remarked that the Speaker "never had been for aid for salaries and I don't believe he really is this time either." Spokesmen for the National Education Association developed a proprietary interest in the original bill, which blocked reasonable compromise. The Catholic hierarchy had turned Majority Leader McCormack and the Catholic Democratic members of the House Rules Committee against the Administration bill for public-school financing. And the efforts of Secretary Ribicoff, his Health, Education, and Welfare lawyers, and the White House legislative staff to reach a compromise on the Church-State issue resulted in a bitterness and confusion that doomed the bill.

In 1960 an aid-to-education bill similar to the one the President proposed to the 87th Congress had passed both House and Senate, only to wind up in the Rules Committee pigeonhole. Some of the members who had voted for the bill had been defeated in the 1960 elections, but lobbyists for the aid bill calculated that this loss would be more than offset by the votes of Southern Democrats who had meanwhile shifted their support to the measure. They counted close to 70 of the 99 Southern Democrats on their side as the session began. But when the vote came on the vastly weakened proposal that finally emerged, only 32 of the 99 Southerners still stood with the President. Unbiased observers believe that the vast majority of those who fell away—and they weren't all Southerners—did so because of the religious issue and the equivocation of the President's men. "A month ago," one Western liberal was quoted as saying the day before the vote, "I was willing to die for the education bill. But there's been so much maneuvering and so much controversy that I don't care what happens." And another Democrat remarked that "White House tactics have been so Machiavellian, so tortuous that it makes me sick."

Mr. Kennedy must have felt equally frustrated, but for a different reason. He had won a Presidential campaign in which he promised Federal support of public schools with complete separation of Church and State. (Kennedy had favored, Nixon had opposed, the inclusion of aid for teachers' salaries.) He had forced reform of the House Rules Committee to permit the keeping of that and other promises. And now the obduracy of leaders of his own church and the ineptitude of members of his own Administration were about to prevent it.

A month after his Inauguration, President Kennedy sent a message to Congress outlining his program for aid to education. None of the elementary or secondary school funds it would provide would be allocated for "constructing church schools or paying church school teachers' salaries," Mr. Kennedy pointed out, "in accordance with the clear prohibition of the Constitution." Three days later Archbishop Karl Joseph Alter of Cincinnati issued a statement on behalf of the Board of the National Catholic Welfare Conference. Speaking in the name of the Roman Catholic bishops of the United States, he said, "In the event that there is Federal aid to education, we are deeply convinced that in justice Catholic school children should be given the right to participate. Respecting the form of participation," he went on, "we hold it to be strictly within the framework of the Constitution that long-term, low-interest loans to private institutions could be part of the Federal aid program." In conclusion, the Archbishop made what many interpreted as an improper threat of interference. "In the event that a Federal aid program is enacted which excludes children in private schools, these children will be the victims of discriminatory legislation. There will be no alternative but to oppose such discrimination." That was generally taken to mean that if parochial schools were left out, the Catholic bishops would oppose the Federal-aid program.

It certainly seemed to be the way some strategically placed Catholics in Congress construed his meaning. Majority Leader McCormack began energetically promoting a special aid plan for private schools. Democratic Representatives James J. Delaney of New York and Thomas O'Neill of Massachusetts, previously in favor of Federal aid, quickly formed a coalition with five of their Republican colleagues in the Rules Committee to block the Administration school bill. And because the earlier Rules-reform drive had stopped before it was complete, the power of the Rules Committee Chairman was still great, and Representative Howard Smith, who instinctively opposes Federal aid for almost anything, was able to help the blockaders work their will and did. The education department of the National Catholic Welfare Conference went to work organizing the "opposition" to "discrimination" which Archbishop Alter had promised. By March, *Newsweek* magazine reported, the Catholic campaign against the bill had started rolling.

From N.C.W.C. Headquarters in the Capitol, pamphlets containing the Bishops' statements and other arguments were mailed by the thousands to parochial-school superintendents and to groups of Catholic laymen. Families were urged to write their Congressman. Thousands followed campaign advice to send pictures of their progeny along with the simple message: "Why doesn't my child count?"

"We darned near had a first-class holy war in my district," says one Congressman. "In the late Spring I began to be bombarded with letters. One letter compared Kennedy and me to Gomulka; we wanted to destroy religion." . . . As another member of the House put it, "Great slugs of form letters and yard-long petitions streaming across your desk aren't likely to be very persuasive in themselves. But they do alert you to the fact that something is cooking in your District."

The grass roots letter-writing campaign so unnerved many House members, in fact, that all they want now is to forget the whole thing. As one put it glumly last week: "You are wrong, whatever you do on a bill of this kind."

Why were the bishops making life so hard for one of their own? Mr. Kennedy himself seemed to raise the question when he remarked, but without rancor, that the matter of aid for parochial schools "was not made an issue in recent years until this time." Writing in *The Nation's Schools* at the height of the battle over the school bill in the House, Dr. Edgar Fuller, Executive Secretary of the influential Association of Chief State School Officers, offered one explanation: "In Washington, one often hears that the hierarchy is not holding out for parochial school aid primarily to borrow and build, but rather to develop a record of Federal-Church financial relationships to nurture precedents for constitutionality and eventually to substitute grants for loans. Such observers note that only a minor fraction of the funds available to Catholic schools have been claimed under the National Defense Education Act since 1958."

Would the hierarchy co-operate in finding a compromise? Secretary Ribicoff and some White House aides thought it essential to give them every opportunity. The relationship between Church and State was not a matter on which one could effect a give-and-take understanding with the Southerners, as O'Brien had learned to do from his experience with the minimum-wage and depressed-areas bills. As a Catholic, the President could hardly explore so sensitive an area personally. And in any case, at the time the school bill was pending, Mr. Kennedy was totally involved in deciding what was negotiable with Khrushchev in the Berlin crisis. The problem would have to be left to Ribicoff. Three times in three months, the Secretary of Health, Education, and Welfare shifted administration strategy on the school bill in the hope of finding the formula all could accept. And once he seemed to come close. Cardinal Francis Spellman himself indicated that the Constitutional distinctions the Administration was trying to draw between loans and grants might be an acceptable one. But what the Cardinal would concede, Congressman Delaney would not. And in the Rules Committee the Administration bill stayed.

On the basis of House reaction to Ribicoff's efforts at compromise, it would appear that the former Governor of the more than fifty per cent Catholic state of Connecticut did not reflect national thinking on what was negotiable with the Catholic hierarchy. There was as much disgust as disagreement in the 170 to 242 vote by which the House rejected a last-minute bill that Representative Frank Thompson, a leading school-aid supporter, patched together and Education Committee Chairman Adam Clayton Powell called up under the irregular Calendar Wednesday procedure. Following the action, Thompson said he saw "very little use to try again until after the next Presidential election because the forces against it are too great despite the proven need." President Kennedy told his news conference the next day that the defeat of Thompson's bill "indicates it would be difficult to find a satisfactory formula," but, he promised, "we will be back next year."

BLARNEY, BLUDGEON, AND BOODLE

Conventional political warfare succeeded for the Kennedy Administration when one of three other forces was present: Speaker Rayburn's personal prestige (which he laid on the line in the Rules Committee fight and subsequently); the continuing economic recession (which made it vastly easier to gain approval of domestic economic measures in the first months of the Administration); and Soviet hostility (which caused Congress to permit acceleration of military appropriations at lightning speed and institute three new projects—the Alliance for Progress, the Peace Corps, and the Disarmament and Arms Control Agency).

But without one or more of these elements of auxiliary power, blarney, bludgeon, and boodle were not strong enough to prevail. And so, in the closing months of the first Kennedy session, Congress got out of hand. The additional actions Kennedy wanted from Congress involved issues on which convictions were strong and ran against the Administration position. The House could not be manipulated into agreement on an aid-to-education bill when a majority of members felt that separation of Church and State was the core question. And, similarly, the Administration failed to carry the House when it was persuaded it would be abdicating Congressional authority to give the Executive Branch reorganization power over regulatory agencies, or the right to finance foreign-aid developments directly from Treasury funds. And this time there was no *deus ex machina* waiting in the wings.

The day after the losing vote on the school-aid bill, Mr. Rayburn went home to Texas, never to return. The economy turned upward in the spring, and Khrushchev withdrew his December deadline on Berlin.

Republican support for Administration bills fell off sharply. (Mansfield could still count on 12 to 16 Republican votes on most roll calls in the Senate, but in the House in late August only 6 of the 174 Republicans supported the school-aid compromise.) Democratic liberals had not shown great force. Former leaders of the Democratic Study Group, Lee Metcalf and Stuart Udall, who had gone on to the Senate and Cabinet, were much missed. The Democratic leadership, minus Rayburn, was flabby. How flabby, former Representative Udall helped to demonstrate. When House leaders told the now Secretary of Interior that they did not have the votes to put through his cherished bill authorizing construction of Federal power lines in the upper Colorado Basin, Udall refused to accept defeat. On the first count, the Administration was 28 votes behind. Udall rounded up pro-public-power Southerners from Tennessee Valley Authority states, and Rural Electrification Administration officials worked on Western Representatives, and the bill passed with 41 votes to spare.

It was not only the Democratic Whips who could not count. Speaker *pro tempore* John McCormack, presiding over the final all-night session before adjournment, reported standing votes adding up to less than a quorum, something a proper presiding officer never does by accident, regardless of the number of empty seats facing him. And the confusion and disorder that prevailed with McCormack in the chair threatened to disrupt proceedings entirely.

But when it was all over, and the House had outraged the Senate by adjourning and going home (at 4:20 A.M. on September 26) without a by-your-leave, there was a good deal to which the Kennedy Administration could point with pride. Speaking for the Democratic Senatorial candidate in New Jersey in November 1961, the President recalled that when he had been there in his own behalf in September 1960, he had talked about the need for a "decent" minimum wage, better Social Security and unemployment insurance, and a real attack on slum housing, polluted rivers, and depressed areas.

"In 1960, every one of those bills had been stopped, stymied or vetoed," he said. "Today, every one of them has been passed."

"Now we are making progress," Mr. Kennedy went on. "And there is no disputing the fact that this progress in these ten months has been helped by harmonious cooperation between a Democratic Congress and Democratic Administration."

They could expect, in the future, Mr. Kennedy told his New Jersey audience, that the Administration would lead the way to medical care for the aged under Social Security in the 1962 session of Congress—"That is a must for next year." So, he subsequently told meetings of business and labor, was a new international-trade bill to permit the President to negotiate reductions in tariffs where needed.

Would the "harmonious cooperation" of 1961, about which Mr. Kennedy boasted in New Jersey, continue in 1962? Medical care and trade were issues more analogous to support for public schools

and foreign aid than to the issues with which the Administration
had had success in the first session of Congress. Strong convictions
would again stand in the way of compromises on those two measures, as well as on tax reform, the other top item on Kennedy's
"must" list of legislation for the second year—in preparation for
the midterm Congressional elections.

Certainly, the problems that had been most vexing to the President in dealing with Congress would not fly away. The House
would continue to dominate the Congress by its power of veto over
the Senate. The South would continue to dominate the House by
means of the seniority of its members on committees and the majority power it could exercise in coalition with nonurban Republicans. The new leadership to be installed in the House as a result
of Mr. Rayburn's death was bound to be weak for some time to
come. Accustomed to having Mr. Rayburn at the helm, the House
would take a while to adjust to whatever pace the new Speaker
and Majority Leader set; more important, after years of Rayburn
dominance, the House would no doubt try for a little of the relaxa-
tion the Senate began to enjoy after Lyndon Johnson and his
ferocious energy moved to the other side of the street. The split in
the Democratic Party would remain the central fact of political
life for the man in the White House. And that split would almost
surely widen as Democratic conservatives proceeded to test the
mettle of the new men in charge of working the Administration's
will on the Hill.

Close study of the record showed that Administration blandishments had made inroads on the conservative coalition in the Senate
—in 1961 the coalition won in less than half the roll calls where
it came into play, as compared to sixty-six per cent in the last
Eisenhower Congress. But House records told a different story. A
postadjournment study by *Congressional Quarterly* revealed that
in seventy per cent of the 1961 roll calls where the coalition appeared, it won—a rise in power from the last Eisenhower Congress when the percentage of coalition victories in the House had
been fifty-seven per cent. And, although the worst immediate damage the coalition inflicted was in defeating school aid and restrict-
ing foreign aid, its potential threat to the whole Kennedy program
was all too obvious.

An analysis of Congressional roll calls in 1961 in which a majority of voting Southern Democrats joined a majority of voting
Republicans to oppose the position taken by a majority of voting
Northern Democrats showed that the President's party is divided
on many key issues: civil rights, depressed areas, temporary un-

employment compensation, minimum wage, school aid, housing, foreign aid, Mexican farm labor, election reform. And think how that list could grow in the remaining three years of Kennedy's term.

Given all this, was there some better immediate strategy for dealing with the House than the one the President followed in the first session?

The answer seems to be no—as long as the proportion of rural to urban-minded Representatives remains so high. The differences between a slightly-left-of-center Democratic President and a Senate of the same party have diminished as the size of the city vote has increased. More and more Senators owe their election to the same constituency that elected the President and are bound by the same considerations on legislation. *Congressional Quarterly* finds that conservative-coalition victories in the Senate are now highly dependent on help from a Northern Democratic minority because the full theoretical strength of the coalition is only 59 of the 100 votes in the Senate. But in the House in 1961 the coalition's full strength, according to the same analysis, could reach 285, or 65 per cent of the 437 House votes. And that picture will not change materially until some way is found to force the rural politicians who control most state legislatures to reapportion Congressional districts fairly.

There was no obvious short cut to building a working majority for the Kennedy Democrats in the House. Conceivably, they could add to their number by the 1962 elections—although they would be bucking the tradition that the Presidential party in power loses seats in its midterm test at the polls. But the President's vast general popularity and the fact that he intends to campaign personally all across the country held out the hope that his Congressional strength would increase in 1963. If Kennedy were to gain firm control in Congress before his four years are up, however, it would apparently have to be by the strategy with which he began his term as President.

Mr. Kennedy's aim then was to preempt the center, as Thruston B. Morton, then Republican National Chairman, sadly pointed out at the time. If Kennedy could draw in the Rockefeller Republicans and win back the Democrats he lost on the religious issue in 1960, he would be set, barring catastrophes one could not anticipate. That meant conveying a strong sense of his own moderation, avoiding at all cost the tags of "big spender," "fiscal irresponsible," or "union lover." That course would antagonize some, but it should win over more.

In early February, less than two weeks after Kennedy's Inauguration, Walter Lippmann thought he could see where logic was leading the new President, who prides himself more than anything else on being effective politically. "The center in American political life is an enormous majority of the people," Mr. Lippmann pointed out, "and the party which controls the center is virtually unbeatable."

The Republicans controlled it most of the time from the Civil War to the Taft-Roosevelt Schism of 1912. The Democrats controlled it from the Great Depression to the Korean War. Eisenhower had a chance to take command of it and to inaugurate a new Republican era. But he did not know how to go about it.

"But this young man Kennedy," Lippmann concluded, "understands perfectly the meaning of the center. He intends to lead it, and he knows how to go about doing it."

The first year suggests that the last sentence was accurate prophecy.

· IV ·

Attorney General Bobby

"Dammit, Bobby, comb your hair," the President-elect remarked as he turned toward the door to face the newsmen gathered on the sidewalk outside his Georgetown home. John F. Kennedy was about to announce the appointment of Robert F. Kennedy as Attorney General of the United States. Bobby obediently smoothed his locks before they went out together to meet the press with news that would make nepotism a byword in the papers for days to come.

The choice of his brother for this sensitive job, by far the most controversial of Kennedy's Cabinet appointments, apparently was one of his first and firmest decisions. The Senator initially broached the idea of the Attorney Generalship to his campaign manager at Hyannis Port soon after election day. Bobby, it seems, demurred, went away for a rest, thought it over, and still resisted the assignment. His inclination immediately after the election, the younger Kennedy told friends, was to get out of Government entirely for a while, travel around the world, perhaps write about what he saw for the newspapers. But his father discouraged that—why run away from the only field in which he had experience simply because his brother was now President? He thought then of going into the Department of Defense to get the lagging missile program moving, or into the Department of State in a Milton S. Eisenhower kind of role, trouble shooting around the world. Those jobs would attract less attention and perhaps muffle the cries of nepotism, but how would a Secretary of Defense or a Secretary of State like having the President's younger brother looking over his shoulder?

Discussing Bobby's concern about the possible damage to his Administration from criticism of a Cabinet appointment for his brother, the President-elect reportedly remarked that Bobby had

to realize that the criticism would die down as his value became
apparent.

When his brother began to press hard for an answer, Bobby
went outside his family for advice. On a single day he consulted
Eisenhower's Attorney General, William Pierce Rogers, Supreme
Court Justice William O. Douglas, his former boss, Senator John
L. McClellan, and J. Edgar Hoover. Only Hoover really urged
him to accept.

At dinner in Palm Beach a few nights later, the younger Kennedy told his brother no. The next morning at breakfast, the accepted story goes, the older brother told Bobby his mind was made
up, he wanted to hear no more about it—Bobby was going to be
Attorney General.

Why was the President so insistent? Later events suggest that
he knew how much he would want to rely on Bobby and foresaw
that it would be simpler all around to place him in the front rank
in his Administration. Below-Cabinet status for his top adviser
would create the problems Roosevelt and Wilson had in relation
to Hopkins and House. It would be simpler to deal with worries
over nepotism now than complaints about his brother's behind-
the-scenes role later. The answer was to give Bobby a place in the
Cabinet, with access to information and participation in decisions
at the highest level.

But was the President's 35-year-old brother the man to put in
charge of the United States Department of Justice? Some strong
Kennedy supporters thought not. Perhaps the sharpest condemna-
tion of the appointment came from Professor Alexander Bickel
of Yale Law School who wrote in the *New Republic,* which had
come out for J.F.K. before Los Angeles, that "Robert F. Kennedy
is not fit for the office." Analysis of Bobby Kennedy's role as Chief
Counsel of the McClellan Investigating Committee convinced Professor Bickel that "Mr. Kennedy appears to find congenial the role
of prosecutor, judge and jury, all consolidated in his one efficient
person." . . .

No doubt he sought to serve the public interest as he saw it. The
question is merely how truly he sees it. And the answer on the record
is that he has tunnel vision; he sees the public interests in terms of
ends with little appreciation of the significance of means. . . . The
meaning of due process, of the adversary process of accusation and
defense before judges disinterested in the immediate outcome, is that
the Government suffers itself to concede it possible that it may be
wrong. Mr. Kennedy's assured righteousness is in vivid contrast. . .

The Attorney General of the United States is the nation's chief

aw officer. More than any other executive officer he is required to
uffer himself not to "know" all the things Mr. Kennedy is certain of.
More than any other executive officer, he is required to regard means
is above ends, process above result. The Attorney General exercises
he only civilian control over the F.B.I., whose vast files contain much
inprocessed "knowledge." He presides as a judge—very often as a
ourt of last resort—over myriad deportation cases. He decides in
incontrolled discretion whom to prosecute and when, and that is a
uasi-judicial function.

Walter Lippmann, for once missing the point, assumed that
3obby had been named to the Cabinet "for the same reason that
'arley was placed in Roosevelt's Cabinet, Hannegan in Truman's,
3rownell and Summerfield in Eisenhower's." He did not disap-
rove of rewarding a campaign manager with a Cabinet post, but
e doubted the wisdom of putting a politician in charge of the De-
artment of Justice. Lippmann was ready to concede that among
1ose who had worked closely with Bobby, there was "no ques-
on of his exceptional competence as an administrator and as a
iw enforcer." But he was reserving judgment: "There are some
ho say that he has not yet acquired a sufficiently highly refined
1d mellow sense of due process.

"We shall see."

THE PRESIDENT'S REASONS

But the President had special reasons for placing his brother in
at particular post. First, it was the only Cabinet position for
hich Bobby had any training or experience at all—he was a
wyer, he had served an apprenticeship in the Department of
istice soon after graduation from law school, and, as a result of
s racket-busting experience on Capitol Hill, he did understand
e menace of organized crime. In addition, the President had vast
spect for his brother's ability to master any job. "In planning,
tting the right people to work, and seeing that the job is done,"
told an interviewer a short time after Bobby's appointment, "he
the best man in the United States. That was the big difference
tween our campaign last fall and Adlai Stevenson's in 1956,"
r. Kennedy said. "I didn't have to worry about anything except
1at I was going to say, which was enough of a challenge. He
ngs the same aspects to the Justice Department."
The President was confident that Bobby would prove himself
the general conduct of the office (and be a credit to the family).

But he would make unusual requirements of his Attorney General—political acumen, zeal, and unswerving boldness in action—qualities that even Bobby's enemies must concede Bobby had showed in abundance in conducting the rackets investigation and in running his brother's campaign.

Kennedy's Attorney General would be the man in charge of buying time for the President to try out the strategy he had decided to use in dealing with Congress. Kennedy was deeply obligated to the Negroes of the United States for their support in 1960 and well aware that he and other Democrats would need that support again in 1962 and 1964. Negro leaders wanted action that only Congress could authorize—specifically a law requiring all school districts to file plans for desegregation that would bring about compliance by 1963 with the Supreme Court decision of 1954. But Kennedy had decided on a policy of wheeling and dealing with the conservative coalition in Congress on his first-year domestic program instead of trying to force the Southern wing of his party into submission. That ruled out a compliance bill for school desegregation or any other significant civil-rights legislation in 1961. Kennedy's task was to accomplish so much by Executive action that the demand for immediate legislation could be kept under control. Power to enforce existing civil-rights law lay in the Department of Justice. And the hand that would wield it was the Attorney General's. A Kennedy in that position could convey not only the color of Presidential authority but the personal moral force of the President as well.

The problem was clear.

Between 1950 and 1960, the decennial census showed, 1.5 million Negroes moved out of the one-party South where they were not a significant political factor. By the time of Kennedy's election three out of every four Negroes in the United States were living in cities. New York City's Negro population had passed the one million mark, and the Negro community in Los Angeles would number one million by 1970. Politically significant numbers of Negroes had also congregated in Illinois, Ohio, and Michigan.

Voteless Washington, D.C., stood first among major urban centers in proportion of Negro population, according to the 1960 census, with 53.9 per cent. After the capital came Detroit with 28.9 per cent, Cleveland with 28.6 per cent, St. Louis with 28.6 per cent, Philadelphia with 26.4 per cent, Chicago with 22.9 per cent, Cincinnati with 21.6 per cent, Pittsburgh with 16.7 per cent, New York with 14 per cent, Los Angeles with 13.5 per cent, and Buffalo with 13.3 per cent. A transitional move inside the South

from the farm to the city had swelled the proportion of the Negro
population to 38.3 per cent in Atlanta, to 37 per cent in Memphis,
to 37.2 per cent in New Orleans, and 22.9 per cent in Houston.

The Gallup Poll estimated that seven out of ten Negroes voted
for the Democratic ticket in the election that put John F. Kennedy
in the White House, a gain of seven points in Democratic strength
among Negroes since 1956.

Southern Negroes who had moved from the farms to the cities
where some of them were allowed to vote almost certainly carried at least two Southern states for the Democrats—Texas and
South Carolina. Loss of the large Texas electoral vote would have
lost Kennedy the election; the statewide margin for the Kennedy-
Johnson ticket in Texas was only 45,000, and it is estimated that
more than 100,000 Texas Negroes voted for the Democrats. Kennedy beat Nixon by less than 10,000 votes in South Carolina, and
more than 40,000 Negroes voted Democratic.

It had been Kennedy's strength in the great Northern cities to
which Southern Negroes had migrated that produced hairline victories for the Democrats in the eight states experts consider critical
to success in any close election—New York, Illinois, Pennsylvania,
Michigan, Maryland, Missouri, Minnesota, and New Jersey. All
but one—Missouri—went to Eisenhower in 1956. All eight went
for Kennedy in 1960, on the strength of the big-city vote. The
Republican National Committee, using Philadelphia as a labora-
tory, made a precinct-by-precinct study of why this happened.
The study revealed, among other things, that their candidate won
only 18 per cent of the Negro vote, leaving 82 per cent for Kennedy.

If any group had reason to expect remembrance of past promises once Kennedy was in the White House, it was the Negroes and
their allies in the cause of equal civil rights.

WHAT THE NEGROES EXPECTED

What would Negroes expect the Democratic President to do?
What had drawn them to Kennedy? In part, surely, it was the 1959
economic recession. Negroes, as always, were first to be fired, and
Kennedy had successfully labeled this a Republican recession. But
undoubtedly it was in large measure the way Kennedy stood up on
the issue of civil rights. Both party platforms had strong civil-rights
planks, and both candidates spoke forthrightly on the issue—
Kennedy more often than Nixon. The dramatic difference came

toward the close of the campaign when Kennedy intervened in the case of Dr. Martin Luther King, Jr. Learning that the leading spirit in the Southern integration movement had been imprisoned in a Georgia jail on a traffic charge, Mr. Kennedy telephoned Mrs. King in Atlanta to express his personal sympathy. Mr. Nixon made no comment on the incident at all.

Two million copies of a four-page pamphlet bearing the heading " 'No Comment' Nixon vs. a Candidate with a Heart, Senator Kennedy" were quickly printed and distributed by the Kennedy forces—250,000 copies in Chicago alone. (Kennedy carried Illinois by only 8,000 votes.) Dr. King's father, also an Atlanta minister, declared that "I had expected to vote against Senator Kennedy because of his religion. But now he can be my President, Catholic or whatever he is. . . . I've got all my votes and I've got a suitcase and I'm going to take them up there and dump them in his lap." And the Reverend Ralph Abernathy, the younger King's associate in the successful Montgomery, Alabama, bus boycott, sounded a call that may have made the difference in more than one part of the South. "I earnestly and sincerely feel that it is time for all of us to take off our Nixon buttons," he announced. "Now I have made up my mind to vote for Senator Kennedy because I am convinced he is concerned about our struggle. . . . Senator Kennedy showed his great concern for humanity when he acted first without counting the cost. He risked his political welfare in the South. . . . We must offset whatever loss he may sustain."

They did.

And as a new Congress made ready to begin work, and John F. Kennedy prepared for his Inauguration, Dr. Martin Luther King, Jr., made it clear that Negroes knew what they were entitled to. "The Negro vote elected Kennedy," King told a rally of his newly formed Emancipation Proclamation Association, "and we must not hesitate to remind him of that." The new President could be assured that they would also remind him of what he and his party had promised on their way to the White House.

Kennedy's campaign talks and the plank in the Democratic platform pertaining to civil rights had promised to do specific things at definite times. At Minneapolis, a month before election, someone in the audience asked: "What legislation do you have in preparation on the civil rights issue?" "I think I will say two or three things," Kennedy replied. "First, there is a good deal that can be done by the Executive branch without legislation. For example, the President could sign an Executive order ending discrimination in housing tomorrow. Second, the President could ompel all companies which do business with the Government, and after all that is nearly every American company, to practice open, fair hiring of personnel without regard to race, creed, or color. . . . In addition, the Department of Justice can pursue the right to vote with far more vigor. The Vice President's Commission on Contracts has been completely ineffective. It has not instituted one suit outside of the District of Columbia. So I would say that the greater opportunity is in the Executive branch without Congressional action"—a broad hint of decisions yet to come.

"The things I would ask the Congress to do are really twofold," the candidate continued. "First, to pass title 3, which gives the Attorney General additional powers to institute suits to provide for constitutional rights. Secondly . . . provide technical assistance to school districts that are trying to desegregate." The platform had included an added commitment to insure compliance with the Supreme Court decision on public-school desegregation by 1963 by enacting a law requiring it in 1961.

Time was of the essence, Kennedy had said. "If there is anything that history has taught us," he told a National Conference on Constitutional Rights in New York in the final critical week of the campaign, "it is that the great accomplishments of Woodrow Wilson and of Franklin Roosevelt were made in the early days, months, and years of their administrations. That was the time for maximum action. . . . Now is the time to prepare for what we must do in the winter of 1961. . . . October is the month to prepare for action in January, February, and March."

"Several weeks ago," Mr. Kennedy told the civil-rights leaders from 42 states, "I asked Senator Clark in the Senate and Congressman Celler in the House to join together and organize a committee of House and Senate members to prepare legislation for the new year to implement the commitments made in the platform. . . . I assure you that the new Democratic Congress, and I hope a new Democratic Administration, will press for action to implement their work."

On this point promises and present strategy were out of step. The President still believed in the need for the legislation he had specified, and he intended in due course to call for it. But he was changing the timetable. His Administration would be fully occupied in its first year simply in enforcing civil-rights laws already on the books, Kennedy believed. Legislation could wait at least a year.

When Kennedy carefully emphasized the possibilities for progress in extending civil rights through Executive action during the

campaign, he was not unmindful of the choice he might make a
President about how best to deal with Congress. Some of thos
possibilities were in his personal powers under the Constitution
"Many things can be done by a stroke of the pen," the candidat
had airily asserted. Still more could be done by strict enforcemen
of laws that had been applied loosely or not at all. That power la
in the Attorney General and his Department of Justice. If Ken
nedy's Attorney General won the confidence of those chiefly con
cerned with civil rights and maintained a strong impression of for
ward motion in this field, the President could stall on supportin
new civil-rights legislation until after Congress had approved hi
social and economic program—and that required Southern votes

ABILITY

This could be done only by an Attorney General with the kin
of energy and drive Bobby had put into the Presidential campaig
and the same disregard for whoever or whatever got in the wa
(Richard Rovere, in the *New Yorker,* wrote from Los Angele
after the tumult and the shouting had died, of "the respect, som
times close to awe" that politicians showed for Bobby. "Loy
members of Bobby's staff," he reported, "delight in describing h
indifference to rank and age in his large task force of Governor
Senators, Harvard professors, labor leaders, and grizzled vetera
of earlier political wars. 'In the Stevenson campaigns, everyor
was a general,' one man said one day last week, 'but now there
only General Bobby.' " And Rovere quoted an "unimpeachab
source" as saying, "I think [Bobby] is quite capable of telling Go
ernor Ribicoff to stay after school and of ordering John Kenne
Galbraith to write 'Procrastination is the thief of time' five hu
dred times.")

For the tactic to succeed, the Attorney General would also ha
to demonstrate a sincerity and conviction that would most like
emerge once Bobby became personally involved in the ne
cause. (New friends and associates are customarily struck by t
Puritan streak that runs through the younger Kennedy's charact
—his tendency to see things as clearly "right" or "wrong" ar
fight compulsively for the "right" when, and as, he sees it.) I
achieving so much by Executive action that those demanding mo
progress on civil rights would feel like ingrates, Bobby might
able to buy the President time to carry out his strategy with Co

gress, for the first year at least. If the cries from city Democratic leaders grew loud, Kennedy would have to shift and take the initiative on civil-rights legislation before the '62 elections. But the President could play '61 his way—if "the best man in the United States . . . on planning, getting the right people to work, and seeing that the job is done" was in the place where he could help the most.

THE ATTORNEY GENERAL PICKS HIS MEN

And so General Bobby became Attorney General Bobby, and set out to pick the right people to help. In the top rank in the Department of Justice he placed only three men with whom he was connected through politics, and two of those could just as easily have turned up in the impersonal "talent hunt" process. The new Deputy Attorney General, Byron White, who had served as Deputy to Bobby in the campaign organization, too, had been a respected Denver attorney, Phi Beta Kappa and All-American halfback in college, a Rhodes Scholar, and law clerk to Chief Justice Fred M. Vinson of the Supreme Court.

The Solicitor General, Archibald Cox, had been head of a professional speech-writing factory in the Kennedy campaign—but he had also been an attorney in the Solicitor General's Office for two years under the New Deal, had served in the State Department and the Department of Labor, and had been a member of the Harvard Law faculty since 1945.

In the second rank, as his Administrative Assistant, the new Attorney General retained another campaign veteran, 32-year-old John Siegenthaler, a Nashville newspaperman who had gone the long route to Los Angeles as Bobby's aide.

When I asked Professor Bickel as a principal critic of Robert Kennedy's appointment to state his opinion about Bobby's first ten months in office, he replied in part that generally Robert Kennedy "staffed his Department beautifully . . . It is perhaps, under him, a stronger department than we have had since early New Deal days."

Specifically, in the "hot" area of civil rights, Bobby bore out his brother's judgment that he was the greatest in "getting the right people to work." Deputy Attorney General White was told to find an Assistant Attorney General to head the Civil Rights Division who was a "hard-nosed lawyer" interested in the enforcement of civil rights but not a "professional civil rightser." He should be "uncommitted" enough to run the gauntlet of Mississippi Senator James Eastland's Judiciary Committee, which must agree to his confirmation, yet dedicated enough to Constitutional principles to take the punishment the position, once it was his, would bring. The job called for a smart, principled lawyer who would not be intimidated by those who objected to enforcement of civil-rights laws and would not run from their fire.

Harris Wofford, one of the talent-hunt team, well acquainted with the whole civil-rights field in and out of Government, suggested an unknown 38-year-old Washington lawyer, Burke Marshall. Wofford knew Marshall's reputation from Yale Law School, of which both were graduates, and he knew about his work from four years' association with him as a fellow lawyer in the Washington firm of Covington and Burling. White's check produced strong secondings of Wofford's suggestion. Marshall clearly met the essential requirements. The Attorney General did some checking too; then, sight unseen, telephoned Marshall and offered him the job.

SENATE APPROVAL

What manner of man would now be in operating command in the civil-rights sector under General Bobby came out clearly when Marshall appeared before the Senate Judiciary Committee to answer questions about his fitness for the office.

Time: 11:00 A.M., Thursday, March 2, 1961.
Place: Room 2228, New Senate Office Building, Senator James O. Eastland, Mississippi (Chairman) presiding.
CHAIRMAN EASTLAND: The next is the hearing this morning for the purpose of considering the nomination of Burke Marshall, of Maryland, to be an Assistant Attorney General. Senator Johnston, you may proceed.
SENATOR JOHNSTON (S.C.): Mr. Marshall, how long have you been practicing law?
MR. MARSHALL: Since 1951, Senator.
SENATOR JOHNSTON: What has been the nature of your practice?
MR. MARSHALL: I have been all of that time with a law firm called Covington and Burling here in Washington; it is a large law firm. The practice is mainly business law. My only practice has been in the anti-trust area.
SENATOR JOHNSTON: Anti-trust?

MR. MARSHALL: Anti-trust; yes, sir.

SENATOR JOHNSTON: I believe you have been assigned over here as Assistant Attorney General under the Civil Rights Section. Isn't it something along that line?

MR. MARSHALL: That is correct, Senator.

SENATOR JOHNSTON: What experience have you had in that field?

MR. MARSHALL: Virtually none, Senator. I have really had no experience in that field.

CHAIRMAN EASTLAND: Tell him of your affiliation with the American Civil Liberties Union.

MR. MARSHALL: I was a contributing member, I think it is called, Senator, to the Union until I received the appointment as Assistant Attorney General. . . .

SENATOR JOHNSTON: Have you had any connection with N.A.A.C.P.?

MR. MARSHALL: No, Senator, none.

SENATOR JOHNSTON: Have you contributed at any time to it?

MR. MARSHALL: No; I have not. . . .

SENATOR JOHNSTON: And you have had no connection with any civil rights cases or matters of any kind?

MR. MARSHALL: That is correct, Senator.

SENATOR JOHNSTON: When did you first learn, then, that you were going to be appointed to take over this kind of work?

MR. MARSHALL: The Attorney General called me up. He said he wanted a lawyer to supervise and conduct the legal work of the Civil Rights Division in the Department. He asked me if I would be willing to do it, and I said I would. . . .

Then Eastland drove to the heart of the matter:

CHAIRMAN EASTLAND: Well, now, what is your policy? Are you going to solicit complaints?

MR. MARSHALL: In what field do you mean?

CHAIRMAN EASTLAND: Voting rights.

MR. MARSHALL: No; the Department of Justice does not solicit complaints in any field. I will expect, however, that we might, as the Division has in the past, make record demands where there has not been a complaint.

CHAIRMAN EASTLAND: Repeat that, now and let me get it . . . where you have no aggrieved parties, you might sue?

MR. MARSHALL: No what, sir?

CHAIRMAN EASTLAND: Where you have no aggrieved parties who made complaints, you would bring suits anyway. Is that what you say?

MR. MARSHALL: Well, Senator, I do not want to give the impression that we would file any suit in any case where we did not believe that we could prove, in the trial, that voters had been discriminated against in violation of the statutes, but if your question is concerned with filing suits where there was not a specific complaint before even an investigation was started, I would say that the answer is "Yes, we will file suits." I would expect to file suits in some cases where the investigation started without a specific complaint.

CHAIRMAN EASTLAND: Who would start the investigation?

MR. MARSHALL: The Department.

CHAIRMAN EASTLAND: You started an investigation, now, that would be under you, would it not?

MR. MARSHALL: That would be on my recommendation. . . .

CHAIRMAN EASTLAND: All right. Now, what criteria would you use in selecting an area?

MR. MARSHALL: Well, I think one important criterion that we would refer to would be the statistics on registration and voting. If the statistics on registration and voting in particular cases showed a heavy imbalance against race, I think that we would consider that to be sufficient to start an investigation.

CHAIRMAN EASTLAND: Do you contemplate the initiation of requests for the inspection of voting records in any area outside of the South? . . .

MR. MARSHALL: . . . I have not seen any evidence of discrimination on account of race which would warrant the records demand outside the South. . . .

That colloquy between the Senator from Mississippi and the slight, soft-spoken young lawyer who would do much of the pick-and-shovel work in the Administration's first-term civil-rights program marked a new beginning. To tell the Chairman of the powerful Senate Judiciary Committee that the United States Department of Justice was headed for his state of Mississippi to see that Negroes were permitted to vote may not have been a shot heard around the world, but it sounded loud in that committee room that morning.

To teach Marshall his manners, Southern Senators delayed his confirmation for two weeks and seemed prepared to filibuster longer when the Attorney General walked, unannounced, into the third committee session on Marshall's fitness and silently took a seat. A few embarrassed moments later Marshall was approved.

But there was general puzzlement at the new Administration's attitude. As Eisenhower's Attorney General, William Rogers had gone to great lengths to avoid crossing swords with Chairman Eastland, whose committee has legislative jurisdiction over all the main concerns of an Attorney General: Federal courts and judges, judicial proceedings, revision and codification of the statutes of the United States, national penitentiaries, civil liberties, immigration and naturalization, and interstate compacts generally. Rogers and Eastland met frequently in the manner of two friendly powers. And although of the opposite party, Rogers was usually able to get whatever he wanted through Eastland's committee. Many in the Justice Department thought that Attorney General Rogers' reluctance to bring suits as "Friend of the Court" to prevent infringements of voting rights of Negroes—none at all were brought in Mississippi—was in deference to Eastland's tender feelings on the subject, a view the present Attorney General seems to share. "I have an impression," Bobby Kennedy said soon after taking office, "that people in the Department of Justice wanted to do more [in civil-rights cases], but were held back by a general hands-off policy in the past administration. This won't be true in the future."

SOUTHERN TOES

Again Bobby was cast as the "nay-sayer" for the Kennedys. While the President wooed Southern support for his emergency antirecession measures in Congress, his brother proceeded with long-range plans that would diminish the power of those same Southerners. It was like Los Angeles. Looking back at the impression left after the nominating convention, a *Look* reporter asked the new Attorney General in an early interview: "Do you have any comment about such adjectives as 'cold,' 'ruthless' and 'arrogant' that some people have applied to you publicly?" "If my children were old enough to understand," Bobby replied, "I might be disturbed to have them find out what a mean father they have. I've been in a position where I have to say no to people, and at times I've had to step on some toes."

The toes he would have to step on now would be Southern ones. He could expect howls, for he would have to step hard enough to hurt. Shrewd opponents of equal rights for all citizens under law among the Southerners were well aware that voting equality was a deadlier threat to their White Supremacy civilization than economic or social equality. It was also harder to oppose. Among reasonable men there was a broader consensus on the need for strict enforcement of voting rights than on any other phase of civil rights. For example, among possible crusades, it appealed most to Bobby's natural conservatism. The right to vote was basic, and opening the polls to qualified Negro voters was something the Kennedy Administration wanted to encourage.

Eastland had asked the central question and Marshall had given a truthful answer—guaranteeing the right to vote would be a prime objective.

VOTING RIGHTS

The new Attorney General put much of his early attention on backing up his new Assistant. While Marshall and his staff dug into Division files for voting-rights complaints to pursue, Bobby was boning up on civil-rights law. "This is not a field in which I have had a great deal of experience," he told a visitor. "It is, therefore, getting my immediate attention." Before February was out, the Attorney General was on Capitol Hill asking Congress for funds with which to finance "expanded and more aggressive programs in the field of civil rights."

What more aggressive programs did he have in mind, a member of the House Appropriations Committee asked?

MR. KENNEDY: I think a great deal more could be done in the voting field than has been done in the past for one reason or another.

MR. BOW: Have you some plans to go forward with that?

MR. KENNEDY: Yes . . . we have fourteen or fifteen counties in the United States where there are more Negroes than white people, and yet not one Negro is registered. We have in many instances complaints that Negroes have attempted to register to vote in an election where there have been problems and difficulties created for them in their attempt to vote. We intend to take whatever steps can be taken and should be taken under the law to insure that they have the right to vote.

I have had a number of conversations and conferences with the leadership of many of these states where this is a problem. And I have pointed out to them that in a certain county or a certain area it would appear that the Negroes were discriminated against. In a number of instances they have indicated that they themselves would take steps to insure that the Negro is permitted to register. Where they will take the steps themselves, where we can do it on an amicable basis, this will be done and kept out of the courts; but where steps were not taken by the local authorities or by the states, we, ourselves, will have to move.

Meanwhile Marshall and his lawyers were combing the United States Code for other unenforced or not fully enforced statutes with which to help desegregation along. For, to Marshall, voting was only the door by which to enter. In his subdued way he showed excitement as we discussed his work one afternoon in early October. There was probably no other job in the Administration he would have taken, Marshall volunteered. This was an exciting place for a lawyer—a man could see his accomplishments. He new no other area in which it was similarly possible to "work a ocial and economic revolution through law." If Senator Eastland ould hear him now!

The Attorney General intended to enforce the civil-rights laws, nd it would be the first time an Attorney General had, Marshall aid. He saw Bobby almost every day and was confident he meant vhat he said. The Attorney General had done everything his As- istant had asked him to do, and the Attorney General's brother ad done everything the Attorney General had asked him to do. There was no lack of backing. It had been that way from the first lays of the Administration, even before Marshall was sworn in.

REBELLION IN LOUISIANA

Bobby, like his brother, had some immediate problems inherited rom the previous Administration—there was a rebellion in Louisi- na as well as in Laos. During the Attorney General's appearance pefore it in February, the House Appropriations Committee asked or a report on the New Orleans school situation.

MR. KENNEDY: We have been working on that very hard over the period of the last ten days. These things are never finally settled, but I think we have achieved a very satisfactory result, the result being that the Governor has in fact recognized and the legislature has in act recognized that these two schools will be operated on a desegre- ated basis. The teachers are all being paid now, as of yesterday, in- luding the teachers from these two schools. That is what the argu- nent and fight has been over the period of the last few months. We ave kept up the pressure. We indicated to them down there that the Department of Justice was going to back up the court, that the Federal iovernment, was going to use its full power to insure that the court's lecisions were carried out, and that we would follow contempt cases vhere there has been contempt of court, and bring those before the ourt and let them be adjudicated.

I think these conversations and the strong position that the Govern- nent took over the period of the last ten days has had a very salutary ffect.

I do not wish to come here, Congressmen, and say that is the end f the problem in New Orleans, because we shall have more problems n September. We shall have more problems in other places in Louisi- na, come next year, and we shall have more problems in all of the tates wherever this is a very sensitive problem and difficulty.

As those "problems and difficulties" began to present themselves or day-by-day solution, it became clear that circumstances had

created a remarkably effective three-man civil-rights team in the
Department of Justice. General Bobby contributed relentless en
ergy and the instinctive knowledge that much had to be done by
persuasion; Marshall contributed wisdom, intelligence, and the
analytical powers of a good lawyer; Siegenthaler added a humane
approach, plus knowledge and experience of the South and Southerners that the other two lacked.

THE CIVIL-RIGHTS TEAM

President Kennedy's good fortune in getting the right people
to apply his civil-rights strategy did not end there. Harris Wofford
whom he had taken into the White House as a Special Assistant
had worked in the civil-rights division of the Kennedy campaign
organization, and earlier with the Civil Rights Commission estab
lished by the Civil Rights Act of 1957. He had knowledge of the
people and the interconnecting problems those newer to the field
had yet to learn. Wofford, his Yale Law School classmate Ber
Bernhard, who moved up from Deputy to Staff Director of the
Commission on Civil Rights, their friend and fellow Yale man
Burke Marshall, and the Executive Director of Vice President
Johnson's Equal Employment Opportunity Committee, John Feild
were soon holding weekly meetings to co-ordinate their work. They
met in Marshall's office in the Department of Justice—signifying
as everyone understood, that General Bobby was commander in
chief for civil rights. And they were in daily touch with each other
and with lobbyists representing the private civil-rights organiza
tions.

Word spread by the grapevine that Kennedy's men had authority
to act in emergencies. "The direct accessibility of Bobby Kennedy
John Siegenthaler, or Burke Marshall through the simple act of a
telephone call from a citizen in distress is no small achievement,"
a Negro leader in the mid-South wrote to me by way of report. "I
do not know how many little emergencies have been met in this
way, but I have been told that they have taken place with more
than occasional frequency."

The President and his brother had a good working team, and
although there had never been a formal pre-Inaugural task force
on civil-rights policy, as there had been in most other areas, the
strategy the team was to follow was clear: No request for further
civil-rights legislation in 1961; full use of every Executive power

in areas beyond those of Federal employment and Armed Forces which Roosevelt, Truman, and Eisenhower had entered; full enforcement of all existing laws, starting with all-out support of the right to vote; a special effort to appoint qualified Negroes to high office; and use of the President's personal prestige in behalf of the principle of desegregation.

Bobby did not underestimate the power of the last. Laws alone wouldn't work in the civil-rights area, he said. "There has got to be—and there is going to be—leadership from the White House. That is going to make the difference."

THE PRESIDENT'S PART

The President started doing his personal part the morning after his Inauguration when he telephoned the Coast Guard to ask why there had been no Negroes in its section of the Inaugural parade. At an early Cabinet meeting he queried department heads on their hiring policies toward minorities, and followed up with orders that one official in each department be assigned to promote employment of qualified members of minority groups. He used the New Orleans school incident a few weeks later to declare, as President Eisenhower never had, that the decision of the Supreme Court on public-school desegregation was morally just and right as well as legally binding. He forbade segregation at any function held under Government auspices—for business or pleasure. When Charleston, South Carolina, refused to serve as host to a nonsegregated meeting of the Civil War Centennial Commission, the President directed that the meeting be held elsewhere. He ordered surplus foods sent to the Negroes of Fayette and Heywood Counties, in Tennessee, to relieve suffering caused by the economic boycott that the white community imposed when Negroes tried to register to vote.

GOVERNMENT APPOINTMENTS AND THE NEGRO

Part of the pre-Inaugural casting operation that Sargent Shriver, Harris Wofford, and Adam Yarmolinsky conducted from the Democratic National Committee offices they had occupied during the campaign was a conscious effort to place Negro employees at all levels in Government. Helping them was Louis Martin, a former *Afro-American* reporter, now assistant to Democratic National Chairman John M. Bailey. They chose nominees with care —there was no difficulty in riding out the attack made on the first Negro appointed to a quasi-Cabinet position, Robert C. Weaver, who was named to head the Housing and Home Finance Agency. George L. P. Weaver, who had formerly worked in a professional capacity for trade unions, became Assistant Secretary of Labor for International Labor Affairs. Pierre Salinger chose Andrew Hatcher, a Negro newspaperman from San Francisco, as his White House Press Assistant. And Carl Rowan, also a reporter on the *Afro-American* and later for the Minneapolis *Star and Tribune,* became Deputy Assistant Secretary of State for Public Affairs. (When the Cosmos Club, composed largely of intellectuals and professional men, refused membership to Rowan, the President's name was withdrawn from the list of nominees for admittance.)

Bobby struck a personal blow for equal rights by resigning from the exclusive Metropolitan Club of Washington when it refused to welcome a Negro as his guest; he followed up with a major effort to bring Negroes into the professional level in the Department of Justice and into the Judiciary. When he had been in his new job only a few days, the Attorney General toured the Justice Building with John Siegenthaler at his side. After they had popped in and out of dozens of private offices, Bobby remarked "I don't see any Negroes, John—check into it." A check disclosed that there were only nine Negro attorneys in the entire department. The Attorney General immediately wrote letters to the Deans of fifty law schools asking them to recommend young Negroes qualified for Department of Justice work. He received the names of 150, and they were invited to apply for positions. The number of Negro attorneys in Justice had increased from nine in January to fifty by the end of the year, and for the first time there was a substantial file of Negro applicants on which to draw for future openings in the department.

There were higher appointments Bobby could make, too. Ceci Poole of California and Merle McCurdy of Ohio became the first Negroes to be appointed United States Attorneys in the continental United States. Negroes were given the positions of Employment Policy Officer and Chief Assistant United States Attorney for the District of Columbia. A Negro was named to the Municipal Court of the District of Columbia. And the new Attorney General nominated the first two Negroes ever appointed to be District Judges in the continental United States—Wade Hampton McCree of Michigan and James B. Parsons of Illinois.

All these appointments helped create a good initial impression on the Negro community. But it was the naming of the General Counsel of NAACP, Thurgood Marshall of New York, to the United States Circuit Court, the second highest court in the land, that topped everything else Kennedy was to do in his first year as far as solidifying his position with Negro makers of opinion. That one act did much to make up for the President's refusal to join the fight to reform the Senate rules or to give his blessing to bills to carry out the school-desegregation plank in the Democratic platform. For to some Southerners—even some in Congress—the name Thurgood Marshall was synonymous with the devil. Mr. Kennedy had bent his rule about dealing with Congress in this instance. And that had its desired symbolic effect.

Civil-rights leaders, Negro and white, were mollified by the appointments. But this long-overdue recognition of Negroes in Government service, although a welcome promise of better things to come, was no substitute for the legislative action for which they had agitated so long.

THE STRATEGY OF CONCILIATION

There had seemed to be a meeting of minds during the campaign, but apparently Kennedy had had second thoughts. Six weeks after the election, NAACP Secretary Roy Wilkins sadly reported to a meeting called on behalf of changing Senate rules that an "atmosphere of super-caution" on civil rights had "pervaded" all discussions with the President-elect and his staff since Election Day. Presumably there was need for a new understanding. The more sophisticated among the leaders of the fifty-odd organizations expressly concerned about civil rights understood and sympathized with the President's problem of a narrow margin in Congress and the basic split within the Democratic Party. They would go along with his strategy of conciliation for purposes of his domestic program so long as he could show a rapid rate of progress on civil rights. But they had their constituencies to satisfy, too—believers in civil rights to whom the necessity for Congressional action was an article of faith.

Under similar circumstances in 1960, when civil-rights proponents tried in vain to strengthen the bill under debate, Senate Majority Leader Johnson had held out a goal—if not a promise—that made the final Civil Rights Act of 1960 easier to take. That mild measure was only a beginning, Johnson had argued, as did Attorney General Rogers in a separate session. The important point was that it would be the second civil-rights bill passed in two consecutive Congresses. This seemed a pledge that every Congress would be a civil-rights Congress, or so it had been understood by the proponents of civil rights. They had countersigned that promise and conveyed it to their followers. And their expectation was that Kennedy would be bound by it.

It was against this background, shortly after the convening of Congress, that Wilkins and Arnold Aronson, Chairman and Secretary, respectively, of the over-all co-ordinating organization known as the Leadership Conference on Civil Rights, conferred with the President. Kennedy, as I have already said, had established no pre-Inaugural "task force" on civil rights, as he had in most other fields of policy. Wofford had assembled a cross section of ideas on what the new Administration might do. And Vice President Johnson, with the help of former Undersecretary of Interior Abe Fortas, had prepared a much-improved approach to the problem of preventing discrimination in employment in the Federal Government and by contractors working for it. But the civil-rights "lobby" had not had its day in court. The President invited its emissaries to outline what they would consider an effective civil-rights program. By February 3 he had their memorandum outlining it. On February 6 Wilkins and Aronson were back at the White House discussing their proposals with the President's Special Counsel, Ted Sorensen, Sorensen's deputy, Myer Feldman, Deputy Attorney General Joseph Dolan, and other White House aides. The February 3 memorandum from the Leadership Conference officials contained recommendations for both Legislative and Executive action. Sorensen broke the news that legislation was out. Would Wilkins and Aronson please return to their member organizations and prepare another analysis of what the President, acting on his own authority, might do? They would, but reluctantly, and they insisted that some of the pledges in the Democratic platform could be redeemed only through legislation.

The word spread. Having refused to join the fight to limit filibusters in the Senate, the President was now going back on his pledge to support specific new civil-rights bills at the first opportunity. The leaders, with a few exceptions, were more tolerant of the President's decision than their followers. And when the annual conference of the National Civil Liberties Clearing House gathered in Washington in late March, the mood was stormy.

Those who came together at these annual meetings were the war horses of the liberal organizations of the country. Harris Wofford, now of the White House, had been one of them. At the last conference he had been a delegate. This year "Hon. Harris L. Wofford, Jr., Special Assistant to the President" was listed as a principal speaker. He was there to explain the course the President had chosen. Among friends, who could not question his *bona fides,* Wofford could be brief and to the point: They were faced with new questions, he said. Were they "and all the organizations and people who are working to protect civil rights and civil liberties responding to the new possibilities" under the new Administration?

We may have learned too well the habits of opposition. Decades of disappointments—of frustration over "the consistent omissions of a Government frozen in the ice of its own indifference"—may have taken their toll on the champions of civil rights.

Are we on guard to avoid a tendency to prefer to lose a long, loud fight for a Congressional civil rights bill rather than to win a quiet, steady campaign for effective executive action? Is the readiness to protest and take a stand on an issue matched by an equal unreadiness to follow through with the careful next steps necessary? . . .

I do not mean that the new avenue of executive action will be easy. This course has plenty of contradictions and it will not . . . resolve the built-in political contradictions. The need for the enactment of vital measures for the general welfare—such as the bills for education, health care, housing and a decent minimum wage—may still at any given moment have to be weighed against other actions to advance civil rights. Since these social measures have the most direct impact on our racial minorities, so many of whom are at the bottom of our economic ladder, the weighing process is sometimes painful.

You may on occasion disagree with the result of the weighing of priorities. But for your disagreement to be effective you will need to look at the process through a political lens that takes into account the major contradictions shaping this problem.

Let me put this in shorthand: It took the combination of Lyndon Johnson and a strong civil rights plank—the combination of faith in a new South and determination to end racial discrimination everywhere—the combination of a strong appeal to the South and a strong civil rights campaign—the combination of a large part of the white South and of Negro voters, North and South—to elect Kennedy. It will take such a novel and winning combination to move this country ahead on the new frontiers at home and abroad, in civil rights here and in human rights everywhere.

What they must expect—as allies of the party in power—began to sink in. The waters calmed. And while the Leadership Conference group reviewed their recommendations and dug more deeply into the possibilities for Executive action, the White House went ahead. Months later, at the end of August, the Wilkins group presented a second memorandum of 61 pages to the President outlining in detail a carefully prepared program "To End Federally Supported Segregation and Other Forms of Racial Discrimination" that would take years to carry out and would drastically alter relations between races. But the time between would not be wasted. No new studies were needed to discover that the next big job was insuring equal job opportunity for all races.

At the height of the 1960 recession the National Urban League found that the rate of unemployment among Negroes was three times that among whites. Negroes would continue to be "last to be hired and first to be fired" until the Federal Government made a drastic effort to eliminate discrimination.

JOHNSON TO HEAD COMMITTEE ON
EQUAL EMPLOYMENT

In the 1960 campaign Kennedy had attacked Nixon for his do-nothing record as Chairman of Eisenhower's Employment Committee. There had not been a single contract cancellation outside the District of Columbia for violation of Eisenhower's antidiscrimination order while Nixon was chairman. One of Kennedy's early actions at Palm Beach was to appoint Vice President-elect Johnson to the post Nixon was vacating. Then, on March 6, President Kennedy signed Executive Order 10925, creating a new Committee on Equal Employment Opportunity under Johnson with much broader enforcement powers than Eisenhower, Truman, and Roosevelt had given predecessor groups.

The Johnson committee began by emphasizing the "positive." Rules implementing the President's order authorized cancellation of contracts in cases of violation and the filing of regular compliance reports by Government contractors. Johnson and Executive Vice Chairman Jerry Holleman, former president of the Texas AFL-CIO, moving carefully, decided against imposing a heavy burden of paper work on employers at first. Emphasis was on obtaining voluntary agreements against discrimination rather than on processing complaints. And the major targets were companies employing large numbers of workers.

By January 1962, more than 50 of the largest defense contractors in the country had signed "Plans for Progress" with Vice President Johnson, in the presence of the President at the White House. The Plans were detailed agreements to equalize opportunity for 1.3

million jobs in these companies. But more than half of the 50 biggest defense-contracting firms had yet to be persuaded. Johnson was pushing his staff to win them over to voluntary agreements and, at the same time, to prepare to move into the tougher area of enforcement.

Militant minority groups had been agitating for cancellation of at least a few contracts or imposition of at least a few sanctions on flagrant violators of the Executive Order in such industries as textiles. Senator Richard Russell of Georgia, the author of a statute prohibiting use of Presidential funds to support Presidentially created agencies like Johnson's for more than one year, surely would not like that. Johnson had been in no hurry to move into an area that might upset the man who could disarm Johnson's enforcement army. But in December Johnson's Committee on Equal Employment Opportunity acted. In 1962 it would require all firms holding Government contracts of $10,000 or more to file regular reports giving proof of compliance with the President's Employment Order, the first large-scale effort the Federal Government had ever made in that direction.

In a short time the invigorated Employment Opportunity Committee had made a surprisingly deep and favorable impression. In October, I asked a Southern Negro leader who is not usually thankful for small favors to pass private judgment on the Johnson committee's performance to date. It has been a "clear, strong, and consistent program," he said. "There has been swift and thorough follow-through from the big contractors, such as Lockheed, to the Governmental agencies themselves. . . . Policy directives have gotten down to the least significant Government agency and the smallest Government contractor. . . . The one big area yet to be dealt with is the State Employment Services which are about 90 per cent federally subsidized."

Civil-rights organizations were not moved to decorate Johnson for his year's achievements in equalizing employment opportunities. But his name was no longer a synonym for obstructionist as it had been among those groups during his days in the Senate—a transition devoutly to be wished by a politician with Johnson's ultimate ambition.

DISCRIMINATION IN VOTING

The Department of Justice, too, made a fast start. On Inauguration Day only six cases to end discrimination in voting were on file in Federal courts—three years and three months after the Right to Vote Bill had been passed in 1957—and inspections of voting records were under way in only six counties. The Civil Rights Commission had cited 100 counties as the principal areas of voting discrimination in the South, and Burke Marshall went to work in those.

Four cases were brought in Mississippi, the first such suits to be filed in Senator Eastland's state. Successful judgments were obtained in three of the six actions left over from the Eisenhower regime—including an order restraining a white registrar in Macon County, Alabama, from delaying and obstructing Negro registration. (In three months Negro registration had risen to half that of white registrants.) Federal officials began investigating voting records, as Marshall had told Eastland they would. After nine months investigators had completed the job in 19 counties and were at work in 50 more of the 100 hard-core areas where Negroes, according to the Civil Rights Commission, were being prevented from voting. Eight new court cases had been filed—including one that gave new heart to Martin Luther King and other leaders who were trying to bring about greater Negro interest in voting.

The right-to-vote provisions in the 1957 and 1960 civil-rights laws afforded no protection to those who took the initiative in registering and voting—sometimes a dangerous step. That was one reason—among many—why an NAACP registration campaign had moved slowly. When the first Civil Rights Act passed in 1957, the NAACP talked of registering three million Southern Negroes by 1960. In 1961 they were not halfway to the goal. In two Tennessee counties, the Department of Justice found that white landlords had evicted Negro tenants who voted, and white merchants had refused to sell to Negroes who were registered to vote. A Civil Rights Commission investigation disclosed that the registrar in one Mississippi county, a former chain-gang boss, customarily walked along the line fingering a sawed-off pool cue as Negroes filed in to register.

The fact that in small towns voting often takes place in areas that are usually off limits to Negroes, such as white schools and churches, was a restraining factor. It was common practice for election officials, especially in rural areas, to make literacy and other qualifying tests more difficult for Negroes than for whites.

Even these subtler methods were sufficient to deter most Negroes from trying to vote for fear that protest would bring harsher physical or economic reprisals against which they had no protection.

If the number of Negro voters was to increase significantly any time soon in the South, Negro leaders needed assurance that the Federal Government would find new ways to protect those who tried to exercise the vote. Martin Luther King received assurance at the top. After one meeting between the Attorney General and Dr. King, a Kennedy aide remarked that the two men got along very well. "King only asked for maximum effort," he said, "and so does Bobby." When the registration clerk in rural Walthall County, Mississippi, cracked a Negro registration worker over the head with a pistol and then had him arrested for disturbing the peace and "bringing an uprising among the people," Burke Marshall had a case through which to demonstrate the Government's good faith. The Department of Justice promptly sought an injunction against the State Criminal Court to block trial on the disorderly conduct charge.

"The blunt truth," Mr. Marshall said in his brief, "is that Negroes who have lived all their lives under the white supremacy conditions which exist in that area of Mississippi cannot be expected to try to register if, in addition to being threatened and beaten, they will be prosecuted in state court with all that such a prosecution entails.

"Such prosecutions not only are expensive, but it is becoming increasingly difficult for Negroes accused of offenses in the civil rights context even to secure competent legal assistance.

"There are scarcely a half-dozen Negro attorneys in the entire state of Mississippi. Because of the tremendous political and economic pressures brought to bear by the State of Mississippi, it is difficult if not impossible to secure competent white counsel for Negroes in cases such as this."

The Federal District Judge refused to halt the state prosecution. Marshall appealed the case, and the Federal Circuit Court broke new ground in ruling that Federal courts should use their power to stop state court prosecutions designed to harass those who attempt to register. The Federal Government had new authority to protect those who could not protect themselves. Martin Luther King's plan for "stand-ins" at registration places throughout the South by Negroes eligible to vote would have legal cover when it began.

All this was months in the making. The Walthall County decision did not come until October. But Negro leaders were aware of the preparation and the spirit that were going into the voting drive in the Department of Justice. Thus they were loath to be constantly calling to the Administration to go a little faster. That is, until the Freedom Rides began.

THE FREEDOM RIDES

On May 5, 13 white and Negro men and women, members of the Congress of Racial Equality, left Washington, D.C., by bus. Purpose: to challenge segregation in the buses and in the waiting rooms, rest rooms, and restaurants of bus stations between Washington and New Orleans. Calling themselves "Freedom Riders," the 13 progressed with only minor incidents down through North and South Carolina, across Georgia, and as far as Anniston, Alabama, where the mobile sit-in demonstrators met a mob that beat them and set fire to their bus. Organized hoodlums again hauled the riders off the substitute bus that carried them on to Birmingham. No police help came, though the city hall was just around the corner.

When bus drivers refused to haul the Freedom Riders on to Montgomery for fear of further attacks, the group reluctantly abandoned the bus and flew to New Orleans where they disbanded.

In spite of the change in plans, CORE headquarters and the riders, proud of their foray, were preparing a celebration in Washington when word came of a new development. Inspired by the CORE riders, a group of students belonging to the Nashville Non-violence Movement had resolved to join the caravan. But by the time seven of them reached Birmingham, the original party had gone. Determined to carry on, the Nashville group tried to board buses for Montgomery until they were taken into "protective custody" by the police; they were then driven to the Tennessee state line and released. But the seven borrowed a car and drove back to Birmingham.

Meanwhile, 12 more adherents of Martin Luther King's version of passive resistance had arrived. A Department of Justice representative had tried to deter the reinforcements by pointing out to their 22-year-old organizer, Diana Nash, how explosively dangerous the situation in Alabama had become.

"It was as if I were talking to a wall," the department man said later. "She never listened to a word." Miss Nash explained in her turn that there was no need to listen: "We aren't going to stop, not now. Why, those people in Alabama think they can ignore the

President of the United States, and they think they can still win by beating us Negroes over the head.

"We saw this as a chance to go ahead and the kids wanted to go. All the kids knew that death was a real possibility on this trip."

On Saturday, May 20, in Birmingham, the Nashville group was allowed to board a bus for Montgomery.

In the five days between the bus-burning in Anniston and the departure of the Nashville group for Montgomery, the Department of Justice in Washington had been humming. Free travel had not been possible in Alabama since bus drivers refused to transport the CORE riders to Montgomery. FBI reports on the situation in Alabama and talks with leaders of the Freedom Riders caused the Attorney General to ready a civilian force for an emergency. Learning from Little Rock that uniformed troops still evoke bitter memories in the South, Eisenhower's Attorney General, William Rogers, had trained a group of deputy Federal marshals in riot techniques. Attorney General Kennedy gave orders to prepare them for action. Meanwhile, the atmosphere in his office was reminiscent of the good old days of the campaign. Lights burned late into the night, telephone calls backed up on the switchboard, secretaries worked in shifts, the Attorney General sat in shirt sleeves at his big desk trying to reach everyone who could conceivably help to get the buses rolling again—Alabama's Governor John Patterson, police officials, bus owners, union representatives. After days of receiving word that Patterson was out of town, the Attorney General asked the President to see if he could get the Governor to answer the phone—the Governor still was not taking calls. Finally a telegram came from Patterson asking the President to send a personal representative to discuss the situation with the Governor of Alabama.

On the night of May 18, John Siegenthaler, aide to Robert Kennedy, received the Governor's pledge that he could and would fully protect everyone in Alabama under any contingency and his assurance that he needed no Federal assistance to do it. Specifically, the Governor guaranteed the safe passage of the bus due to bring the Freedom Riders to Montgomery the next morning. Siegenthaler phoned Robert Kennedy from the Governor's office to report the agreement. And at Patterson's suggestion Justice officials notified the Greyhound Bus Company of the safe-conduct guarantee.

Up to a point it was carried out. State highway patrol officers flanked the bus all the way to the Montgomery city limits to prevent hijacking; a state-owned plane kept surveillance overhead. But at the city limits the protection ended. Not a single policeman was in sight when the bus drove into the terminal, although the FBI had notified the Montgomery police of the need for special protection for the students on board.

The armed mob that was there swarmed over the students. The crowd, witnesses say, could have been any group of lower-middle-class Southerners and their wives on an outing. "There was a really gay atmosphere about the whole thing, like taking the children to a parade . . . their attitude was one of real jollity and when one of the women would scream 'Go get him!' it was exactly the same yell you hear at football games."

When the President's representative, Mr. Siegenthaler, driving by, saw a Negro girl being pursued down the street by attackers and tried to rescue her, he was beaten unconscious and left to lie on the sidewalk for half an hour. A few of the Freedom Riders escaped by rushing into the Federal Building where an FBI agent hid them in the cellar.

The next day 400 deputy United States marshals arrived, led by Deputy Attorney General Byron White. And Martin Luther King, flanked by veteran leaders from the previous year's "sit-in" campaigns, arrived, too. Before the day was out only the presence of the marshals had prevented an even larger and wilder mob from attacking a rally of the Reverend King's followers, and the Governor had admitted failure by declaring a state of martial law and summoning his Alabama National Guard to keep order.

Those Freedom Riders who did not land in the hospital hid out in private homes while the Reverend King, CORE leaders (who had hastily rejoined the Ride), and Nonviolence leaders from around the country met to decide where to go from there. A tough young veteran of the 1959–60 "sit-ins," the Reverend James Lawson, Jr., was called in from Tennessee to organize a refresher course in the "philosophy and techniques" of nonviolent action to prepare the young Freedom Riders for what they might encounter in Mississippi and Louisiana.

Siegenthaler, dismissed from the Montgomery hospital after his head wounds were patched up, hurried back to Washington where Robert Kennedy was trying to anticipate the next guerrilla attack.

On May 24, with fantastic precautions, National Guardsmen of Alabama and the state police of Mississippi escorted the Freedom Riders to Jackson, where they were quietly arrested.

On May 29, the Attorney General requested the Interstate Commerce Commission to issue regulations at once requiring the full desegregation of terminals of buses engaged in interstate traffic. On the same day, martial law was ended in Montgomery.

THE ATTORNEY GENERAL PLANS AHEAD

The President reserved his personal influence, presumably against a larger crisis. But with his backing, Robert Kennedy acted in the Alabama incidents in a way to leave no room for doubt as to his courage and resolution. Unquestionably, the United States marshals, standing in their thin line between the mob and the Negro church, saved lives that Sunday in Montgomery. The Attorney General himself, the Southern Regional Council said in retrospect, "more than any other person or agency defended public order and common sense during these travails." And when the worst was over, he looked and planned ahead. "This is just one incident in a long struggle," the younger Kennedy said the morning after the Sunday violence in Montgomery. "It's going to continue not for weeks and months but for long into the future." With this prospect in mind, the FBI fanned out over the South trying to spot potential oubreaks and deal with them before they occurred. And Kennedy's men kept lines of communication open to the activist groups wherever they could. At this point, the Attorney General told the public, a cooling-off period was called for.

But there was not the faintest chance of that. The Rides were gathering momentum every day. Students held sympathy demonstrations on Northern campuses. And professors from Eastern universities where no Negro served on the faculty traveled by Greyhound to help liberate Mississippi. The constituted leaders of the nonviolence movement had not planned this eruption. Fledglings had led it, and the problem now was to keep matters from getting out of hand. The older leaders first had to get back in front again if the young crusaders were to follow them.

"The moment has come," Martin Luther King told the embattled Negroes in the First Baptist Church after the riot was broken up in Montgomery, "for a full-scale—non-violent—massive assault on the system of segregation in the South." His colleague, the fiery Reverend Fred L. Shuttlesworth of Birmingham, put it less elegantly that same night: "Let's go on and get it all now . . . no more compromise." Back in Atlanta the next week, King announced there would be a temporary lull in the Rides, but no "cooling off."

The Freedom Rides fixed attention on a phase of civil rights left out of Kennedy's basic plan, "the most difficult of all," Yale Law School Dean Eugene Rostow called it—"the task of organizing large-scale affirmative action by the states to initiate progress toward equality without the prod of a specific court order." The area of transportation was one in which the Government had done practically nothing to eliminate segregation. "Court decisions should have a 'multiplier' effect throughout society, as lawyers instruct their clients to conform voluntarily to the reasoning of the judges," Dean Rostow pointed out. And "Normally, this is the case. But it has not yet become the rule in the field of civil rights, where the law is seeking to accomplish far-reaching changes in customs and habits.

"The Freedom Riders succeeded in dramatizing one aspect of the contest between law and the resistance to law," Dean Rostow wrote in *The Reporter* in June, "the failure of the Interstate Commerce Commission, through appropriate administrative action, to require full desegregation of the facilities of interstate travel, including buses and bus terminals."

THE ATTORNEY GENERAL AND THE ICC

Having been shown his duty, the Attorney General turned his attention to the field of transportation, and not a moment too soon. Martin Luther King and all the hierarchy of the desegregation movement were in full cry for the immediate pulling down of every "White Only" sign in every waiting room, restaurant, and rest room in every interstate transportation terminal in the South.

In June, the Department of Justice petitioned the ICC for regulations requiring desegregated facilities in terminals used in interstate bus travel. On November 1, such an ICC order became effective in more than 100 terminals. But it had taken persuasion. Bobby used all the legal arguments and all the political finesse he could summon. In getting Commission agreement to the department's petition it was helpful that among the members were one Democrat appointed by the new President and one Republican interested in being reappointed when his present term expired.

While waiting for the ICC bus ruling, Mr. Marshall was looking for ways to attack the segregation problem in rail and air terminals. At Bobby's direction, Marshall and other Justice officials began conferring privately with the operators of rail and air lines serving the South. Would they not voluntarily desegregate their terminals without waiting for courts or regulatory agencies to order them to do so? After a series of talks in September, 18 railroads agreed to ban segregation in the railroad stations of 12 Southern states.

The air terminals at Columbus, Georgia, and Raleigh-Durham, North Carolina, voluntarily did the same. But beyond that the air terminals presented a legal problem. There was no specific provision against the segregation of airports in the Civil Aeronautics Act. Marshall had given this subject considerable thought. He had found in the files inherited from his predecessor a letter from the President of Tuskegee Institute listing the distinguished Negro visitors, many of them foreign officials and educators, who had passed through the segregated Montgomery, Alabama, airport in the previous twelve months. Could not the Department of Justice do something, Dr. Foster wanted to know?

Marshall brought suits in Montgomery and New Orleans to resolve the legal questions involved. The decision for the Government handed down by Federal District Court at the end of the year provided a basis for legal action against all other segregated air terminals if necessary. The first reaction from Montgomery city officials was the announcement that the airport restaurant and rest rooms would be locked, benches in the waiting room would be removed, and drinking fountains would be plugged. On second thought, they were not.

Meanwhile pressure to "get it all now" had forced many of those who had been sympathetic to the President's problem with the Southerners in Congress a few months before to take on a new militancy.

The President came home from his saddening experience with Khrushchev in Vienna to demands that he issue a single Presidential order ending racial segregation in every form once and for all. Martin Luther King told the National Baptist Convention of the U.S.A. that the Negro "cannot wait" any longer—he would, he said, make an appeal to the President for a new Emancipation Proclamation within a month. (When he did call on the President to make that request, Mr. Kennedy responded by saying, "Let me show you where the first one was signed," and leading the way to the Lincoln bedroom in the White House. The talk resumed, by mutual consent, not on the Proclamation but on specific areas of possible action.)

WHERE DISCRIMINATION, NO FEDERAL FUNDS

The Leadership Conference completed its brief, detailing myriad ways of advancing equality under law by Executive action alone, in ways the President was far from ready to pursue.

Specifically, civil rights leaders urged the President to establish policy whereby Federal grants to the states would no longer be given "as a support for the continuation of segregation and other forms of discrimination."

The memorandum said, "The essential thesis of this and of our previous memorandum—the thesis that the Federal government should in no way be a party to discrimination—represents no new radical principle. . . .

"The time has arrived for a full implementation of this principle, to the end that the Federal Government will no longer participate in any program that requires it to be a partner in supporting discrimination but will instead require that all Federal programs be administered in such a manner as to ensure equality of opportunity."

What the Leadership Conference wanted the President to do took 61 pages to describe. In receiving it, Mr. Kennedy again leaned on Lincoln to ease the situation. He felt, he said, as Lincoln had when the doctor told Lincoln he had a small case of smallpox. "Well," Lincoln remarked, "at last I have something I can give everybody."

Congress could not be so lightly put off. A Democratic Senator from Pennsylvania and a Democratic Representative from New York City were not unmindful of the desire for civil-rights legislation among their constituents. In May, Senator Clark and Representative Emanuel Celler completed the assignment given them by the President during the campaign. They had put the party's civil-rights planks in legislative form and had introduced six bills to implement the pledges, Senator Clark wrote the President. The principal bill would speed public-school desegregation by requiring every school board operating a racially segregated school to adopt a desegregation plan within six months of the bill's passage and to file the plan with the Secretary of Health, Education, and Welfare. In case of violation, the Attorney General would be authorized to seek an injunction requiring compliance.

There was little reason for Clark and Celler and the minority groups to expect the White House to press for this or the other five measures Clark and Celler had introduced. The sponsors did hope for benevolent neutrality. Clark had discussed his bills with the President, who encouraged him to proceed. But the day after Clark's announcement the press reported: "The White House disassociated itself today from civil rights legislation introduced by two Democrats yesterday in Congress." The President had made it clear, White House Press Secretary Pierre Salinger stated, that

he did not think it necessary at this time to enact civil-rights legislation. The morning of Clark's anouncement United Press International had incorrectly referred to the Clark-Celler measures as
"Administration bills." Prominent Southerners had been calling the
White House to protest, hence the blunt repudiation.

NO FURTHER LEGISLATION NOW, BUT—

The Administration was working on accomplishing what it could
under existing law, Salinger added. Small consolation though it
was to the sponsors of the bills, the accomplishment was considerable. In April, Bobby Kennedy had made by far the strongest move
since 1954 on school desegregation. Earlier he had departed from
the Eisenhower position that the Department of Justice would
intervene in a school case as Friend of the Court only on a court
invitation by entering several Louisiana cases on his own motion.
Now the Department of Justice was asking the Federal Court in
Richmond to force the reopening, in Prince Edward County, Virginia, of public schools that had been closed to prevent desegregation. The new position was that the Government had the duty to
enter any school case where its help was needed. Four times the
President had thrown his personal weight behind efforts of local
parents, teachers, and school officials to achieve peaceable compliance with Supreme Court decisions. And Bobby and his men
worked quietly and efficiently throughout the summer to achieve
an orderly transition in Atlanta, Dallas, Memphis, Little Rock,
and New Orleans when schools would be integrated in the fall. In
Memphis, the Justice Department found it necessary to threaten
suits and actions.

Secretary Hodges was enlisted to write letters of encouragement
to fellow Southerners. Bobby telephoned friendly and unfriendly
local officials, encouraging or persuading, as required. Without
publicity, Marshall and Siegenthaler traveled from city to city,
meeting with school and police officials in anticipation of trouble.
In September, the five Southern cities desegregated their schools
without incident.

During September and October, the Civil Rights Commission issued four reports pointing the way ahead. The Commission recommended that: segregated school districts be asked to submit desegregation plans within six months; a sixth-grade education be
considered evidence of literacy as a test for voting; unions be pro-

hibited from excluding or segregating Negroes; and segregation in all Federally aided housing be prohibited by Executive Order.

"STROKE OF THE PEN"

The last was a repetition of a recommendation the Commission had made in 1959. Senator Kennedy had twitted President Eisenhower for failing to carry it out in 1960. President Kennedy's failure to do so had been a bone in the throat of civil-rights organizations since January 20. What explanation could they offer for Mr. Kennedy's refusal to do what he had declared any President should and could accomplish by a "stroke of the pen"?

The problem, more than usually, was the Southerners in Congress. Housing subcommittees in Senate and House were headed by Alabamans—Senator John J. Sparkman and Representative Albert Rains. Both were vehemently opposed to an Executive Order. Such an action would destroy public housing in the South, they told the President, and seriously set back urban renewal and construction financed by the Federal Housing Administration. Their aides told the press that both men, strong public-housing supporters and also men whom the President was counting on to support his fight for a new trade bill, would surrender their committee chairmanships in the event of a housing order from the White House.

Several times the President postponed the day. Restless Negro groups threatened marches on Washington to demand action. The President's advisers on minority matters strongly favored signing a housing order before Congress reconvened for the 1962 session—Bobby, Marshall, and Wofford all voted yes when the President asked their advice on the matter. But he evidently had not felt the pressure as keenly as they. Critics of his rate of speed melted in the President's presence, aides noted. At a Peace Corps Advisory Council meeting, while timing on the housing order was under discussion at the White House, Dean Rostow of Yale and Harry Belafonte, the Negro singer, were discussing the delay when the President walked in. "You should hear what they are saying," a Kennedy aide remarked. But to the President they spoke only praise. Belafonte commented on how much the President had been able to accomplish. Rostow suggested a statement the President might make. Had Rostow read what Kennedy had released to the press that morning? "No." "Well, read it first," the President said as he moved on.

In Kennedy's judgment there was more to be gained by delaying than by desegregating housing in advance of the 1962 debate on trade. But if there was to be no Executive action on housing in 1961, could there not be some accommodation with the civil-rights groups on the question of legislation in the new year? The President thought there could be. But what moderate new proposal would be worth the cost of the division that would result in Congress? Setting a Federal standard of literacy for purposes of voting would be least likely to stir up a major ruckus on Capitol Hill. But would such a bill accomplish enough to make the effort worth while? Department of Justice lawyers believed it would be no great stimulus to voting. But Roy Wilkins and Martin Luther King and the Civil Rights Commission, all of whom the President consulted, thought such a law would make a significant difference. That and Presidential approval for elimination of the poll tax as a prerequisite for voting—a generally noncontroversial proposal—accordingly went into Kennedy's second State of the Union Message.

THE ATTORNEY GENERAL'S FIRST-YEAR RECORD

Bobby Kennedy's first year as Attorney General had been good for him and good for his brother. His competence, as the President had foreseen, stilled talk of nepotism in connection with his work as chief law officer of the Government at least. (Such criticism had turned to the larger uses to which Bobby was put after Cuba, when the President launched him in the new role of personal emissary abroad.) And the time was not far off when, if ambition had not grown cold, Bobby could run for elective office in his own right. Ambition was already running high in his immediate circle in 1961. "We know what a great President he would make," one of Bobby's assistants said to me in the autumn. "1968 may not be the year, but if Ted [Sorensen] could think and plan ahead, why shouldn't we?" Lyndon Johnson, he said, realized, if others did not, that Bobby was a potential threat. "People repeat to us all the time remarks Lyndon makes to discount Bobby."

With some exceptions, Bobby had lived up to his brother's great expectations in the conduct of his office. By his fortuitous choice of a principal aide, Bobby had brought about an important revision in race-relations philosophy in the Department of Justice. Eisenhower had repeatedly declared that law could not improve relations between the races, that the hearts of men must change "Acceptance of what the law requires is the beginning of change" was the philosophy Burke Marshall brought to his job as Assistant Attorney General in charge of Civil Rights. And knowledge that the law is going to be enforced is vital.

"Implying that it will not be enforced until there has been some other social change has an adverse effect on the situation," said Marshall. "The law has to lead the people sometimes."

The public record was first rate. Litigating activity had been vigorous and imaginative, particularly in civil rights. Civil liberties were another matter. It was in that area that doubts about Bobby's appointment had initially centered, and the first-year record did not allay them. American Civil Liberties Union officers and other libertarians opposed the bill Attorney General Kennedy sent to Congress that would have sanctioned wiretapping in national security and kidnaping cases without approval by a Federal judge. The bill, rejected by Congress, would also have given state officials the right to tap telephones with the sanction of state courts. (Bobby had first indicated he would ask only limited authority to wiretap and then only with Federal sanction.) The same organizations and virtually every major legal, religious, and welfare agency opposed the Walter Immigration Bill, approved by the Department of Justice, limiting due process for aliens seeking to stay deportation through the courts.

But there is another, less visible record, as to which the evidence will emerge only in years to come, when, for example, litigation against the department emerges in the higher courts. We do not know whether corners have been cut in the conduct of criminal prosecutions, or how the Attorney General has been performing his quasi-judicial supervisory and adjudicating functions in the field of immigration and naturalization in which some of his predecessors sinned outrageously. And we do not know whether the record number of judicial appointments for one year were relatively good or relatively disastrous, as were those of the Truman Administration.

But Attorney General Bobby bought the time his brother needed to try to work his will with a difficult Congress in its first session. In large part by the force of Bobby's leadership and his personal performance, the Administration held the confidence of Negro citizens in 1961. Elections for Governor in New Jersey, for Mayor in New York City, and for Congress in San Antonio, Texas, registered no loss of minority support for the Democrats.

As the Kennedy Administration entered its second year, there was still leeway for advancing civil rights by Executive action. But the consideration for Southern sensibilities that had led Kennedy to close the door on Legislative action at the beginning of his term had begun to make itself felt on Executive considerations before the first year came to a close. In three specific areas where the Presidential pen held the final power, Mr. Kennedy had not responded to pressure to ban segregation: in federally supported housing programs, in the National Guard, or in colleges and universities receiving Federal grants-in-aid. The price of patience in 1962 would be greater than in 1961. A sterling performance by Bobby was not likely to be enough to keep the Democrats in the big cities happy.

· V ·

The Economic Challenge

In mid-March 1961, a few days before John Kenneth Galbraith was to leave Washington to take up his duties as Ambassador to India, we sat together in what once was Cordell Hull's office in the Old State Department Building next door to the White House. We were discussing not his new interests as a diplomat but his lifetime concerns as an economist.

During John F. Kennedy's years in Congress and during his campaign for the Presidency, the Harvard professor had been his most intimate adviser on economic-policy matters. Galbraithian thinking and phrasing could be found in Senatorial speeches and campaign addresses. But now Kennedy's economic mentor was moving on to other fields and would soon be 8,000 miles away. He would no longer be across the street and available to the President for consultation as he had been during the early weeks of the Administration. Nor could he stroll down the corridor to the offices of the President's Council of Economic Advisers, or down the block to see Secretary of the Treasury Dillon, or up to the Capitol to advise and consult and argue his point of view with the men who make economic policy in Congress.

He would be absent, moreover, when the President began to implement his plans for dealing with the current recession and then with other great problems that lay beyond it.

Seldom have economic questions been discussed more thoroughly or cogently in a campaign than by Kennedy in 1960. In no other field did he have advisers who were stars of such magnitude. There were differing views among them—it was a rare leader among the "modern" school of Keynesians who did not add his two-cents worth to some Kennedy speech or statement. Neoclassicists were heard from, too. However, by Election Day men who took their liberal economic views seriously were persuaded that the

146

Democratic nominee was in their camp. It took more than a page merely to list references to the problem of unemployment in the index to the compilation of Kennedy's campaign speeches published by the Senate, and more than two pages to list the times he talked about the need for long-term economic growth. On the basis of that emphasis, Leon H. Keyserling, Chief Economic Adviser in Truman's Administration, said on the eve of the election that Senator Kennedy was endowed with qualities which would help to "lift the concept of a great national purpose under freedom from a pretentious generality into a splendid performance."

Kennedy had promised to reverse the recession and restore an expanding economy. Many voters had undoubtedly favored him for that reason, and apparently they were going to get action. One of Kennedy's first acts after the election was to invite Professor Paul A. Samuelson, a political moderate widely respected in his field and President of the American Economic Association, to bring in recommendations. By January 1, the President-elect had Samuelson's report: First of all, it said, the current recession, which had grown worse since the election, would not shortly cure itself, as some were saying. The Government should immediately extend unemployment benefits, begin to ease credit, and give relief to the most distressed areas. It should make a modest beginning on a public-works program to pump money into the economy—in the range of $3 to $5 billion in fiscal 1961—and then be prepared, if the situation grew worse or failed to improve, to do much more: spend heavily on public projects and perhaps cut income taxes temporarily. The one out of every sixteen workers who were unemployed as Kennedy took office must be put back to work.

These men must be kept at work. At the same time one million additional jobs must be made available each year for young people coming into the labor force. This was where "growth" economics came in. Professor Samuelson's report pointed out that, between 1950 and 1957, the United States economy had grown only at about 2.5 per cent per year, almost the lowest rate of any large industrialized nation, lower than Germany, Japan, France, or England, and little more than ⅓ of the growth rate of the U.S.S.R. Had we progressed even at a modest pace in those years, the report said, "not at the dramatic sprint of Western Europe and Japan or at the rush of the controlled totalitarian system," the United States could have anticipated in Kennedy's first year a total national production of ten per cent—about $50,000,000,-000—above what was in sight, and a budget surplus of $10,000,-000,000.

"We take office," the new President asserted in his first State o
the Union Address, "in the wake of seven months of recessior
three and one half years of slack, seven years of diminished eco
nomic growth and nine years of falling farm income."

KENNEDY'S FIRST RECOMMENDATIONS

Then, as the first of many special messages, Mr. Kennedy o
February 2 sent Congress a "Program for Economic Recovery an
Growth." The first steps he asked it to take toward recovery wer
so modest as to alarm the liberals. They were based on Samue
son's advice, but they were adjusted to Kennedy's strategy of psy
chologically disarming Congress and the country by avoiding an
appearance of being a "big spender."

President Kennedy's first Executive Order had directed th
distribution of more, and more varieties of, surplus foods to th
needy. Immediately afterward, following Eisenhower's example i
the preceding recession, Kennedy had ordered a speed-up of ac
tivity on Federal projects, advanced the date for return to th
public of dividends on Veterans Life Insurance and tax refund
and taken steps to speed up housing programs and lower Feder
mortgage rates. Those mild stimulants were already wearing o
and unemployment was still continuing to rise toward the 5.5 mi
lion mark. What was needed now, the President told Congres
were measures that would have more general impact on the eco
omy. He recommended temporary extension of unemployme
compensation, liberalization of Social Security, aid to children
unemployed parents, aid to depressed areas, and an increase in th
minimum wage. The price tags on these first-step measures, plu
the cost of a substantial increase in defense expenditures, total
$1.3 billion in fiscal 1961 and $3 billion in fiscal 1962. That wou
mean deficits of $2.2 billion in 1961 and $2.8 billion in fiscal 196
—or spending over two years about what the Samuelson report ha
recommended be spent in one.

As reassurance to the liberals, Kennedy concluded his speci
message with the pledge that "If these measures prove to be i
adequate to the task, I shall submit further proposals to the Co
gress within the next seventy-five days."

Almost at once the debate began between those who favor
even more massive spending in the first year than Samuels
recommended (they projected a deficit of $6 to $8 billion rath

ʜan the $5 billion Samuelson had contemplated) and those who,
ɔr fear of inflation, favored even less spending than the $1.3
ɪllion Kennedy had recommended.

THE HELLER VIEW

Although the President had not included a tax cut in his first
ɪrescription for recovery, Chairman Walter W. Heller and the two
ɪther members of the President's Council of Economic Advisers,
ames Tobin and Kermit Gordon, were not giving up on that or
ɪn even more drastic measures. Appearing before the Joint Eco-
ɪomic Committee of Congress four days after Kennedy's February
 message, Dr. Heller gave his long-term view of the job of over-
ɪauling the economy. "An economic upturn would be only the
ɪeginning, not the end, of the solution of our economic problems,"
ɪ told the committee. "The recession followed an incomplete re-
ɪvery in which the American economy fell substantially short of
ɪ potential levels of employment, production, and income. Indeed,
ɪe gap between what we are producing and what we can produce
ɪached eight per cent at the end of 1960. [Some reckoned it much
ɪider.] Today, it may be even closer to the ten percent gap that
ɪveloped at the worst stage of the 1958 recession. Taking up this
ɪack of some $50 billion in economic activity, rather than merely
ɪversing the economic decline, is the real challenge of economic
ɪlicy in the months ahead."

Heller went on to emphasize the "disturbing slowdown in the
ɪte of growth" and to discount fears that antirecession projects
ɪould exacerbate an inflationary boom—the danger, he said, was
ss in 1961 than in any previous postwar recession. The pro-
ɪams the President had announced "can be a major factor in
ɪrengthening the American economy in the months ahead," Dr.
ɪeller granted. However, he hastened to point out that the Presi-
ɪnt had promised that "If economic developments in the first
ɪarter of this year indicate that additional measures are needed,
ɪwill promptly propose such measures." And Dr. Heller was ready
ɪ propose to the President what measures he should propose.
ɪny program for economic recovery might consider a speed-up
ɪ government construction and related projects, an expansion of
ɪusing programs, and tax reduction. Temporary income tax cuts,
ɪ particular, provide a fast method for enlarging the private in-
ɪme stream and speeding recovery." These measures, together

with policies the council favored "to initiate further steps to promote faster economic growth" such as "tax incentives to stimulate business investment and expanded programs in education, training and research to build up America's human capital," would, he said produce a 1961–1962 deficit of approximately $8 billion.

JOSEPH W. BARR

What impelled the council to favor a recovery effort of that magnitude was the history of the three post-World War II recessions—a story of economic ups and downs in which the "ups" leveled off and the "downs" deepened. The council's concern was widely shared by economists. And some months later, in October Secretary Dillon's assistant, Joseph W. Barr, was to tell the National Association of Supervisors of State Banks that "this history draws a picture of a shortening period of business expansion leaving an ever larger residue of unemployed," and that the trend was "ominous and must be reversed."

"The 1953–54 downtrend," he asserted "was preceded by period of expansion that ran for forty-five months, and at its peak left only 2.7 percent of the working force unemployed. The 1957 58 downturn was preceded by a period of expansion that ran for thirty-five months, but which left 4.2 percent of our labor force unemployed at its peak in July, 1957. The 1960 downturn followed an expansion that ran only twenty-five months and which registered an unemployment figure of 5.1 percent at its peak in May 1960." Of course, the peak did not actually come until March 1961, when unemployment stood at 6.9 per cent, but Mr. Barr had caught the drift. Six months before, however, when the Economic Advisers, and notably Dr. Heller, were trying to make an early start on the problem, Mr. Barr's boss had not been so prescient.

SECRETARY DILLON VS. SECRETARY GOLDBERG

Asked about the recovery outlook at his first news conference as Secretary of the Treasury—this was early in February—Mr. Dillon bravely reported the Administration was "confident that the immediate recession will end," hopeful that it will be "fairly soon, and therefore saw "no reason for drastic action at this time." That would still be the case, Dillon indicated, when the situation was reviewed in April if there were signs that "the upturn is in sight or is beginning."

The number of unemployed had continued to grow in January, and the President had sent Secretary of Labor Goldberg to view the situation at firsthand in hard-hit cities and towns. Mr. Goldberg had got as far as the shutdown steel mills of South Bend, Indiana, on February 10, when he frankly announced: "We are in a full-fledged recession. I think it is time to say it in no uncertain terms." On his return, and in the ensuing debate, Goldberg allied himself with the President's Economic Advisers, and against Dillon.

It was against this background that I asked Ambassador Galbraith what economist Galbraith would do under the circumstances. He would be in India when the May deadline the President had set for a second look rolled around. Assuming no sharp improvement in the employment situation, what further steps would Galbraith take then if he were President?

THE GALBRAITH PROGRAM

Without hesitating, Kennedy's old friend ticked off his answers on the fingers of his left hand. He would

1. Lower interest rates drastically—to one per cent on short-term loans and to four and one half per cent on long-term loans. "This would be my first big chip."
2. Extend still further the period in which an unemployed worker may draw compensation pay, make this extension permanent, and increase, also permanently, the rate of pay.
3. Increase old-age pensions.
4. Invest heavily in school construction.
5. Increase Federal spending—"This is the second big chip"—to the extent of several billions more for public projects than Samuelson had suggested.

He was not, he said, in favor of cutting income taxes as a means of recovery. Tax cuts, he admitted, had the great advantage of a speedier effect than spending, but a greater disadvantage, in his view, in that they destroy the Federal power to allocate income to the public sector of the economy. If we cut taxes now, he feared, that would be the accepted formula for getting out of the next recession. Given the choice of living with some unemployment for a longer time or changing the tax system to provide quick relief, he would choose the former.

His five-point plan, Galbraith reckoned, should return the United States to *fuller* employment—that is, with no more than

3½ to 4 per cent of the work force unemployed—at the end of 1961. If less were done, or the decision to take these actions were delayed beyond the spring of 1961, then of course recession would linger longer.

KEEPING OUT OF THE RECESSION TROUGH

Once out of the recession trough, the way to stay out and to achieve long-run economic stability, he went on, was to maintain low interest rates and a proper level of spending—*and* to control prices and wages. This last he would achieve in a permissive way, perhaps through the new Labor-Management Advisory Council the President had just announced. That council was the joint inspiration of Galbraith and Secretary of Labor Goldberg, but their conceptions of it differed. Goldberg thought of the council basically as a conciliation device to prevent strikes. Galbraith's hope was that it would develop into a means for impressing both labor and management with the need to hold the price-wage line.

Whether it did or not would depend a lot on Galbraith's related hope that the regular three-way conferences he had helped institute between the President's Chief Economic Adviser, the Secretary of the Treasury, and the Secretary of Labor would develop into an operating triumvirate, preferably with the Chairman of the Council of Economic Advisers predominant. Galbraith had recommended Professor Walter Heller of the University of Minnesota for the CEA job, and although he and Heller differed on some points —Heller, for example, favored a temporary tax cut to speed recovery—Galbraith considered Heller "the ablest economist ever to serve on the President's Council."

With Heller and Goldberg leading the way toward as much spending as Dillon would vouchsafe to Congress as noninflationary, the President might be persuaded to recommend more public projects to cure the recession. The outlook was less bright for lowering interest rates as drastically as Galbraith thought was necessary for growth and stability. Given the strong determination of the Chairman of the Federal Reserve Board, William McChesney Martin, Jr., not to go along with any plan based on a steady lowering of both short-term and long-term lending rates, it would take a passionate counterdetermination on someone's part to prevail against him. Certainly in the first phase of a difficult Administration the President could not be relied on for that. If there was to be a crusade for lower interest rates, it would have to be led from

some other quarter than the White House. "But who is there to do
it?" I asked Galbraith. "Albert Gore could," he replied.

WHO CAN HEAD THE CRUSADE?

Galbraith was, of course, referring to the junior Senator from
Tennessee, who had learned his economics on the Banking and
Currency Committee as a member of the House and had gone on
to become one of the most expert members of the Committee on
Finance in the Senate. Well liked and respected by his colleagues,
persuasive in debate, effective in making difficult issues simple to
understand, Gore had the passion, the prestige, and the understanding to take the leadership in the interest-rate fight. He also
had a proper ambition to get ahead in national politics that would
keep his passion burning bright. In addition, he had entree to the
new President.

Gore and Kennedy had been seatmates in the Senate and became personal friends. Senator and Mrs. Gore were in the dinner
party of eight at which Kennedy met Jacqueline Bouvier. At Kennedy's request, Gore had served with Senate Foreign Relations
Chairman William Fulbright and Clark Clifford, Special Counsel
to former President Truman, as private advisers to the candidate
on key matters during the Presidential campaign. These three men
met every weekend in Washington: usually at Gore's apartment,
sometimes at Fulbright's home (to escape notice at the Capitol),
and threshed out strategy advice that was then relayed directly to
Kennedy. Almost every day in the last weeks of the campaign,
phone calls, messages, and draft speeches flew back and forth
between the group of three and the candidate. After the election
the close consultation between these men and the President-elect
continued. When Congress reconvened after the conventions, Gore
spent a private hour with Kennedy at Kennedy's request, going
over economic-policy questions. Then, on November 22, from his
farm at Carthage, Tennessee, Gore wrote a long private letter to
the President.

SENATOR GORE'S ADVICE

The Senator argued that the most important appointment to be
made was that of Secretary of the Treasury, and that the choice of

Douglas Dillon, who was rumored to be in the running, would lead to disaster.

Gore wrote:

Ordinarily, the Secretary of State is the most important [appointment], but not so with your administration. This is true because the central theme of your campaign and the key to regaining, or the failure to regain, U.S. prestige and power in world affairs depends primarily not upon diplomacy but upon dynamic economics. This involves not only domestic economic goals but international trade, balance of payments, foreign aid, military security, and political leadership. . . . Without proper economic policies, no other policies can be successfully implemented.

Under current conditions of the world power distribution and given the population growth of the peoples of the world, including our own, as well as the rising expectations of individuals the world over, the primary requirement of the economy of the United States at this moment in history is quantitative and qualitative growth.

The United States had all the necessary ingredients for growth, he said—"the natural resources, the physical space, the climatic diversity, the capital, the managerial structure, the technicians, the labor, and the individual will." What had been lacking in recent years, the Senator argued, was "the government ingredient." The Government, "as agent for the whole society, must implement clearly defined economic policies."

The present difficulties with balance of payments, and the consequent gold problem, are symptoms, really, of the failure of the present administration to keep the United States on the "move." You made this case to the American people magnificently [in the campaign]. Why then, should you consider even for a fleeting moment for appointment to the key post of Treasury one whose chief claim to fame is that he has been a member of a team that failed its most important test? This applies not only to Mr. Dillon, who is an affable easy-goer, but to other conservative Republicans who have been mentioned.

That kind of appointment, in Senator Gore's opinion, "would be a signal that you had given up the goals of a truly Democratic Administration in domestic affairs and, consequently, the progress necessary to restore United States position and prestige abroad." It "would mean, for instance, that glaring tax loopholes would not be closed; that fiscal policies, monetary policies, and economic policies would not be very different from the present [Eisenhower administration. This would not be your intention, to be sure, but it would be the likely consequence."

Having explained to his friend the President-elect what kind of Secretary of Treasury he did not need, the Senator from Tennessee went on to tell him what kind of economic policies he would need. "It is generally recognized that the active use of fiscal measures, in conjunction with other measures (tax and monetary policies) can do much to smooth out the business cycle and prevent disruptions in employment and production, thus guarding against loss of production and helping to insure growth." Like Galbraith's list of essentials for recovery and growth, Gore's included changes in fiscal and monetary policies. But from his greater experience in Government, the Senator put tax policies at the head of the list, for the reason that "in recent years, fiscal policy has not been actively pursued. Indeed, a proper use of fiscal measures has been impossible because the Internal Revenue Act of 1954 established a level of revenues far too low to permit sufficient flexibility." Gore was referring to the income-tax cut President Eisenhower had allowed his Secretary of the Treasury, George N. Humphrey, to put through in the early days of his Administration.

"Because of the top priority given tax favoritism and high interest rates" by Secretary Humphrey, "deficits have been overly large and frequent, even in years of comparative prosperity," Gore pointed out. "Government spending, both necessary and desirable, has been curtailed both in years of prosperity and in years of recession." (The publication of Sherman Adams' memoirs shortly afterward revealed that even on the question of increasing the national-defense budget, Eisenhower had given Secretary Humphrey a final right of veto.)

CLOSING TAX LOOPHOLES

It followed that "The first requisite is to raise the general level of revenue. Without this," Gore stressed, "it appears to me that our administration will be in an economic strait jacket." With more income, the President could be more flexible in his use of fiscal and monetary measures. The place to begin increasing income, he said, "is by closing certain tax loopholes." And he included a little list:

1. Tighten up on excessive deductions for expense accounts and other so-called business expenses of questionable validity.
2. Eliminate the dividend tax credit.
3. Basically modify the formula for tax deduction which is called

percentage depletion but which bears no relationship whatsoever
to depletion of a resource.

4. Repeal restrictive stock option provisions.
5. Repeal or basically modify the foreign tax credit provisions.
6. Repeal capital gains treatment for certain lump sum tax repay-
   ments.
7. Repeal estate and gift tax exemptions for certain pension payments.
8. Provide for withholding at the source tax on interest and dividends received.

"These loopholes of tax favoritism," Gore assured Mr. Kennedy,
"can be closed without an extensive or drastic overhaul of the tax
structure."

Senator Gore was especially emphatic on point number 5 and
spoke boldly about the ticklish subject of taxation (or lack of
taxation) of profits earned by American businesses abroad. He
was later to convert the President to his point of view after lengthy
private explanations. "The foreign tax credit is overly liberal," his
letter asserted, "and leads to the exportation of too much capital
abroad. This, in the short run, leads to balance of payment difficulties and, in the long run, to the loss of employment at home and
increased imports from abroad."

Then there was the question of tax cuts for industry to encourage expansions and so increase tax income in the future, which was
being strongly urged on Kennedy. The trouble with that, Gore
pointed out, was that "At the present time it appears that the
shortage is not in production facilities but in purchasing power.
Should expansion of production facilities be needed, the matter
should be thoroughly studied before taxes are cut. Past experience
has not been encouraging." When Humphrey gave the corporations substantial tax cuts in 1954, Gore pointed out, "instead of
modernizing they raised dividends and increased their liquidity.
Moreover, a large share of expansion has been accomplished by
internal financing, that is through higher prices and thus bigger
profits. There is undeniable need for improved efficiency in production, but tax reduction for this purpose requires careful study
and treatment, else the desired results may escape us."

KENNEDY'S MODEST BEGINNING

All these opinions and interpretations were well known to the
President when he decided on a far more moderate beginning to

reverse the recession than most of his trusted advisers wanted. He heard them repeated frequently while he was taking a second look. But, as always, there was more than economic advice for the President to consider. There was his judgment of what the public would support, against what new contingencies he should hedge, and how far he could carry Congress with him. With respect to a cut in income taxes to speed recovery, there was little question: Galbraith's arguments and Gore's concern with increasing Federal revenue had their effect, and Congress unquestionably would take a dim view of the proposed plan to give the President authority to lower or raise rates to counter recessions without asking Congressional approval in each instance. He would not ask that.

As for expanding public works, Mr. Kennedy had a natural allergy to spending for its own sake. In the Senate, he had felt a greater affinity for Paul Douglas for his "responsible liberalism" on economic matters than for the Humphrey-Clark wing of the Democratic Party. The difference, oversimplified, was that the latter group saw so many public needs unfulfilled that almost any Federal spending seemed justified, while Douglas and Kennedy felt that unless spending could be allocated to the most urgent sectors, they were willing to wait until it could be. Douglas, for example, would not approve some highway construction on the ground that schools were needed more. And there were those, too, who said it was already too late to spend the United States out of the current recession—the peak was past and large spending now would only contribute to inflation. The theory behind the billion-dollar public-works bill Senators Clark and Humphrey were urging was that the first signs of recession should trigger public-works spending to restore balance in the economy. The time for that, it was argued, had been October 1960, not now.

In March, as he laid down his suggested first steps for recovery, the President could feel new contingencies in the wind. Laos and the Congo were boiling, and a showdown on Berlin could not be far away. Laos alone made certain another budget request to train guerrilla forces and increase conventional-arms capability. If there was to be any thought of a balanced budget at all, what all this would cost had to be kept in mind.

And then there was room for a certain scepticism as to how scientific the men of modern economics really were. John Maynard Keynes had taught how to deal with depression—by the free flow of credit and injections of public spending—but were the economists really sure when to turn off the Keynesian faucet to forestall inflation? The President resolved to go slow and see to what extent the business cycle would work its own cure.

Kennedy seemed to think he had more to lose politically by outraging those who would draw back in horror from the billion-dollar public-works bill that Clark and Humphrey were proposing with the support of organized labor than by disappointing its sponsors. Why begin by antagonizing the inflation-conscious inhabitants of suburbia who had been suspicious of him in 1960 and whom he wanted to win over? Why not try in one degree or another all those spending methods that did not require huge new appropriations, and see if unemployment fell to less than six per cent by the end of the year? After all, the Samuelson report had sanctioned going slow. "One cannot realistically expect to undo in 1961 the inadequacies of several years," Samuelson had written. "It is not realistic to aim for the restoration of high employment within a single calendar year." The President seemed to assume that the adverse balance-of-payments problem he had inherited would stir sufficient sympathy to silence some of the critics on the left. Of course, if unemployment increased and the outlook darkened before the 75-day period for the second look expired, more would have to be done, but if at the end of the year moderate measures had not lowered unemployment to less than six per cent, he would have proved that he had tried everything else first and could then ask Congress to open the spending throttle wide.

That was how some of those privy to the economic discussions going on in the White House read the President's intentions in early April, and the Administration's attitude toward the public-works proposal in the Senate bore them out. When hearings were scheduled on the Clark bill, the White House indicated it had no burning desire to take part. In fact, word was passed that if asked to take an official position on the measure at that time, it would have to register opposition. The organizers of the hearings therefore postponed an invitation while the Administration presumably wrestled with the statistics.

"GROWTH-SCHOOL" ADVISERS

President Kennedy had consciously picked personal advisers from the "growth" school of economics, men who believed in a larger Federal role in managing the economy and a more militant use of the spending power to achieve growth and full employment.

When he was chosen as Chairman of the CEA, Dr. Heller, to make sure that Kennedy understood what philosophy he was getting, warned the President that he would want a voice in the picking of the members and would choose, for one, Professor James Tobin of Yale, a "modern" like himself. Kennedy replied that he wanted the situation understood also, and that if Heller had refused the position, Tobin would have been Kennedy's second choice.

But the President meant the CEA to be "advisory," in keeping with its name, and in line with his general policies of administration. And it quickly became clear that to advise was not always to prevail. However, his three economic wisemen reported, by the way, that Mr. Kennedy was facile and quick to grasp concepts they discussed. Some of his old friends from the Senate and House do not rate the President so high. "Jack has never had any practical financial experience, you know," one of them says. "His personal affairs have been run by bankers and accountants who mail him checks and forms to sign. He never had to master economics." But the man who probably knows John F. Kennedy's public mind better than anyone concurs in the council's estimate. When I asked Ted Sorensen in what subjects the President is least learned, he made no mention of economics. "Agriculture," the President's counsel answered after a pause, then added with a smile, "And Catholic theology."

Just as consciously Kennedy had chosen, as head of the august Department of the Treasury, a solid ex-Republican, trusted as sound by bankers and business in general. Douglas Dillon proved his loyalty to his new boss and perhaps risked his reputation for "fiscal integrity" with Mr. Eisenhower, by declaring that there is nothing sinful about deficits per se. Dillon told Congress, and later the National Press Club, that a deficit is good business after a recession, not inflationary, but "inevitable and appropriate." As a practical man who had accepted the new economic philosophy, Dillon's word had steadily increasing weight at the White House.

Off in the wings, there was always the autonomous Federal Reserve Board whose chairman brooked no interference with what he considered the Board's right to regulate the flow of credit. Eager to avoid a clash, the President and his men were maintaining a watchful attitude toward Chairman Martin, leaning over backward not to offend.

Budget Director Bell and Ted Sorensen tried to establish the White House as neutral ground. But sharing Kennedy's built-in reservations about spending and having his boss's future political

welfare always in mind, Sorensen impressed the "growth" group
as neutral against them.

At issue during April and early May was whether to settle for
mild recovery—lay aside basic high unemployment and low economic growth rate to worry about later—or, something more radical, go to the root of the problem. A second look failed to convince
the members of the Economic Council, Secretary Goldberg, and
leading liberals in Congress that the program the President had
announced in March had put us "firmly on the road to full recovery and sustained growth" in May. More stimulation was
needed—in their view, an income-tax cut and much more Federal
spending for public purposes.

Heller had been encouraged to work out more palatable ver-
sions of the Clark bill, and for a time the proponents of over-all
spending to bolster demand thought that the President had decided
their way. Then came the Cuban failure and resultant tougher
talk from Premier Khrushchev. Then Major Yuri Gagarin orbited
the earth.

SPACE AND DEFENSE AS SPENDING SUBSTITUTES

Kennedy as candidate had dwelt on our loss of prestige from
being second to the Soviet Union in space. In his first two months
as President, he was preoccupied with moving the first phases of
his domestic program ahead in Congress. But on March 22, the
President, Vice President Johnson, whom Kennedy had named
Chairman of his Aeronautics and Space Council, and the director
of the Council, Edward Welsh, met to thresh out the budget requests for space activities left over from the Eisenhower Administration. The next day the three conferred again with the President's
Science Adviser Jerome Wiesner and Budget Director Bell, after
which the President approved a $126-million increase in National
Aeronautics and Space Administration funds to develop "big
boosters," the immediate point of lag between the United States
and Russia.

Because the President had approved only part of NASA's pending supplemental budget request, the press generally misinterpreted
Kennedy's action as a cutback in the NASA program. In fact, the
$126 million was earnest money for what would become a $40-
billion undertaking over ten years to beat the Russians to the
moon.

This was not known to most of the public-works advocates while the "second look" debate was going on. Nor was it realized how quickly the Russian response to Cuba would multiply Pentagon requests for more of everything with which to wage conventional war.

The battle to solve the 1960 recession by peaceful means was lost in the fourteen hours of May 21 when Yuri Gagarin was circling the earth. The immediate demands for funds to overtake the Russians in space and to match their nonnuclear military power would by themselves require as much in deficit spending as Kennedy's converted Republican Secretary of the Treasury would vouch for—and only a little less than the Federal Reserve Chairman might regard as signaling the need for tightening up on the money supply.

The President indicated in a press conference how his mind was adjusting to all this. Had the second look persuaded him that we should be doing more? "I think we could make a judgment as to what additional efforts should be made in retraining and more public works, based on our judgment of the economy, and also what other expenditures we have to make in fields of national security," Mr. Kennedy replied. But Heller and the Economic Council were not reconciled to substituting armament and space spending for public projects. The latter were more efficient stimulants to recovery and, more important, led to economic growth. Spending for defense might stop a headache, as had been demonstrated in 1939, during the New Deal; but our trouble now was that persistent pain that called for seeing a doctor. Senators Humphrey and Clark joined them in arguing that the space and arms programs would not affect unemployment before February or March of 1962. If the President would request a large public-works program before June, the Senators said, they would undertake to put through an emergency program to relieve unemployment in the meantime. A large investment program would cost big money now but bring in big money later, Chairman Heller reminded the President. He would guarantee a balanced budget in 1963 if Kennedy would follow his recommendations now.

UNCERTAIN SUPPORT IN THE SENATE

The President did not rush to accept either offer. Senate leaders had come close to a costly cropper on the most elementary bill to limit economic suffering. Assuming he wanted to take the chance, how did Mr. Kennedy know his Senate leaders were any better at their business now? Kennedy's own legislative man had had to ride to the rescue to prevent a symbolic defeat on the first recovery measure to reach the Senate floor in mid-March—a bill to extend unemployment compensation for those who had been out of work so long that the period in which they were entitled to draw benefits had expired. Waving the banner of "preserving State responsibility," Senator Byrd had stormed the Finance Committee and written in a provision that negated the Administration bill. By a vote of 11 to 2, with only Senators Gore and Douglas opposing, the committee, following Byrd's lead, voted to base payments on the amount of state contributions to the Federal Trust Fund rather than on the number of unemployed. The President's close friend, Senator Smathers of Florida, supposedly in charge of defeating the amendment in committee, was not even present when it came up.

With the committee vote so lopsided against the Administration, there was general discouragement at the prospect of defeating the Byrd provision on the floor. Then Albert Gore got mad. As State Labor Commissioner he had set up the original unemployment-compensation program in Tennessee, and Senator Byrd was striking at the equalization provision that was the heart of such a measure. Senator Gore called the White House to say, in effect, beat this amendment or you will lose your whole program. Senate staff work had been so bad that Senator Morse and others were out of town on speaking engagements without being paired. And Secretary Goldberg, whose department was primarily concerned, was touring centers of unemployment. Reached by telephone in the field, Goldberg was back in Washington by evening for a meeting with O'Brien and Senate leaders. Communications with the Senate had apparently failed completely, for Senators Clinton P. Anderson of New Mexico and Vance Hartke of Indiana, staunch Administration men, had voted with Senator Byrd in committee, never having had word not to. Getting the word, they now reversed their stand. O'Brien got on the telephone to Governors of states standing to benefit by the bill and asked them to call their Senators. Southerners were given an alibi to use at home: unless they went along on equalization of unemployment compensation, Northern Senators would vote against them on health and education measures—and Southern states take more out of Federal funds than they put in.

The bill was saved. But the incident showed little promise of a precision operation on the Democratic side that would guarantee victory for the controversial works bill.

As for Dr. Heller's guarantee of a balanced budget in 1963, the President understood modern economics well enough to know how rapidly recovery could increase Federal income—he explained it dozens of times in his campaign. But Kennedy had an added problem not yet worked out in the books. Aside from the question at what point constructive spending turned into destructive inflation, there was a troublesome new factor. In the last three years of the Eisenhower Administration, so much gold had flowed out of the United States that we had accumulated a deficit of almost $11 billion in our international balance of payments.

In other words, what the United States Government had spent and what United States business had invested abroad in those three years exceeded all our export and other earnings overseas by about $11 billion.

Little was said publicly about this dramatic change in the international economic position of the country until the 1960 Presidential campaign was over. Then "balance of payments" joined the other pigeons that came home to the White House to roost. The knowing ones in Washington were well aware of the bearing the new problem would have on all economic actions in the future. But few, in February, when the President sent Congress a special message on "Balance of Payments and Gold," appreciated the central part this technical and abstruse matter would play in Kennedy's decisions during his first year and, probably, for some time to come.

FEAR OF INFLATIONARY EFFECTS

There were long-run ways to correct the balance between what went out and what came in—they involved a drive to increase exports by granting credit and guarantees; and to make savings in foreign-exchange costs by persuading other countries to share in the expenses of United States troops overseas and to buy more of their military equipment from us.

One faster way was to abolish the tax exemption that encouraged business to invest abroad, particularly in tax haven areas. (In the first session, the House Ways and Means Committee refused to report out a bill Kennedy sent to Congress to accomplish that.) Steps to improve the international-reserve mechanism through working with other governments and their central banks and organizations like the International Monetary Fund would take time.

Meanwhile, what happened to the flow of gold would be largely in the hands of international bankers and would depend upon their confidence in the soundness of the United States dollar. And that, President Kennedy's Secretary of Treasury and Federal Reserve Chairman assured him, was a psychological matter. If the men who controlled the movement of currencies around the world decided that the Kennedy Government was "responsible" and was moving toward a balanced budget, confidence would be restored and the full value of the dollar assured. Let those sharp-eyed men in "The City" and the Paris Bourse and the banks of Brussels and Amsterdam detect inflationary tendencies in the new Administration and heavy withdrawals of gold would begin before you could say "fiscal integrity."

Professor Samuelson and all three of the President's economic advisers had assured him that he need have no fear of inflationary effects from heavy public-works spending in 1961—even a mighty lift would not take up all the slack in the economy. And many economists were pointing out that a restoration of a healthy rate of economic activity in the United States would lead other nationals to put their dollars to work here rather than repatriate them through gold conversion. But Chairman Martin of the Federal Reserve thought otherwise. It was inflationary nonsense to try to put people back to work by general spending, he insisted. This was persistent "structural" unemployment, calling for technical adjustments and for "special measures" designed to aid problem industries and young, old, and unskilled workmen, not a general attack. And Martin had a carrot and a stick.

In testimony in Congress, Martin indicated that if the Administration wanted to fight unemployment by "special measures," the Federal Reserve would co-operate by insuring the supply of "easy money" during the process. But if Kennedy chose the over-all attack, he could not expect the Federal Reserve to accompany him far along that inflationary road.

During the three months while the second look was taking place Secretary Dillon and Assistant Treasury Secretary Robert V Roosa, a former international expert in the Federal Reserve Bank of New York, brought in reports of talks with friends in the banking community here and abroad that fortified their initial arguments. And the assessment his new associates made of Martin was that he meant what he said and would not be easily moved.

The President's natural preference for the specific and definite in spending—"You don't have to be a wastrel to be a liberal" had been a stock saying among his set in the Senate—probably inclined him to the pin-point approach to unemployment that Martin recommended. The fact that there would be a goodwill dividend in the credit field from Martin if he took that course certainly did not prejudice Kennedy against emphasizing the problem of "structural unemployment" in his program.

Eisenhower's economic adviser during his first term, Professor Arthur F. Burns of Columbia University, was vigorously arguing before committees of Congress and in written debate with members of Kennedy's council that unemployment would automatically fall to around four per cent within a year without any further stimulation by the Government. But this view did not impress the President. Whatever the economic argument, it was certainly risky politics.

Economic boldness of the kind his council favored could be risky politics, too. If his problem was to pull out of the recession by small steps that would not lead to inflation or give the impression of irresponsibility abroad, what better advice could Kennedy heed than that of Dillon who understood the men he was trying to impress? In Dillon's favor was the word that had come from Paris while Kennedy was picking his Cabinet—that Dillon's selection for the Treasury post would bring an immediate slowdown in the then rapid outflow of gold from the United States.

Kennedy chose the middle way—between the counsel of his own economic advisers and Eisenhower's.

URGENT NATIONAL NEEDS

Before leaving for his initial meetings with President De Gaulle and Premier Khrushchev in Paris and Vienna, the President addressed a Joint Session of Congress on May 25 on the subject of "Urgent National Needs." The additional spending program he requested would boost the 1962 deficit to $5 billion, as Samuelson had originally recommended. But the vast bulk of this spending would be for armaments, foreign aid, and space exploration. Spending for space and defense would not have as far-reaching an economic effect as the public-works projects the council advised, but they would be much easier to get past Congress.

On May 25 the President let Congress in on what he saw ahead; more foreign economic assistance and military assistance—"The present crisis in Southeast Asia, on which the Vice President has made a valuable report—the rising threat of Communism in Latin America—increased arms traffic in Africa—and all the new pressures of every nation found on the map by tracing your finger along the borders of the Communist bloc, in Asia and the Middle East—all make clear the dimension of our needs"; more funds for United States Information Agency operations in Latin America and Southeast Asia and to increase army "paramilitary" forces; more Federal financing for Civil Defense; and finally, funds for a costly new undertaking, "before this decade is out, of landing a man on the moon and returning him safely to earth."

There had been only a slight upturn in business between January and June. Unemployment still stood at the same 6.8 per cent, or close to five million, and virtually the same as since February. But Kennedy's voice was vibrantly confident as he declared that the emergency was over. There was one burden he would not carry with him to Vienna and his meeting with Khrushchev. "The recession," he assured the world in his May 25 message, "has been halted. Recovery is under way."

The President did take note of the fact that "The task of abating unemployment and achieving a full use of our resources does remain a serious challenge." Large-scale unemployment during a recession is bad enough, he remarked, but "large scale unemployment during a period of prosperity would be intolerable." But the only long-range proposal was a four-year program for training and retraining several hundred thousand of the "structural unemployed" in hard-hit areas. Otherwise, reliance for putting millions back to work and creating new jobs for a million more every year was to be placed on "the occupational demands of new American leadership in space, aid, trade and defense." The emphasis fell on what a satisfaction it should be to us all "that we have made great strides in restoring world confidence in the dollar, halting the outflow of gold, and improving our balance of payments" during the last two months, and on the fact that "if the budget deficit now increased by the needs of our security is to be held within manageable proportions, it will be necessary to hold tightly to prudent fiscal standards."

Reading the message to Congress, the President was pressed for time: the paragraphs in the complete text of the message that dealt with the importance of economic growth to sustain new efforts in the world and in space were among those he chose to omit.

Few among his usual supporters saw the same economic visions as the President or shared his satisfaction with the course he had set. The Democratic majority in the Congressional Joint Economic Committee could not bring itself to go as far in assessing recovery. They were "pleased" that in his several policy messages the President had adopted "principles of modern economic thought which this committee had frequently endorsed." The 1960–61 recession was, the committee believed and hoped, "at a turning point." But the majority report issued in May pointed out that "of all the expert witnesses we have heard, the most optimistic expected that, by the end of the year, six to seven per cent of the labor force will still be unemployed and unemployment would not be reduced to as low as four per cent by the end of 1962. These expectations are based, moreover, on the assumption that the administration's legislative program will be promptly enacted. . . . Although a moderate rise in production is expected throughout the remainder of the year—and beyond—this will hardly do more than provide jobs for the normal growth in the labor force. In other words, while the economy is expected to run faster, it will run only fast enough to stand still." What he was recommending, the Joint Economic Committee gently warned Kennedy, would not produce the results he had promised. "Certainly no dollar should be spent merely as a recessionary cure," the committee agreed. "Rather, every dollar spent should be prudently spent for proper and useful accomplishments." But, at the same time, the majority report concluded, "We cannot help noting that the total effects of all the actions so far taken and proposed will be small as compared to the gap between the nation's expected economic performance and its economic potential."

THE GAP BETWEEN PERFORMANCE AND POTENTIAL

In a letter to AFL-CIO President George Meany and the Trade Union Council a few weeks later, the President conceded that "Many economic problems will continue to confront us," but, he repeated, "we have now emerged from the recession." The best supporting statement Secretary Goldberg could manage on the occasion was that he saw "some hopeful signs." But Mr. Meany's flat response was that "real recovery is nowhere in sight."

In June Leon Keyserling, by now deeply critical of Kennedy's course, predicted the present slow rate of growth was insufficient to provide the number of jobs needed to absorb the growing labor force, and that unless it was accelerated unemployment would rise six to seven million in four years. Dr. Samuelson, looking ahead, calculated that on the basis of planned programs, unemployment would persist at a six per cent level throughout most of 1962.

Employment, in the first six months of Kennedy's Administration, increased no more rapidly than it had under Eisenhower in 1960. Yet the shouting about it had died down to a murmur. The disenchantment with Kennedy's economic policies was more real than apparent. Senators Clark, Humphrey, and Gore and others from Congress were not bashful about speaking up to the President or arguing with him in private. Their explanation for not attacking publicly the President's seeming willingness to live with quite a lot of unemployment for a considerable time to come was: "It's hard to take public issue with one of our own."

Labor leaders were equally loath to attack the man they had helped to elect. They reasoned, as Kennedy had reasoned with respect to Congress, that it was the better part of valor to stay friends and try to influence him. And besides, Meany and Walter Reuther and David J. McDonald and international union presidents in general were enjoying the unusual privilege of being invited to the White House socially. Mr. and Mrs. Walter Reuther were on the guest list for the select Mount Vernon gala in honor of the President of Pakistan. Labor chiefs had occasionally seen Eisenhower; Truman had them in for regular conferences; but now they were treated like friends, entitled to knock on the front door or telephone when there was something to communicate. That made a human difference. The President and those around him realized, too, the importance of institutional problems to union men. When situations arose that could cast reflections on specific unions or on the trade-union movement in general, the Administration was ready with a sympathetic and sophisticated ear—and that played a role in softening criticism.

Organized labor had been the strongest single voice for the billion-dollar public-works proposal. Meany, an early and effective supporter of J.F.K. for President, wrote to him personally to ask support for the Clark bill. He got a straight and thoughtful answer: The President had to think not just about the here and now of domestic economic affairs—he had to look ahead to possible new military contingencies around the world and the problem of paying for them without severely unbalancing the budget—a harbinger of other decisions to come, when the second look gave way to the third.

SECRETARY DILLON'S INFLUENCE

Kennedy's Secretary of the Treasury had played a central role in the second-look decision. Some think that without his support the President would never have vetoed the advice of so many others around him. Certainly Dillon's first six months as a former Republican in a Democratic Cabinet were full of surprises—for his former Eisenhower colleagues and for some of his new Kennedy associates. He early revealed a tolerance for deficit spending that perhaps partially inspired his former chief's sad statement in the spring of 1961: "I look in vain and with deep concern for fiscal responsibility in today's public affairs." In addition to declaring that the early deficit forecast for 1961 as not only "inevitable" but "appropriate," Dillon added the assurance that it held out no threat of "classic inflation." For his part, he said, a $6-billion deficit would not be too much if that were required to get out of the recessionary rut.

The chorus of consternation in Republican circles was loud enough to move Dillon's friends to rise to his defense. A semi-official explanation of Dillon's activities found its way into the Sunday New York *Times* over the by-line of Arthur Krock.

Setting up a proper straw man, Krock reported that "Senator Byrd of Virginia, who is the Chairman of the [Senate Finance] Committee, has said that the succession of recommendations by the President to Congress that Dillon has approved come too rapidly for sound analysis. But he thinks they might increase spending by $10 billion so far."

Galloping to the rescue, Krock reported that "Inquiries by this correspondent, however, produced a strong challenge of that impression [of acquiescence]. In official quarters the following account was given of [Dillon's] curbing activities in the private fiscal councils of the Administration."

1. In the period between the President's messages of March 24 [sic] and May 23 to Congress, Mr. Kennedy took the "second look" he said he would at budget requirements. Any additions or revisions, he had promised, would confirm to the fiscal principles he outlined on March 24—spending for economic growth and maximum employment "within a setting of reasonable price stability," and each expenditure "evaluated in terms of our national needs and priorities"—according, of course, to his definition of these.

2. During the "second look" there was pressure on the President

    inside the Administration, in Congress, and from special-interest groups for more than twelve anti-recession and social welfare spending measures that would have added a minimum of $10 billion to the $3.7 billion deficit of the 1961–62 budget as revised. The deficit, therefore, instead of rising only to $3.7 billion from the $2.8 billion envisaged in January, would have grown to $13.7 billion at least. Among the strongly backed proposals were these: $4 billion for public works. A make-work repair program for roads damaged last winter. A large increase in the appropriations for housing, house repairs and loans. An expanded food stamp project. Remission or reduction of income taxes. Repeal of the excise taxes. Funds to assist the "structural unemployed." Job training for the unskilled. Funds for a Youth Conservation Corps.

3. Secretary Dillon successfully opposed all of these except the last four enumerated, which accounted for only $175 million of the budget rise from $2.8 billion to $3.7 billion. And the President supported him in every instance.

"This certainly is proof that Dillon, next to the President, is the most effective restraining influence against avoidable spending," Krock quoted the anonymous "high administration official" who had produced the data as saying, adding "as it is the duty of the Treasury to be."

Dillon may have crossed over to the other side, Krock was explaining to the disappointed Eisenhower Republicans, but they could take consolation from the fact that there was "evidence that he holds a check-rein on the more lavish spenders and uses it." Mr. Krock might have mentioned the checkrein others held on fiscal and monetary policies, too.

Heller's influence was not proving predominant in economic decisions, as Galbraith had hoped. Heller, Goldberg, and Senate liberals believed unemployment reflected a generally weak condition in the economy that could be relieved by stimulation of over-all demand. Federal Reserve Chairman Martin insisted that the root problem was persistent "structural unemployment," and that attacking it the over-all way would mean that "massive monetary and fiscal stimulation . . . likely would have to be carried to such lengths as to create serious new problems of an inflationary character—at a time when consumer prices already are at a record high." Martin indicated to Congress that he would co-operate in a low-interest-rate policy for the duration of efforts to solve the "structural" problem, but not through an extended period of general spending. The only part of the original Clark-Heller approach that Kennedy carried over intact into his May 25 message was the provision for retraining the victims of structural unemployment.

TIGHT VS. EASY CREDIT

Having sided with Dillon and Martin on the size of the deficit, and the approach to curing unemployment, the President also moved less decisively than Heller, the Council, and his friends in Congress liked in employing the second available tool for increasing demand. Reversing the Eisenhower tight money policy continued to be the stated goal—there was a strong restatement of it in the May 25 Message on Urgent National Needs.

"The full financial influence of the government must continue to be exerted in the direction of general credit ease and further monetary growth while the economy is recovering," Mr. Kennedy said. "Some further downward adjustments in interest rates, particularly those which have been slow to adjust in the recent recession, are clearly desirable," he went on in the spirit of campaign pledges. "Certainly to increase them would choke off recovery," he concluded lamely, but realistically, in view of what the Chairman of the Federal Reserve Board had been revealing about his inner thoughts on the subject.

It was Democratic doctrine that Federal Reserve policies had prevented full recovery by tightening credit too soon after recent recessions had been reversed. The Administration was eager to prevent a rise in interest rates this time, at least until unemployment fell to four per cent. The President and Secretary Dillon personally turned their not inconsiderable charms on Chairman Martin with that purpose in mind, and it was Administration policy to speak nothing but good of Martin and the Board. Dr. Heller always expressed the friendliest feeling when asked about the Council's relations with the FRB. And in twenty-seven appearances before Congressional committees during the first six months, Secretary Dillon was never trapped into a word of criticism of Board operations.

Martin, however, made no secret of his belief that for the FRB to supply sufficient reserves to permit banks to hold interest rates down very long after recovery began would bring inflation. "I do not believe anyone expects the Federal Reserve to engage in operations that will promote a resurgence of inflation in the future," he had told the Joint Economic Committee in early March. It came as no surprise when in early June, on a repeat visit to the committee, Martin testified that "If business continues to rise, interest rates will tend to rise. We [the Federal Reserve] can moderate but we can't control interest rates. . . . I don't want to see artificially low rates." By early August, the *Wall Street Journal* was reporting a "possible autumn clamp down on credit whether the White House likes it or not." The *Journal* warned that the Federal Reserve would be watching the money market and ready to apply brakes to the supply. "Hot protests would almost surely come from Democratic 'easy money' advocates in Congress," the report continued. But "any similar outcry from the Administration depends largely on which set of advisers Mr. Kennedy listens to."

"Officials in Mr. Dillon's Treasury are showing increasing concern over inflation possibilities," the writer explained, "and are privately discussing the role of tighter credit in heading off higher price trends. The Council of Economic Advisers, in contrast doubtless would show greater reluctance to depart from an 'easy money' policy." Federal Reserve, however, was nominally independent of the White House. "Reserve Board Chairman Martin hopes any Federal Reserve policy change will win the President's support," the *Wall Street Journal* added, "but he is determined to go ahead without it if necessary."

Senator Gore had foreseen this situation and had given the President his private advice about it in his November 1960 letter. "It should always be borne in mind that the Federal Reserve System was established to operate the mechanics of the banking system, not to formulate national economic policy," Senator Gore wrote. "It is absolutely necessary, in my opinion, to lay down strong guide lines for the Federal Reserve System in the field of monetary policy. A strong President can require that monetary policy be coordinated with fiscal, economic, debt management, foreign and related policies." How? The President did not have the power to remove Martin, appointed for a seven-year term, nor was it practical to induce public pressure on him in so technical a matter. A direct challenge, in the form of increasing interest rates when the Administration believed they should be lowered, could only be met by legislation, Gore believed. The President, with full drive, could induce Congress to pass a Federal loan program that would force banks and loan companies to lower their interest rates to compete with Government credit. I discussed the matter with the Senator in early June. "I can hooray them," he said, speaking of his colleagues in Congress, "but only the President can move them. I have told him that but haven't persuaded him." Perhaps

Martin would persuade him by fulfilling his threat and insisting on putting on the credit brakes as soon as the budget was balanced and the normal cycle of prosperity had returned, even though the basic unemployment problem remained unsolved.

In June, Heller impressed visitors as wistful and unfulfilled. By his standards, spending was still too low and credit too dear. But the Council and other loyal advocates of a faster route to recovery put on the best face they could, pointing with pride to the sta-bility of the price index—steadier than in past periods of upturn after recession. And they made much of the President's reiteration of his interest in economic growth at a press conference after his return from meeting Khrushchev. In his opinion, Mr. Kennedy said, a gross rate of growth of 4.5 per cent was "well within our capabilities."

THE RATE OF ECONOMIC GROWTH

It had been a long time between such declarations lately, and understandably the frustrated Council was grateful for even this slight sign that the wind might blow its way. But the context in which his modest aim was announced made it scarcely cause for great rejoicing by men who held the Council's views.

In an opening statement to his June 29 press conference, Presi-dent Kennedy referred to Premier Khrushchev's comparison of the United States to a worn-out runner living on his past performance, and his prediction that the Soviet Union would outproduce the United States by 1970. The best the President had to offer by way of rejoinder was that "If both countries sustain their present rate of growth, 3.5 per cent in the United States and 6 per cent in the Soviet Union, Soviet output will not reach two-thirds of ours by 1970 and our rate will be far easier to sustain or improve than the Soviet rate, which starts from a lower figure.

"Indeed, if our gross rate is increased to even 4.5 per cent, which is well within our capabilities," the President went on, "it is my judgment that the Soviet Union will not outproduce the United States at any time in the 20th Century."

Economic specialists among the reporters present at the Presi-dent's conference that day raised eyebrows in surprise. Coming from a supposed "growth" man, the emphasis was wrong. Mr. Kennedy's statement hinged on the "if" of our achieving a 4.5 per cent rate, not on the difficulty of doing so or the urgency of

doing much better, in view of the great gap between our present
2.5 per cent annual increase in production in recent years and the
Soviet Union's present 6.7 per cent. This was upside down from
the way Candidate Kennedy had approached the problem in the
Labor Day speech in Detroit's Cadillac Square that opened his
campaign for the Presidency. "This can be the most prosperous
country in the world . . . but we have to grow, and under a Republican leadership this country is standing still. . . ."

There were two facts to remember, he said then: "The Russian
economy is growing at three times the rate of ours." And "Last
year the United States had the lowest rate of economic growth of
any major industrialized society in the world.

"I don't like to see the United States second to any country. We
are going to make the United States first."

Nine months later, there was no more talk of going from close
to last to first among industrial nations in the rate of economic
growth as well as in present ability to produce. The urgency had
gone out of Kennedy's feelings about the need for increasing
economic strength. And, in fact, that aim had taken a reduced
priority among his immediate goals. Pressure from the right to balance the budget to preserve confidence in the dollar, in the absence of any great demand for action from the left, led this centrist
President to settle on business recovery, "and, we hope, a reduced
unemployment rate," through government spending on arms and
space. The larger, long-range problems he would have to leave to
worry about later—when, he hoped, a new Congress would be
friendlier or international tensions would have lessened and relieved budgetary strain.

Dr. Heller saw hope in the fact that the President continued to
consider a 4.5 per cent rate of growth "well within our capability"
even after looking into Mr. Khrushchev's eyes at Vienna, but the
New York *Herald Tribune* got the story differently from people
in the Administration with other views. The President was barely
back from Europe when a financial writer reported in the *Herald
Tribune* that "The Kennedy Administration has apparently accepted a 'conservative' approach to near-term fiscal policy in the
belief that it will be able to promote social programs in the year
ahead out of revenues generated by a prosperous economy.

"Thus, general references by the President to 'fiscal restraint'
mean specifically that for the sake of budget balancing, he is willing to defer spending on health and welfare programs for a
time. . . ."

The bill for the new forms of security Mr. Kennedy had felt

alled upon to order after Vienna was going to be sizable. By August, budget experts estimated that the President would have to equest another $3.5-billion defense appropriation to pay it. That lid not include Federal funds for community fallout shelters since t that time the policy was still every family for itself. Nor did it nclude a number of other more-than-likely contingencies already n the horizon.

THE "THIRD LOOK" AT ECONOMIC CONDITIONS

The world situation was not only going to get worse before it got etter, as Mr. Kennedy had forewarned the country in his Inugural Address—it was going to get more expensive and probbly stay that way. It was time for a "third look" at the economic ituation and what the Administration should be doing about it. The third look was well under way before the Communists built The Wall. And the men who were doing the looking had new riteria to guide them. "Officials in a half dozen separate agencies round town . . . for the first time are focusing more on inflation langers than on problems of unemployment and business slack," he *Wall Street Journal* reported on August 8. And the financial ressure was just beginning.

After The Wall, the President called Reserves and National 3uard units, mounted reinforcements, ordered arms-development rograms speeded up—none of them inexpensive items. Our international balance-of-payments position, which the President had roudly reported greatly improved in May, had suffered a setback n September. And the time had come for J.F.K. to prepare his irst full budget—all that the new Administration could do in the irst year was revise and expand and try to live within the budget or fiscal 1961–62 that the Eisenhower Administration had already repared and presented to Congress before Inauguration. The udget for fiscal 1962–63, on which the Administration began oncentrated work in September for presentation to the second ession of Congress in January, would be Kennedy's own.

The reasons his balance-of-payments-minded advisers had given im in May for making it a balanced budget scarcely needed to be aised again. Nineteen sixty-two was an election year. Kennedy ad been keen to escape a "big spender" reputation in 1961; now e was ambitious to begin 1962 with a reputation as a more ealistic balancer of the budget than Eisenhower—who had run deficits as high as $12.5 billion in a year and left Kennedy a sup posedly balanced budget that his Republican Secretary of th Treasury found on recalculation in February $1 billion in the red Now the President felt he needed a balanced budget at home a much as his financial advisers claimed they needed it to maintai confidence in the United States economy abroad. The way t destroy the argument Republicans would try to use again nex November—that Democrats are wastrels—was to bring a balance budget to Congress in January. At least balanced on paper. Emer gencies could alter cases; and there was always the "supplementa request" route when they occurred. There was no delaying th cold-war commitments, the preparations for increasing conven tional military strength to support the Western position in Berlin no backing down on going to the moon, or on carrying throug our foreign economic aid. And not much more than the Adminis tration had been doing before could be paid for out of Federal in come in sight.

There was no more talk of a drastic direct attack on unemploy ment—which had so stubbornly refused to improve as the level o general business activity had been doing. The President com municated a mood of resignation and preoccupation with othe matters when he met the press on August 30, five days after hi grim Address to the Nation on the crisis over Berlin.

Midway in the conference, a reporter arose to remark on th "very hard core of unemployment" that still remained. "Do yor have any special plans now beyond those you have already sug gested?" he asked.

"Well," the President answered, "we are concerned still abou unemployment, which is four and a half million and on a season ally adjusted rate would be about five million, which is still too high.

"We have had in the last two or three months a tremendou economic recovery, but because of population increases and pro ductivity increases and technological changes, we still have a har core," he explained. "I'm hopeful that as the economy begins t move ahead more that there will be a further decrease in the num ber of those unemployed," the President went on mildly.

He hoped that Congress would take action on job-retrainin where the problem was technological, and if that did not work "then we are going to have to consider what other steps we car take. But we have a large deficit and it's difficult to think that we could usefully increase that in order to affect employment withou adversely affecting the cost of living. That's our difficulty," the President said, almost with a sigh.

Instead of more spending, the President was wondering, had the time not come to raise taxes to cover the extra deficit the Berlin crisis would cause?

The sides divided on this issue as they had on the deficit. Secretary Dillon and Federal Reserve Chairman Martin urged the President to raise taxes to hold the budget line. That would help hold confidence in the dollar on the world market and so aid their efforts to keep a balance in international payments. The Council reminded the President that raising taxes now could repeat the error of 1959 when Eisenhower's experts misjudged the swing and the Treasury suddenly found itself with more than $1 billion surplus instead of the $13 billion deficit of the year before, and recovery was severely damaged as a result. Their advice was to maintain a small deficit of, say, $2 billion to make sure that we did not move too swiftly into a surplus position again as we completed the final climb out of the 1960 recession. Furthermore, would not Congress' answer to a request for a rise in corporation taxes be to cut the foreign-aid appropriation then before it? That argument had weight with an Administration that had dared everything to get this far with that bill. The Council prevailed for once—at a time of great importance. Dillon agreed they were right and reversed his position. And the hunt went on for other ways to achieve the desired result.

UNEMPLOYMENT PERSISTS

The judgment in August was that recovery of itself would now prove a sufficient force to maintain momentum in the economy. The economic indicators in September, however, gave the experts cold chills. Unemployment in September showed no sign of decline. Secretary Goldberg, in Tokyo for a trade conference, cabled that the news was "disturbing" and proof of "a stubborn and continuing unemployment problem." The statistics had been supposed to show improvement after the early autumn hurricanes and strikes. But the figures continued to show that the first eight months of 1961 registered the worst lag in employment recovery in any postwar recession. In the 1949 recovery, the unemployment rate improved 1.2 per cent in eight months. In 1954 the rate also improved 1.2 per cent in eight months. But, in 1961, unemployment remained at 6.8 to 6.9 per cent from February through October. The "down" stage of this recession stayed deeper for a longer time.

It was a gloomy September. "We had a few uneasy moments during the lull," Dr. Heller later admitted in an understatement born of better times. There was definite trouble on the international balance-of-payments situation in October—not to be admitted publicly by the Treasury until late December. And Democrats outside the Administration who could afford the luxury of being unpopular with the White House began to talk dourly of the future. Professor Seymour Harris of Harvard, perhaps the President's stanchest defender among liberal economists, said in September that present efforts were not enough and "a $10 billion deficit may be necessary to bring unemployment to 4 per cent next year." And Leon Keyserling saw gloom if not doom. "Some recent forecasts, with which I agree, indicate that full time unemployment at the end of 1962 may be between five and six per cent of the civilian labor force," he predicted. "This level of unemployment at the end of 1962, near the peak of the current 'boom' (if it lasts that long), might be much higher than during the previous 'boom' year 1959, thus representing continuation rather than reversal of the 'long-term retreat.' " There were some economists close to the Administration, Mr. Keyserling added, "who expect that about 1963, in the absence of much more vigorous and sweeping economic efforts than any now apparently under consideration, we shall slide into what is euphemistically called another 'inventory recession.' "

But November dawned brighter—which created a somewhat false sense of security. And at its end unemployment took its first tumble—only to 6.1 per cent of the 72 million work force, but a substantial drop from the 6.8 per cent average in previous months of 1961. And Administration minds turned again to containing the upturn ahead. While some worked on next year's budget to insure a tight rein on the Government's part, others departed for the boondocks to see that the "private sector" was prepared to do its duty.

THE CAMPAIGN TO KEEP BUSINESS AND
LABOR IN LINE

It did not help the Dillon-Martin effort to build confidence in the Administration abroad to have such lack of it expressed at home by United States business every day. Hostile statements harping on the Eisenhower charge of "fiscal irresponsibility" had grown as the estimated 1961 deficit had risen from the original $1 billion Secretary Dillon had found in the Eisenhower budget to an estimated $6.9 billion by the end of October. (That was after The Wall and a third supplemental Defense appropriation, a bumper crop year, and the consequent higher cost of price supports, and Congressional refusal to raise postal rates.) Business' attitude was important for a second reason. If Kennedy was to have a prayer of holding the price line beyond the autumn by the "permissive means" Galbraith and Goldberg had hoped would work, he was going to have to have more co-operation and less carping from the men who ran United States industry. As soon as Congress had recessed and was out of the way, a Kennedy Administration campaign to explain itself to business began.

Secretary Dillon addressed the bankers in San Francisco, Secretary Hodges addressed the businessmen in Chicago and at Hot Springs, Secretary Goldberg spoke to the Illinois Chamber of Commerce in his home town of Chicago, and the President himself addressed the National Association of Manufacturers and the National Convention of the AFL-CIO in the same week. All the messages were the same: This Administration is for a sound dollar and a balanced budget and against inflation—we expect you (labor or industry) to consider the total economy and not self-interest alone, to maintain a reasonable level of (wages or prices) for the common good. Kennedy's brave effort at jollity in saying to the NAM that he understood some members voted for him in 1960 "under the impression I was my father's son," drew but a few smiles. And some thought it presumptuous of Kennedy to link himself with so illustrious a predecessor when he said, "I suppose that President McKinley and I are the only two that are regarded as fiscally sound enough to be qualified for admission to this organization."

The AFL-CIO was not much more enchanted when the President told its delegates that he expected them to be moderate in their wage demands, asking for increases only where the record of increased productivity or special circumstances warranted. The steel industry had held back from a price increase in the summer and had now to be deterred again in the fall and winter. The campaign began to create a climate in which the steel union would "voluntarily" preserve an acceptable price-wage balance.

One of Attorney General Robert Kennedy's first acts had been to oil up the antitrust machinery in the Department of Justice. This was one tangible way to show labor that there would be an honest effort to control living costs if labor held wage demands down.

Many liberal economists in recent years had attributed the phenomenon of increasing prices during periods of unemployment to price fixing by industry, without regard to supply and demand. The President's brother had picked an assistant to head his Anti-trust Division who was able and eager to crack down on illegal price fixing. And on Capitol Hill the President's former Democratic rival, Senator Estes Kefauver, was directing a parallel assault on technically "legal" price fixing through "administered" prices, far less dramatic but more important for the economy than the "illegal" kind.

THE KEFAUVER-KENNEDY JOINT CRUSADE

Kefauver's committee and Robert Kennedy's staff were moving independently and in a spirit of rivalry understandable in public figures engaged in the same crusade. J.F.K. and Kefauver had always been cool but correct toward each other in the Senate and in political dealings. And that was how Kefauver and Bobby Kennedy behaved now. Both were sincerely concerned with protecting the public interest with respect to prices; and both concerned as politicians with getting the credit. Kefauver had supported Robert's nomination as Attorney General in the Judiciary Committee; he had also supported Judge Lee Loevinger of Minnesota to head the Antitrust Division when Bobby appointed him. Kefauver, since his Crime Committee days, had been a champion of a National Crime Commission, and when Bobby Kennedy was Counsel to Senator McClellan, he also took a strong position in favor. But when Kefauver and other Senators introduced a bill to create such a commission—the same bill that had been introduced in the previous Congress, the Attorney General suddenly turned cool and opposed it. Perhaps in his new position he did not want a group that would cut into his authority.

The issue of scandals in boxing had generated irritations between the two men. Kefauver held hearings, uncovered gangster domination, and introduced a bill for a Federal boxing commissioner. The Attorney General came out strongly against the bill, and when the Judiciary Committee requested his official views, there was no response at all until half an hour before the hearings began; then his office called to say he could not be present. Kefauver asked for his views in writing, received no answer, then

ddenly got a copy of a letter from Deputy Attorney General
yron White to Senator Eastland, dated two weeks earlier, op-
osing the bill. When Kefauver subsequently called on Bobby to
iscuss the matter, the Attorney General seemed more amenable.
fter referring casually to crime bills he himself had before the
idiciary Committee requiring votes, he even suggested ways of
drafting the Crime Commission bill so that he could support it.
Despite these differences, in matters of real substance, the Sena-
r, the Attorney General, and the Attorney General's Assistant
. Charge of Antitrust supported one another.
Bobby Kennedy's interest in prices was no doubt stimulated
y the public outrage over the unmasking of a conspiracy in the
ectrical industry during 1959. In the late spring of that year, the
ennessee Valley Authority issued a press release noting the
ceipt of identical bids on electrical generators. An alert Scripps-
oward reporter, who had been covering TVA for years, inter-
ewed TVA purchasing officials and found them unusually loqua-
ous. A resulting series of three articles was carried nationwide
id came to Kefauver's attention. He immediately announced an
vestigation by his subcommittee, with hearings scheduled for
at fall. And the Justice Department convened a grand jury in
iladelphia.
It still is not completely clear whether Justice would have gone
lead without the Senator's prodding. Word in the department
as that the Philadelphia office had some knowledge of what was
ing on, but could not get the attention of Assistant Attorney
eneral Robert Bicks until Kefauver's move. In any case, the Sen-
or held hearings in Knoxville in the fall. The great mass of
entical bids supplied by TVA was turned over to the Justice
epartment. Mr. Bicks proceeded swiftly, and had no trouble
icovering the price-fixing conspiracy. The case dragged along
itil the 1960 election campaign, when Bicks, whose days in office
esumably were numbered, suddenly bestirred himself. He got ac-
n fast enough so that when Bobby Kennedy took over, there was
tle left for him to do except to commend Judge J. Cullen
aney's decision.
Senator Kefauver had a special hatred for identical bids, which
considered a flagrant violation of sound economic policy. Com-
nies located in different areas, with different costs of production
d different rates of efficiency, had no reason to charge exactly
e same price, although it might be legal to do so. As President,
ennedy directed Government agencies to report the receipt of
entical bids, to reject them, and to call for new ones. As Attorney

General, Bobby Kennedy was active in questioning the value of "secret" bids that contained identical quotations. And following up the court decision against the electrical companies, he put pressure on those companies to sign consent decrees forbidding them to cut prices so punitively as to drive small competitors out of business.

So vigorously did Judge Loevinger pursue the matter, with Kennedy's backing, that the Federal Government sought a court order to make the General Electric Company liable to unlimited fines if it ever tried to fix prices or violate any other mandate of the antitrust laws with respect to anything manufactured by General Electric, from electric toasters to jet engines. There had been thirty-nine antitrust actions against General Electric, thirty-six of them since 1941, and, the department pointed out, "the public is entitled to comprehensive equitable relief . . . without waiting for it to engage in additional conspiracies." This was a new kind of talk which could have an important preventive effect on potential price fixers.

Kefauver had no direct part in this effort, but he was firmly behind Justice. Meanwhile, he was plugging away at the kind of price fixing Galbraith had been concerned about when he talked of the ingredients of long-run economic stability and emphasized the need to control prices. Bobby Kennedy's crusade was directed against the illegal type of price fixing—Kefauver's, as I have noted earlier, was aimed at the "legal" method of "administered pricing." Under administered pricing, one or two price leaders in the industry generally set the price pattern—usually by announcement in the trade press. Other companies follow their lead. In some areas, administered pricing is necessary, but in large segments of the economy it is not necessary and it undermines the operation of supply and demand. Administered pricing permits crucial industries like steel to set prices at will and maintain them for long periods of time. This has brought about a situation in which a big company may decide it wants a 15 to 20 per cent return on its investment and set its prices accordingly. United States Steel could rack up respectable profits even when it was operating at 50 per cent capacity, history showed.

HOLDING THE PRICE LINE

No one in the Administration or in Congress had an easy formula for dealing with the administered-price problem as ap parent as in the case of the steel industry. The President had vigorously employed what was called the "jawbone method" when there were rumors of a steel price rise in August. He seized the opportunity of a press-conference question to deliver a little lecture. "Well, I'm hopeful," he began, "that the steel companies themselves will reach a conclusion that the October increase in wages can be absorbed without an increase in steel prices.

"The inflation which marked our economy before 1958 was, I think, tied very closely to the increases in steel prices. Since 1958 steel prices have remained relatively stable. And it is a fact that during that same period, the cost of living has remained relatively stable.

"Now my economic advisers inform me that it would be possible for the steel companies to absorb the increase—the increase in wages—without increasing prices, and still insure to the steel companies and their owners a good profit.

"I am concerned," the President said, "that an increase in steel prices would set off another inflationary spiral, and also make us less competitive abroad, serve as a brake on our recovery, and also affect our balance of payments.

"So," he concluded, without a hint of blackmail in his voice, "I am very hopeful that these private companies will—and I am sure they will—concern themselves with the public interests that are involved in their decision."

Beyond the "jawbone method," or rather an extension of it, was the Labor-Management Advisory Committee of which Secretaries Goldberg and Hodges were co-chairmen and on which all the top brass of industry and labor served. By year's end there had been many meetings and many position papers, reports, and recommendations but little visible achievement—no legislative suggestions for backing up the recommendations. The committee's structure was better suited to talking than to acting. But it was committed to try, by the generation of public pressure and by threats of more vigorous action, to discourage price increases.

Meanwhile, the Attorney General was moving vigorously against illegal price fixing, bringing up case after case in which consumers were directly affected—in the price fixing on bakery products, milk, moving vans, building materials.

Kefauver had never found a legislative formula for dealing with either the "legal" or the illegal form of price fixing. He had not joined in sponsoring a bill introduced by Senator Joseph C. O'Mahoney (Democrat, Wyoming) during the Eisenhower Administration which would have required key industries to give public notification of contemplated price increases, although Professor Galbraith and some other noted liberal economists testified in its favor. Kefauver held to the hope that intelligent business leaders would realize the situation and reform themselves. He was always calling on them to do so and seemed surprised when they did not. Sometimes, too, his pressure forced prices down—when Kefauver announced that his hearings on drug prices would go into the field of antibiotics, there was a 15 per cent across-the-board price cut in those items. But he did introduce piecemeal remedies in special areas. In electrics, he offered a bill to increase penalties, spread responsibility to top executives, and outlaw identical price bids. On drugs, he sponsored a measure to bring down prices through compulsory licensing, the use of generic names, and modified patent rights.

Meanwhile, Kefauver's subcommittee stayed in the background, ready to pounce on industry with hearings if and when price increases came, while everyone waited to see how well the Labor-Management Committee would perform when a big breaching of the price line came. For come it would, as Galbraith had pointed out succinctly and without evasion just before Kennedy's first year began, and while Galbraith was still a practicing professor. Enactment of an emergency program would not be the major problem of the new Administration, he said. The difficulty was that public opinion was "rather poorly prepared" for the longer-range measures that were required. Take the matter of inflation. "When demand is strong enough to keep the economy at full employment industrial prices can be raised. And when wages are advanced, as in all certainty they will be, then prices will be raised and ordinarily by more than the wage advance, for . . . the whole increase can be attributed to the union.

"Price inflation of this sort was always uncomfortable. Now with our balance of payments in poor tone, it cannot be afforded at all. It is what has been pricing our heavy goods out of overseas markets. If there is enough slack in the economy, prices will remain stable. Monetary and fiscal policy operate by creating such slack, but slack is merely an agreeable word for unemployment and this we cannot afford."

We know that "prayer and incantation will not hold prices stable at high employment," Galbraith said, for "these have been tried in a masterful way. All that remains is some direct approach to the problem of wage and price making, but this, we can be sure, will run into horrified cries about controls. The sad truth," he concluded, "is that although we should have been discussing this

ilemma and the way out for years, it was more convenient not to
o so."

A year later, the discussion had advanced a little further, al-
1ough it was mainly a Presidential monologue about the necessity
f restraint on both sides of the bargaining table. But the word
control," which Galbraith had said out loud, was not even being
/hispered at the White House. Administration efforts continued
o be rather "prayer and incantation" than a "direct approach" to
1e problem of wage and price making Galbraith had called for.
'he public was not much better prepared for a larger public part
1 maintaining economic stability than it had been a year before.
.nd there were new signs of strain.

Organized labor, at its Miami Beach Annual Convention in
)ecember, refused to accept responsibility for holding the price
ne by adopting a policy of restraint on wages. AFL-CIO leaders
:served the right to demand wage increases and to strike for them
'henever they were warranted, in their judgment, by profits, pro-
uctivity increases, or other special factors. And Kennedy's am-
assador to the business community, Secretary of Commerce
Iodges, reported that his diplomacy had not been successful. After
1onths of wooing executives at breakfast, lunch, and dinner and in
ff-the-record talks throughout the country, Hodges had to admit
1at officers of big firms remained hostile to the Administration
nd accused it of hostility to them. If the price pace setters in
.merican industry continued to hold the line, it would not be out
f an overwhelming desire to make the Kennedy Administration
)ok good.

There were signs of strain, but there had been no major price
iflation in Kennedy's first year. Those who took part in the final
:ssions at Palm Beach, where work on the first Kennedy budget
as completed during the Christmas holidays, reported the Presi-
ent in a highly optimistic mood about the domestic outlook. In
ie President's opinion, his aides said, the balance-of-payments
roblem would continue to be with us. (Treasury Undersecretary
obert Roosa a few days before had told the American Finance
.ssociation that the deficit of international payments would worsen
1 the immediate future. And that might mean, Roosa warned, that
ie United States would have to slow economic growth for a bit—
r as he put it, "a temporary interruption of internal expansion
1ay be unavoidable if external equilibrium is to be restored." But
 was notable that this official, rumored as a probable successor to
'hairman Martin at the Reserve Board in due course, went on to
xpress the view that "There is no irreconcilable conflict between

the restoration of a sustainable equilibrium in our basic balanc
of payments and the promotion of greater and more lasting growt
in the domestic economy"; and then put himself in the company c
the "moderns" by pointing out with pride that in the course of th
1961 recovery "the conventional expectation that credit mu:
tighten whenever business recovery gains momentum has been coi
founded.")

President Kennedy was described, the week following Chris
mas, as gratified at the degree of recovery achieved. The mor
than four million officially out of work and seeking it and th
lasting effect of automation on the labor market were deep cor
cerns. Nevertheless at the year's end, investment, consumption
income, production, employment, and profits were all moving uI
ward. (At the close of the year corporations were earning profi
before taxes at an annual rate of about $50 billion.) Most exper
expected the upturn to continue through 1962 and perhaps int
1963. Prices remained reasonably stable. And under Presidenti:
order, Government agencies had tightened up on Federal e:
penditures. Advance indications were that the President wou]
present a budget for 1962–63 that was in balance on paper an
ask Congress to approve tax concessions that would stimulat
business to invest in more efficient plants and machinery; give hii
the power to authorize "stand-by" public works at his discretioi
institute guidance and training programs for the "structural ur
employed," and make trade adjustments with other countries t
bring about a balanced expansion of exports and imports.

BALANCE OF PAYMENTS BECOMES PARAMOUNT

In all of this, the President was assuming that the main shor
term problem facing his Administration was inflation. And the me
around him were in closer agreement on that point than they ha
been on the question of how much spending was needed to cui
the recession. The balance-of-payments question had come to hav
almost as dominant a role in the thinking of the Council of Ecc
nomic Advisers as it had earlier in the thinking of the Treasur
and the Federal Reserve. Professor Tobin in particular was fran
to say that his point of view had greatly altered since his appoin
ment to the Council. He had come to Washington minimizing th
payments problem and now considered it overriding. Dr. Helle
in an interview in mid-December, volunteered with implied aI

proval that "In all government agencies you will find an alertness to the balance of payments overtones of their policies that you never had before."

The corollary had to be de-emphasis on growth. In the same interview, Heller indicated concern about what Roosa later indicated was likely to occur on that score. The question asked was "Suppose you had a situation in which the balance of payments appeared to be growing worse, and at the same time your domestic activity—the rise in activity—was running out of speed, and you felt a need for more stimulation through government spending. How would that be handled?" Walk, don't run to the nearest exit, was Heller's answer, in effect, or—as he put it—"You try, in other words, to relieve and offset the short-run pressure which might force you to take measures that would tend to restrict the domestic economy, until some of your longer-run measures pay off." Or to put it another way, "Hope for the best."

If experience with business cycles repeated itself, the current recovery would not begin to taper off until mid-1963. Secretary Roosa had not estimated how long it might be before the payments deficit fell sufficiently to justify removal of the restraints imposed because of it. Suppose the downturn came early, and payments imbalance lingered late? Perhaps President Meany was not speaking prematurely in mid-November when he asked President Kennedy to clarify his Administration's views on budget policy. The AFL-CIO was concerned, Mr. Meany wrote, that the Administration might have placed itself "in a committed position for a balanced budget in fiscal 1963, with very little room for the flexibility that actual conditions may require." Meany wanted assurance that Kennedy did not mean it when he said that only "extraordinary and unforeseen defense requirements" would swerve him from a balanced budget. Labor felt that his pledge should be extended to include the economic situation as well. Meany's question reflected the findings of labor economists who reckoned that the steam would begin to go out of the recovery as early as mid-1962, when the major force of current defense contracts would be spent. "Frankly," Meany asserted, "we foresee the dangerous possibility that the level of joblessness may be no lower than 5.5 per cent of the labor force in late 1962 and early 1963, when the budget would be moving from a deficit to a surplus. In that event, a continued deficit would be needed to provide the basis for additional demands to reduce unemployment to necessary minimum levels."

There was little reason to doubt that Kennedy would take a closer, sympathetic look at the situation then, if what Meany feared came to pass. But this was scarcely the time to take the edge off his pledge of allegiance to the balanced budget.

THE SLOW RATE OF ECONOMIC GROWTH

Meany was seeking insurance for his constituents in the event of continued illness in the economy. But underlying labor's question was concern over one factor for which the President apparently found no place in his list of economic good thoughts on looking back at the old year. There was not a lot to say about the rate of economic growth, for it was very small—2 per cent for one year, well below the average for the sluggish Eisenhower years. In the campaign, President Kennedy had declared a 4.5 per cent rate of growth "well within our capability," and the Democratic platform had mentioned 5 per cent as a reasonable goal for the early future.

Two per cent certainly did not loom large when measured against the rate of growth in other industrialized nations. In its annual review of the economy of each of its twenty member nations (Western European countries, plus the United States and Canada), the Organization for Economic Cooperation and Development pointed out that between 1955 and 1960, under Eisenhower, United States gross national production rose 13 per cent compared to an average of 23 per cent for all OECD member countries combined. (United States production, too, had risen 2. per cent in the previous five-year period.) In the United States "the rise in output over recent years has been modest, both compared with the previous years and with the experience of other industrialized countries," the report stated. And it went on to point out danger spots ahead—a persistent high rate of unemployment, underutilization of productive capacity, continuing adverse balance of payments; and a slower rate of growth than in many other countries.

Leon Keyserling—by now his was not a name one dropped around the White House with the idea of currying favor—had stronger reservations than ever about Kennedy's economic policies and aired them. Kennedy's policies, in his opinion, minimized the importance of consumer demand, failed to force an easier supply of money, did not expand Social Security, or sufficiently increase the minimum wage or farm income. And he did not like the way the Government persisted in taking random actions toward recovery instead of setting long-range goals toward full employment.

The current recession, Keyserling argued, had borne out his theory of the ever-deepening recessionary trend since the end of the Korean War—a pattern of upturns, stagnation periods, and recessions, with an average annual growth in national production little more than one half of that needed to utilize our growing labor force and productivity per man hour.

He maintained that economic policies being pursued and those apparently in prospect would lift the rate of growth, but not sufficiently to achieve reasonably full use of manpower and plant even at the peak of the coming upturn. In 1959, a recovery year, a growth of 6.8 per cent above the recession year of 1958 was registered; in 1955 the recovery rate was 8.0 per cent. And recovery in both years was incomplete. Now, because unemployment was still so much higher than in preceding postwar recovery years, we would have to grow at least 10 per cent in 1962 to bring unemployment down to acceptable levels, and so rapid a gain would not seem in prospect. He feared that unless more rigorous recovery policies were to be adopted, the coming upturn would leave unemployment higher than at any previous peak since World War II. And thus the succeeding recession would lead to more idle men and machines than there were at the bottom of any recession since the Great Depression.

Such talk was naturally annoying to an Administration that could not concentrate on this one problem as Mr. Keyserling could. But, if two exchanges between the confident Keyserling and Kennedy's friend Senator Paul Douglas of Illinois reached the omnivorous reader in the White House, he must have given at least grudging consideration to the possibility that Keyserling might be more right than he was.

Testifying before the Joint Economic Committee in August, Keyserling commented: "The mild changes in national economic programs which have recently occurred . . . seem to me for the most part desirable. But I do not find them adequate. . . . This may be too dismal a view, although in 1954 I correctly projected the low rates of growth and their main consequences through 1960."

Senator Douglas: "Let me say, Mr. Keyserling, your statement at this point is correct. I remember you speaking in 1954 on this very point. I thought you were exaggerating the dangers at the time. I think the general line of your predictions has been borne out by events."

In an earlier exchange, Keyserling recalled: "When in 1953 and

1954 and 1955, I published studies projecting how low the economic growth rate would be and how much unemployment would rise, I was scoffed at. I did not object to this," he added, "but there has been an amazing corroboration of what I have been saying."

Senator Douglas: "I would like to say for the record that while Mr. Keyserling and I have had our differences . . . I think he was the first man in the country in 1953 and 1954 to indicate that our growth rates were unsatisfactory and to predict that we were in for a great deal of trouble. . . . I think you deserve a great deal of credit, Mr. Keyserling, on this point which has never been paid you."

If Keyserling should be right again, and Kennedy less than quick on his feet, economic caution could lead to political trouble.

SENATOR GORE'S CRYSTAL BALL

But what of the predictions of things to come in Senator Gore's November 1960 letter to the President? The appointment of Mr. Dillon as Secretary of Treasury, the Senator had said, "would mean, for instance, that glaring tax loopholes would not be closed; that fiscal policies, monetary policies, and economic policies would not be very different from the present administration. This would not be your intention, to be sure," Senator Gore declared, "but it would be the likely consequence." A year and a month later, one could bring Senator Gore's prophecy up to date by removing the qualifying word "likely."

The eight "loopholes of tax favoritism," which the Senator had listed in his letter to the President-elect, were still open—Mr. Kennedy had recommended closing only one, excessive deductions for expense accounts, but had done little to persuade Congress to do so.

Short-term interest rates had remained high, as the Administration desired in view of the balance-of-payments problem—three-month Treasury Bonds, quoted at 2.30 per cent in January, were at 2.32 per cent in late October, while the commercial bank "prime" rate for short-term loans was maintained at 4.5 per cent for the year. But the parallel goal of lowering long-term interest rates was still far away. Treasury long-term bonds had gone from 3.8 per cent to 4.04 per cent between Inauguration Day and the end of October, while *Moody's* average corporate-bond yield was rising from 4.65 per cent to 4.72 per cent.

Business expenditures on improved plant and equipment were less in 1960 than five years before. Business had not supported an Administration-proposed incentive tax cut, preferring to hold out for an across-the-board reduction in corporate levies. And the House Ways and Means Committee had held back the only Administration proposal to stiffen taxes—a requested increase in the tax on income earned abroad.

Total national production by the last quarter of 1961 had reached an annual rate of $540 billion, an increase of $20 billion over 1960, primarily as a result of military expenditures. But the experts estimate that, with the economy in full swing, production would have approached $600 billion instead.

Had the precautions against inflation been too stringent? Had the President's economic advisers allowed the balance-of-payments issue to scare them, as inflation had scared Eisenhower's economists, into too timid an approach to recovery? Had the Council gone too far toward rationalizing issues for the President rather than leaving it to him to add the political ingredient? Had they gone along on a "booster" program too small to get recovery off the ground?

Had Kennedy given up the economic goal to which he had dedicated his Administration in the campaign? Had the appointment of Douglas Dillon to the Treasury signaled as much as Senator Gore had declared it would? Did that action, as was predicted, insure that Kennedy's economic policies would not be very different from those of the previous Administration?

· VI ·

Dealing with the Russians

THE PROSPECT BEFORE US

The Friday before Tuesday, December 6, when President-elect Kennedy was invited to call on President Eisenhower at the White House, Eisenhower's chief assistant, William Burton Persons, telephoned attorney Clark Clifford, Kennedy's White House liaison for the transition period, to brief him on the agenda for the meeting. President Eisenhower, Persons advised Clifford, intended to discuss with Mr. Kennedy:

1. NATO nuclear sharing
2. Laos
3. The Congo
4. Algeria
5. (a) Disarmament
   (b) Nuclear test-ban negotiations
6. Cuba and Latin America
7. U.S. balance of payments and the gold outflow
8. "The need for a balanced budget"

The President's agenda for the discussion with his successor, consisting mostly of "emergency" items, supported Kennedy's central criticism of Eisenhower's foreign policy—that it was based on reacting rather than acting. As Kennedy analyzed the problem in *The Strategy of Peace,* "We move from crisis to crisis for two reasons: First, because we have not yet developed a strategy for peace that is relevant to the new world in which we live; and secondly because we have not been paying the price that strategy demands."

In the campaign Kennedy's principal argument had been that Republican "failures" had cost the United States a steady loss of power and prestige in the world. Specifically, he charged the Eisenhower Administration with failing to maintain superiority over the

192

Russians, delaying too long in entering the space race, and failing
to do enough about Latin America and Cuba. A new Democratic
Administration "could reverse the present deterioration," he said.
And he, better than Nixon, Kennedy claimed, could "summon all
the resources of this land to the defense of freedom to restore our
nation's relative strength and leadership."

Now it was time to tackle the details. Clark Clifford had passed
the agenda he received from Persons along to Adlai Stevenson's
unofficial representatives in Washington, attorney George Ball and
his young partner, John Sharon, who over the weekend drew up
briefs on each of the eight points for Kennedy's use in the conference.

The memoranda which Sharon and Ball were able to prepare
on such short notice were condensations of the confidential 150-
page report on foreign policy they and others had helped Stevenson prepare at Kennedy's request during the months between his
nomination and election. That document, it seems fair to assume,
was a statement of the policies Stevenson would have favored had
he been selected to serve as Kennedy's Secretary of State. And on
rereading Stevenson's private advice to Kennedy after one year of
Kennedy's Administration, it is evident that though the new President did not choose Stevenson to preside over his Department of
State, he did choose to follow a remarkable amount of Stevenson's
advance counsel.

There was one Eisenhower characteristic in the conduct of international affairs that Kennedy least wanted to emulate—his
failure to anticipate.

"Peace . . . requires foresight," Kennedy declared in a campaign speech in Syracuse.

The next administration—in addition to meeting our present commitments and facing up to the crises already mentioned—must look ahead
to all the new problems just over the horizon:

The spread of nuclear weapons to several nations, drastically alter-
ing the world balance of power and sharply increasing the chances of
accidental war;

The emergence of Red China as a nuclear power, dedicated to the
proposition of victory through war, and differing with the Soviets as
to the pursuit of their ambitions;

The possibilities of new cracks in the Iron Curtain of Eastern Europe, new Communist moves in Africa, new East German pressure on
Berlin, and new voting blocs in the U.N.;

The possibility of new steps to integrate the economy of Europe and
the economy of Latin America.

"We need to plan for such developments before they happen," said Kennedy. "We need to foresee that they are going to happen. We need to recognize the revolutionary tempo of the world in which we live" and to strengthen "our arms, our diplomacy, our economy and our sense of purpose" accordingly.

Stevenson's carefully thought-out report therefore commended itself to Kennedy. It dealt with the emergency situations the new President would inherit, but it also looked ahead and suggested the necessary components of a new foreign policy. In a world where two-thirds of the peoples were emerging from centuries of domination by a handful of power centers, Stevenson advised that the United States cease attempts to impose its political and economic ideas on those emerging peoples and try leading them by example and at the same time strive for a common front in the Western world that would for the first time make possible an arms-control and disarmament agreement with the Soviet powers.

THE STEVENSON REPORT

The Stevenson report stressed two priorities and outlined plans of procedure in detail.

The first was to make sense out of the confused foreign economic policy of the United States. "Present policies on trade and aid reflect their haphazard and uncoordinated formulation and growth," a supporting paper appended to Stevenson's private memorandum pointed out. "Trade policies are at odds with what aid policies are trying to achieve; private investment activities are at loggerheads with public investment proposals; our trade policy is ambivalent and contradictory; our aid policy is diffuse and uncoordinated." President Kennedy, in response, devoted a major share of his personal energy to clearing up those contradictions and bringing direction to our program of aid in his first year. And he gave the same priority to the issue of trade in laying plans for his second.

The second coequal priority was to create a Western partnership between a United Europe and America, within an Atlantic Community strong enough to negotiate an arms agreement with the Soviet Union. And Stevenson had specific advice on how to get that effort off to a good start.

One of the most important decisions you will have to make concerns your policy on disarmament—as contrasted with arms control measures [Stevenson wrote in his private report to the President-elect in November]. By the term "disarmament" I mean broad and drastic proposals to do away with practically all armament. The most important proposal of this nature was contained in the United Nations General Assembly resolution of November 20, 1959.

The policy of the Truman Administration was similar and stated clearly that disarmament was to be substantially complete, reached by stages, inspected, and "foolproof." This implied that the arrangements were to be such that in case the agreement broke down, none of the parties would be in a worse position relative to the others than at the time the agreement was made.

The present Administration initially rejected this policy, adopting the more cautious line that disarmament was not possible until a climate of world opinion favorable to disarmament had been achieved. The policy of the Administration, accordingly, has been in favor merely of arms control measures, or, at most, partial or limited steps toward disarmament. It was not until November 20, 1959 that the present Administration was compelled by the force of world opinion to reverse itself and vote for the sweeping proposal in the General Assembly resolution. However, attempts were still made to qualify this commitment.

I recommend that in your Inaugural Address, you support the objective of "general and complete disarmament under effective international control." Disarmament is by no means the totality of a policy for peace; it must be surrounded by efforts in all areas of foreign policy to create the conditions which will make the goal of peace achievable. Your Inaugural Address should call upon the nations and the peoples of the world to give support to this effort to save mankind from war.

Your Secretary of State Designate should be guided accordingly and make this policy his most important order of business.

Adoption of the objective of general and complete disarmament should not, however, preclude a test suspension treaty or other partial measures so long as they are not regarded as ends in themselves but building blocks for the goal of complete disarmament.

Kennedy did not bring himself in his Inaugural message to adopt the phrase "general and complete disarmament"—which had special meaning to the Russians. But he did embrace the concept. "Let both sides, for the first time, formulate serious and precise proposals for the inspection and control of arms—and bring the absolute power to destroy other nations under the absolute control of all nations."

And he added the essential formula for turning proposals into agreements—"let us never fear to negotiate."

The semantic distinction was important only to sophisticates in disarmament encounters with the Russians. But it was nevertheless important. For the Soviet Union, as Stevenson understood, would have taken the words "full and complete" as a sign that we were open to serious proposals relating to halting the nuclear-arms race.

Instead of opening a new door at once, however, Mr. Kennedy chose to explore a less controversial area he was already committed to enter—the possibility of a nuclear test-ban treaty, as a first step toward general disarmament.

FIRST STEP TOWARD GENERAL DISARMAMENT

"One of the first things I did on becoming President," Mr. Kennedy told Alexei Adzhubei nine months later, "was to commit the United States to an earnest effort to achieve a satisfactory agreement with the Soviet Union on the cessation of nuclear tests." The record would bear out the President's assertion to the Soviet Premier's son-in-law, the editor of *Izvestia,* who printed his interview with Mr. Kennedy in full.

The first question the newly appointed director of his Disarmament Administration asked the President in their first official conversation was, are you serious about trying to reach a test-ban agreement? If you are, John J. McCloy said, we must ask a postponement of the negotiating talks, then scheduled for early February, in order to better prepare ourselves for them. But if you are only proceeding with the talks because you pledged to do so, and have no real hope of achieving anything, then we can go ahead.

He was serious, the President replied. And so were the preparations for and the conduct of the United States part of the test-ban negotiations that were still in process at the end of 1961.

Halting of nuclear tests, which had been so hotly disputed during the 1956 Presidential campaign, actually occurred October 31, 1958. At that time East and West agreed to a moratorium on testing and agreed to begin discussing ways of arranging a permanent cessation. Representatives of the United States, Britain, and the U.S.S.R. began meeting spasmodically to explore the possible arrangements.

These talks dragged on with little progress for more than two years. They were suspended on December 5, 1960, to allow the new United States Administration to assess the situation and re-evaluate the American position to be maintained at the bargaining table. During those two years, scientists had made considerable gains in the scope and precision of detection devices. Even with this greater accuracy, the West had presumably found no real evidence of Soviet violations of the moratorium on testing. This led the Kennedy Administration to believe that the U.S.S.R. had a genuine interest in arranging for a permanent ban. If it did, the assumed desire of the U.S.S.R. to keep Communist China out of the nuclear club might, it was thought, be an added incentive to the Soviet Union to co-operate.

There was strong evidence, however, that in fact the Russians had lost interest in the kind of test ban we wanted to negotiate.

In mid-February 1961, about a month after Kennedy's Inauguration, Leo Szilard returned to Washington from Moscow where he and 74 other scientists from 15 countries had met in late November in the Sixth Pugwash Conference on disarmament (so called after the town in Nova Scotia where the first such session convened). Szilard had stayed on to talk privately with Soviet officials. Along with Enrico Fermi, Szilard had set off the chain reaction under Flagg Stadium in Chicago that led to the making of the first atomic bomb. But in recent years he had concentrated his energies on convincing world leaders of the necessity for ending the nuclear-arms race. There was exciting news, one of the new men at the White House hastened to tell him on his return—the President had ordered a serious effort to reach agreement with the Russians on a nuclear test-ban treaty! "What makes you think the Russians are still interested?" Szilard asked.

A year before in Moscow Szilard had found great interest in a test-ban agreement. But on this latest visit the Russians seemed more interested in understanding Western ideas on inspection and control arrangements to enforce a general disarmament agreement. In all Szilard's Moscow conversations no Russian had mentioned a test-ban treaty as an important objective.

Another American present at the Pugwash sessions observed the same direction of Russian interest. Professor Jerome B. Wiesner of MIT, soon to become the chief Science Adviser to President Kennedy, explained what he had learned in an unrehearsed report on the Moscow meeting over Boston station WGBH-TV on January 3, 1961. "The Soviets for a variety of reasons . . . have developed what I would call an almost paranoid fear of the consequences of too much openness while military power still exists," Dr. Wiesner commented in the course of the long discussion. "The degree of inspection we would like [to make a nuclear test ban a certainty] involves so much inspection of the Soviet Union that it represents almost as much of a concession on their part as an inspection system for total disarmament." He had gathered from the Russians, Wiesner said, that "it is not a price they are prepared to pay for trivial arms control or disarmament measures." And he added frankly, "if I was negotiating for the Soviets or doing their military planning, I would take this view too."

One highly regarded intelligence source reported to Washington about this time that Khrushchev had agreed, in return for continued Chinese toleration of his policy of coexistence with the West, not to enter into any test-ban treaty until China could develop nuclear capacity of her own.

And United States Ambassador Llewellyn E. Thompson sent a similarly pessimistic prediction from Moscow. The U.S.S.R. could be expected to stall when test-ban talks resumed, Thompson reported—for the reason Wiesner had cited, because of Chinese considerations, and because of reported Soviet concern over nuclear testing by the French.

All this, and perhaps more discouraging information, was known to the President, who, nevertheless, made achieving a test-ban agreement his first major objective in the attempt to "reverse the deterioration" in U.S.-Soviet relations and begin to move toward peace. No apparent alternative was immediately available. And time, the President and his close advisers were convinced, was of the essence.

Mr. Kennedy had explained in his campaign that "If we are ever to hope to negotiate for an effective arms control agreement, we must act immediately, for as each year passes the control of increasingly complex, mobile and hidden modern armaments becomes more difficult and the chances for country after country to possess an atomic capacity [increases]. By 1964 or 1965, we may see a world in which 20 countries have a nuclear capacity and the ability to destroy their adversary, themselves, and perhaps the world."

WE MUST ACT IMMEDIATELY

Professor Paul Mead Doty, Jr., of Harvard, an expert on disarmament whom Kennedy appointed to his Science Advisory Council, was expressing a considerable consensus of informed opinion when he discussed the immediacy of the threat in the Boston television report on the Pugwash meeting. Experience indicated we would see the production of a new generation of nuclear weapons "within Kennedy's first Administration," Professor Doty said. In anticipation, "We're being exposed again to the request from many sides to consider the relevance of a large shelter program," he noted. "If we do that, the Russians will have to do the same in order to maintain some parity." Then after five years when the shelter program is complete, he foresaw, "both sides must look for weapons to operate against it . . . weapons of the 500-megaton variety which will blast out several countries or several states at a time, and completely lay waste the whole possibility of using the land for agriculture, let alone eliminating the people who were there in the first place. One can see this enormous deadly spiral going up and up and up."

Dr. Wiesner interrupted his colleague at that point. He was thinking beyond the next generation of new weapons, too. "People always worry about the period two or three or four years hence," he said. "And this keeps us from having the courage to do a really substantial job in disarmament without a tremendous amount of assurance. But if you look ahead ten years and see where this is taking you, you find that . . . the security you think you buy just won't be there."

If this country proceeded with "an all-out arms race of the kind that we're engaged in," as he projected the picture, "you would first of all . . . go from the present missiles to a massive shelter program to protect yourself—but about the time you finished that shelter program you'd find you weren't protecting yourself against one-megaton or two- or three- or four-megaton warheads—nuclear bombs—but against the 100- or 1000-megaton bombs which we think can be developed if we continue."

The man who was to become Kennedy's deputy adviser on national-security affairs and later chief of policy planning in the Department of State had been at the Moscow Pugwash Conference, too. This was Wiesner's MIT colleague, Walt Whitman Rostow, an expert on international economic affairs and the problems of undeveloped areas. He had gone along because the delegation wanted a social scientist in the group. "As I sat there, a non-scientist listening to the scientists talk about [the advanced stages of disarmament], I sometimes felt I was in a very hopeful new world and sometimes I felt I was mad," Dr. Rostow told the TV audience. "The world unfolding all made sense. There was nothing about this vision that was technologically impossible or even in human terms impossible. The sense of madness arose because simultaneously with our presence in Moscow there was the Summit meeting of the 81 Communist parties, and as we are talking now, we have

Cuba, Laos, and the Congo. And the really great problem of moving sequentially from limited, turn-around, confidence-building measures to . . . creation of scrap heaps with adequate inspection, towards the creation of a world order which can't really stop very short of world law and some form of world government."

If the deadline for halting the race to disaster was "within Kennedy's first Administration," as Professor Doty and many others contended, if the next step would be as calamitous as Wiesner pictured it, and if Rostow's vision was not itself mad, the President had no more urgent business than to begin talks with the Russians.

UNPREPARED

Yet the United States was technically unprepared for even exploratory talks in the broad area of general disarmament—the research and analysis to prepare a position from which to negotiate would alone require many months. In the entire United States Government under Eisenhower, Kennedy was fond of pointing out in the campaign, there had been fewer than a hundred people working on the complex subject of arms control and disarmament. "As a result, we have been unprepared at every disarmament conference that we have attended," Kennedy said at Milwaukee in late September. "At a time when our relative military strength was at its height, in the midfifties, at a time when we had the best chance to reach an agreement on control of arms, there was not a single top person in the entire Government working on this subject. We did not come up with a single major new proposal in the field of arms control, and we cared so little about it that we regarded the entire effort as merely a part of our effort in psychological warfare. . . .

"The Geneva Conference of 1958 . . . was a failure and our chief negotiator said, 'I doubt that we have given up to this time the intense study to the kind of measures which will make the prevention of surprise attacks possible.' "

The only subject on which the United States was halfway ready to proceed with discussions was that of banning nuclear tests. So that was where the Kennedy Administration would begin.

The United States had been pleasantly surprised by the Russians once before—there had been fruitless meeting after fruitless meeting before the Soviet Union suddenly signed the Austrian peace treaty. It could happen again. The intelligence data on the supposed Soviet agreement with the Chinese could be wrong. Such

eports often were. At least we would be demonstrating to the
world our determination to waste no time in getting down to cases
with the Russians.

PLAN TO PREPARE

We would go to Geneva and do our best to get a permanent
est-ban agreement, Kennedy resolved. Meanwhile the President
et in motion the myriad supporting actions he felt were essential
o achieving peace. Secretary McNamara would be concentrating
on building up United States and NATO forces, conventional and
uclear. ("We arm to parley.") Vice President Johnson would
oversee an effort to regain lost prestige by stepping up space activi-
ies. The President, Secretary Rusk, and the White House staff
would man the bucket brigade to put out brush-fire disturbances
wherever they arose—from Cuba to the Congo. They would gradually shift our basic attitude toward neutral nations and our policy
on economic assistance. The Dulles doctrine of "those who aren't
with us are against us" would give way, in theory, to a policy of
ncouraging and supporting independence among the new nations.
And the force of American-dollar aid would be directed less at
reating military force to support United States aims and more at
reating the economic strength to support political independence.
Kennedy's rhetoric was consistent: We would "arm to parley";
we would "never fear to negotiate." There could be no doubt of
he ability of the United States to achieve for itself and others the
tance Kennedy was seeking. Beyond that the test would be one
of Kennedy's understanding, judgment, and will. Would he be
able to appreciate what was going on in the hearts and minds of
others at critical times? Would he calculate correctly his adver-
ary's reactions to his actions? Would he remain adamant in the
ace of assaults on the principle of negotiation?
These tests would come later. In early March what was impor-
ant was to begin changing the climate of suspicion and the feeling
of distrust of United States motives that existed in many parts of
he world.

JOHN J. McCLOY

The President asked Mr. McCloy, first of all, to work out a new
position for our test-ban negotiators; then, while they were talking

with the Russians, to develop plans for an enlarged Disarmament
Agency with sufficient status and staff to support future negotiations properly; and finally to evolve a United States position for
advancing by stages to general disarmament.

On Robert Lovett's recommendation, the President had appointed John J. McCloy to get the disarmament program going. A
Republican, Chairman of the Board of the Chase National Bank, a
former Assistant Secretary of War, former President of the World
Bank, and United States High Commissioner in Germany following World War II, McCloy was above reproach even by those to
whom the very concept of disarmament smacked of "softness."
The man designated to speak for the United States in the test-ban
talks in Geneva—Arthur H. Dean—was also a Republican. A law
partner of the late John Foster Dulles, Dean had performed the
same function in Eisenhower's Administration, and was a tough
experienced negotiator. McCloy, in his turn, chose as his deputy
Adrian S. Fisher, a former legal adviser in the State Department
under Dean Acheson and General Counsel of the Atomic Energy
Commission. He knew the State Department and the Atomic
Energy Commission as well as McCloy knew the Pentagon. (Those
were the three agencies of the Government that had to be kept in
step in moving toward disarmament.)

The date for resuming the test talks was postponed to March
21. But even so there was not time for the new team to work out
a totally new position. The over-all concept of gradual reduction
of armaments that had been agreed upon by Eisenhower and Macmillan was retained as the framework within which the West would
operate, with the nuclear test ban the first step in a multiphase
approach. But we would give a little on the question of inspection.
The West would still ask for twenty on-site inspections per country, as it had in the past, but if the U.S.S.R. showed a general
willingness to negotiate, we would fall back to 17. (The Soviets
had previously insisted on only three inspections, saying no more
were needed since a violation of the test ban would incite public
opinion to such a degree that no nation would risk its prestige by
breaking the agreement.)

The West would continue to ask for a controlled ban on all
above-ground testing and on all underground testing involving
explosions of at least 19 kilotons; for underground explosions of
less than 19 kilotons there was to be a voluntary moratorium and
the only permissible blasts would be those in connection with seismic research toward improvement of detection devices.

The willingness to reduce the number of on-site tests was par-

ially due to improved seismic devices that could identify more
explosions than previously. There would be fewer detectable but
unidentifiable blasts and fewer inspections would be necessary. But
his greater flexibility also reflected the Administration's determination to prove its willingness to reach an agreement.

Planning for the Geneva talks included, in addition to numerous
small-scale consultations, several large conferences of military,
political and scientific advisers, and considerable personal participation by the President.

The presence of many from the Joint Atomic Energy Committee
was primarily attributable to the need for Congressional approval
of one of the steps the Administration was prepared to propose.
Under the terms of the Atomic Energy Act it was necessary for
the President to get ratification from Congress to offer the Russians
the privilege of inspecting "old" atomic bombs that the United
States wanted to use in its experiments for detection devices. This
was one of the concessions the Administration was interested in
making. The Congressmen reportedly were unenthusiastic.

The meetings were also an effort to bring Congressional leaders
in on the preliminary stages of policy making—it would do no
good to conclude a test-ban treaty the Senate would not ratify. But
Senators Clinton P. Anderson (Democrat, New Mexico) and
Bourke B. Hickenlooper (Republican, Iowa) afterward stated their
objection to the "indefinite" extension of an uninspected test moratorium, and they and others criticized the over-all Administration
plan as too nebulous and overly dependent upon gaining specific
concessions from the U.S.S.R.

Since approval was not forthcoming at the March 7 luncheon,
on March 9 Administration leaders appeared before a meeting of
the full Joint Atomic Energy Committee to reassure its members
that no substantial change in the United States test-ban position
was being considered. Secretary Rusk afterward told the press only
that the United States will talk "in the utmost good faith" and
expects to be able to reach an agreement. He refused to outline
the specific modifications under consideration, nor would he say
how long the talks would be allowed to continue. At that time,
pressure was mounting within Congress to set some sort of cut-off
date after which, if no progress had been made at the talks, we
would resume testing. But the Administration was determined to
wait at least six to eight weeks before evaluating the likelihood
or success.

Meanwhile, at the UN, Ambassadors Stevenson and Andrei A.
Gromyko had reached complete disagreement on a proposal by

the neutral nations that would eliminate from the spring session of the General Assembly several major "cold war" disputes: the U-2 incident, Cuba, Hungary, and Tibet. The U.S.S.R. was also insistent that the question of general disarmament remain on the agenda despite the United States' lack of preparedness for discussion of the subject. But at the same time, feelers were going out in Moscow for a Kennedy-Khrushchev meeting. Khrushchev had indicated in January that he would like one, and United States Ambassador Thompson had been authorized to explore the situation further.

ARTHUR DEAN

On March 12, Mr. Dean met with Vice President Johnson, Secretaries Rusk and McNamara, and Mr. Bundy for a final briefing, had a final meeting with the President on the 14th, and left for Geneva on the 15th. In their farewell meeting Kennedy again emphasized that the United States was "determined to do all possible to conclude a safeguarded agreement on a sound and equitable basis" to facilitate further disarmament and halt the spread of nuclear weapons. If he could not impress Congress, perhaps he could at least impress other countries.

At his March 15 press conference Kennedy announced that the United States would be willing to resume disarmament talks with the U.S.S.R. in August, but refused to say whether he would be willing to have a personal meeting with Khrushchev if that were necessary. He also would not say whether Dean had been authorized to decrease the number of inspections to be demanded, or whether a cutoff date had been established, or indeed to say anything more than to stress the good will and seriousness of purpose with which the United States was entering the talks and to praise the reasonable and sound treaty to which the United States proposals could lead. The President continued to hold out the olive branch with one hand and, with the other, fend off those who would snatch it from him.

THE UNITED STATES POSITION

On the eve of the resumption of the talks, the United States position was to continue to insist on inspections, but be prepared o make concessions in areas such as Soviet inspection of atomic explosives to be used by the United States in seismic research, and the duration of the uninspected moratorium on underground blasts of less than 19 kilotons. For the former, Kennedy did not yet have the required Congressional authorization. On the latter, the United States had originally asked for a 27-month moratorium, and the U.S.S.R. wanted one to last for three to five years. The United States was now reportedly ready to agree to three years, and also to accept the Soviet's proposal that the ban also include explosions at very high altitudes and in outer space, despite the lack of assurance of effective controls there.

The Soviets had also been demanding "parity" on inspection teams, without specifying just what they meant by that. The West was willing to accept parity if it meant equal representation of both sides on the teams, but was unwilling to accept the Soviet demand that the inspection teams of each country be headed by a national of that country.

GENEVA

On March 21 the long-awaited 247th meeting of the Conference on the Discontinuance of Nuclear Weapons Tests opened in the Palais des Nations in Geneva. The chairman for the day was the chief Soviet negotiator, Semyon K. Tsarapkin. Although he knew that the West was prepared to open the talks with its offer, he himself took the floor, spoke at great length, and at once dragged the talks back nine months by reneging on an agreement reached the previous July that the control organization be headed by a single, impartial administrator. When he renewed the Soviet demand for a "troika" directorate, Western hopes for an agreement sank.

The U.S.S.R. had been trying to impose a similar concept on the United Nations to replace the single Secretary General, so perhaps this demand should not have been too surprising to the West. But surprising or not, it was totally unacceptable, for it would mean that a test ban would be controlled by one representative from the Soviet bloc, one from the West, and one neutral, each with a veto power with which it could block any inspection authorization.

Less surprising was the Soviet representative's insistence that the communiqué after the first day include a "serious warning" to France about continuing testing.

When he finally got his chance, Arthur Dean stated the West's position.

The lines were drawn, and both sides prepared for the long siege ahead. The speed and brusqueness of the Soviet rebuff were a great shock to Washington. The winter thaw ended on the first day of spring. For the first two months of his term Kennedy had had reason to believe that Khrushchev wanted to reach some kind of agreement with him. During January the Kremlin gave every indication of interest in working with the new Administration, and lessened the pressure on several trouble spots.

At his March 23 press conference Kennedy insisted he was "still hopeful," despite Soviet attitudes on the test ban. Were developments in Geneva a disappointment? He said only that "the kind of response we get to our efforts for peace in this area [will enable] . . . a better answer." As stated before they opened, the test-ban talks would be the yardstick of Soviet intent for the West.

By late March, the Soviet line had really hardened. Gromyko in Washington and at the UN was adamant on Laos and on carrying through on a general disarmament debate respectively. Tsarapkin at Geneva was insistent upon the troika proposal but refused to clarify the Soviet position on several other matters. At sessions where Western proposals were presented, he refused to say anything at all, but gave his opinions to the reporters who walked with him to and from the sessions. Meanwhile, agreement was finally reached on March 30 at the UN to defer the General Assembly's disarmament debate until the fall session and to set U.S.-U.S.S.R. disarmament talks for early August.

Tsarapkin continued silently to await word from Moscow. A week after the talks opened it was obvious that the gap between East and West was undiminished. But during the actual meetings the West refrained from attacking the troika plan, although making it quite clear in statements to the press afterward that the proposal was unacceptable. To press that question so early in the talks would have invited charges of inciting a walkout. The Western intent now was merely to avoid the onus for what seemed to be inevitable failure. The "yardstick" theory was carried further; just as the talks themselves were to be the measure of Soviet intentions in world affairs, so the degree to which the Soviets insisted on their troika plan was to be the inverse measure of how eager they were for a real agreement on a test ban. The crucial phase of the talks during which this would be revealed was to come after the Easter recess, and world opinion, at least outside the Soviet bloc was being prepared for the worst. Meanwhile the three representatives met every day.

By the Easter recess the new United States attitude of "speak softly" had been convincingly demonstrated. Liaison between Geneva and Washington had been good. The President and Rusk remained in intimate touch with proceedings, along with McCloy and Fisher. And the new humility and flexibility in our bargaining encouraged new confidence among our friends, even though it failed to inspire our enemies.

Tsarapkin had been expected to return from the Easter recess bearing long-awaited news of the Kremlin's reaction to Western proposals for a "reasonable treaty." When the talks resumed he praised Western acceptance of three lesser Soviet proposals, but made no commitment on the crucial matter of controlled inspection. The rest of the plan, he said, was still being studied in Moscow. The three points he did take note of were the offer to allow Soviet technicians to inspect test explosives, the acceptance of a ban on high-altitude testing, and the total budget veto. Then the next day Tsarapkin renewed his insistence upon troika controls.

THE TROIKA QUESTION

Apparently Dr. Wiesner had been right. The Soviets were not willing to open their territory to inspection by foreigners in return for a test ban. But Dean's orders were not to allow the issue to wreck the talks. The strategy now was to keep talking and to make t increasingly clear to world opinion that the West was trying very hard to reach agreement. Dean and W. David Ormsby-Gore accordingly refrained from pinning the U.S.S.R. down at the conference table about whether the troika was a *sine qua non* for agreement.

Two United States visitors sat in on the session when Tsarapkin raised the troika question again. Lyndon Johnson had stopped off on his way back to Washington from Dakar, and Senator Albert Gore was in Geneva for a meeting of the Inter-Parliamentary Union. There they took the positions in April that the President and the proponents of resuming tests were assuming in the United States—in preparation for a test of wills that would continue until September.

Johnson held a press conference after the Tsarapkin speech. He stressed the need for an inspection and control system that would be headed by a single, impartial director, and he ruled out the troika plan. But Senator Gore, ranking Democrat on the Joint Atomic Energy Committee and a critic of the President's patience with the U.S.S.R. in these particular negotiations, was not content to leave it at that. He urged that the United States get the U.S.S.R. to "clarify" its position before going any further with the discussion. The United States and Britain had been bending over backward to avoid the impression that they were giving the Kremlin an ultimatum. Gore was trying to pin the Russians down on how far they were going to carry their troika plan, though Western policy was specifically directed at avoiding doing that.

A month later, Gore was removed from the panel of United States Senators who had been appointed observers at the test-ban talks. When Johnson was serving as Majority Leader, he had named Gore to the panel. Angered by Gore's lack of team conduct, the Vice President bypassed Senator Mansfield, whose prerogative it now was to make appointments and replaced Gore with Senators Sparkman of the Foreign Relations Committee and Anderson of the Joint Atomic Energy Committee. If the President was determined to continue with the test-ban talks, his Vice President would remove obstacles where he could. There were still further concessions that could be made under the McCloy-Dean formula. The United States had few direct lines to the Kremlin. If we were ever to make any headway on disarmament, we had to learn the real reasons for Russian reluctance, and we were less likely to find out if we stopped talking.

British opinion, meanwhile, was coalescing behind the Western position at Geneva, perhaps in part because of the new attitude that the United States displayed there, and the new confidence that this in turn gave the British Government. During early spring the unilateralists within the Labour Party suffered a major defeat and five Members of Parliament of that stripe were expelled from the Parliamentary Labour Party. The peace marches that had become recurrent and the protests against basing United States submarines in British waters did not abate, but majority political opinion was clearly lining up behind the Western position. Kennedy and Macmillan, after a four-day conference in Washington, declared on April 8 that they would continue their efforts for a test ban, and a few days later Macmillan reported to the House of Commons that the West still regarded Soviet attitudes at Geneva as the test of their good will, and hoped for "a general detente" if the first phase succeeded.

Four days later the U.S.S.R. launched Yuri Gagarin, and

Khrushchev launched another appeal for "universal complete disarmament under the strictest international supervision."

Five days later exiles launched their United States-backed invasion of Cuba. In the ensuing international uproar, Khrushchev
apparently decided it was time to take personal charge and gave
new orders accordingly. For when Arthur Dean slightly diverted
attention from the Cuban calamity with a new proposal, Tsarapkin
rejected it flatly the very next day. There was no waiting for instructions from Moscow as there had been after new suggestions
were made in the past. Apparently Tsarapkin's orders now were
to maintain a completely negative line while Khrushchev maneuvered to arrange a personal meeting with Kennedy before the new
President regained his balance.

Dean's new offer combined all of the West's new proposals and
agreements to old Soviet proposals in one big treaty and urged this
compilation on Tsarapkin for his government's consideration. But
Tsarapkin rejected the total draft as "nothing new." And in mid-
April Premier Khrushchev made emphatic again, in an interview
with Walter Lippmann, that the U.S.S.R. would never accept a
single, neutral administrator for the control commission.

MOUNTING PRESSURES

Domestic pressure mounted, particularly within Congress, to
stop talking and start testing. Even the President, at his April 21
press conference, admitted to being "very discouraged" about the
talks, but he intended to continue them, he said. He condemned
the troika plan again as dooming the negotiations, and said he was
dismayed by Soviet efforts to stall the talks in order to merge them
with general disarmament talks later. That would mean extending
the uninspected moratorium, as well as creating a much more
complex environment in which to achieve any bilateral agreement.
The President also acknowledged for the first time that he was
considering resuming some tests, since the U.S.S.R. seemed to have
lost interest in reaching agreement on a ban. But, Kennedy said, he
had sent a letter to Khrushchev about nuclear testing on the day
the Geneva talks opened, and had not yet received a reply. He
felt that he should have a reply from the Soviet Premier before
making a final decision.

This was probably the nadir of Kennedy's entire year. The
Cuban invasion had failed, the Communists were gaining in Laos,

210 YEAR OF TRIAL

and his hopes for achieving an agreement on a test ban were pretty well shattered. "I thought the best hope [for reaching any agreement with the U.S.S.R.] was the nuclear testing," he said, "even though it was always true that the obstacles were large." He observed that the Administration had made the most extensive preparations ever for the reopening of the talks, and therefore was extremely disappointed.

If the talks failed, hopes for the general disarmament talks would also be "substantially lessened" and there would be a "proliferation of atomic testing in other countries"—in China within two or three years, reports from Japan were saying. Khrushchev's often-stated desire to keep nuclear weapons from the Chinese, some Kremlinologists thought, was the main reason for letting his test-ban negotiators come, on several occasions, so close to an agreement. Their turnabouts at the last moment, and their hardening of position when successful compromise seemed most likely, were taken as evidence of the influence of Soviet military commanders and the promilitarism wing of the Communist Party. But in April, although there were some rumblings between China and the U.S.S.R., it was still assumed that Khrushchev was at least master in his own house. He could certainly negotiate for a test ban if he wanted to. This was the thinking of some who urged a meeting of the two K's before the United States resumed testing. It was a last chance that should be taken.

Khrushchev still believed in peaceful coexistence, students of Soviet policy said, but he also felt it necessary to establish the "primacy" of the U.S.S.R. in world affairs. By pressing for troika control of all international affairs, and thus giving the U.S.S.R. a say in, and a veto over, everything, he was seeking to assure for the Soviet Union a position in a balance-of-power world equal to that of the previously dominant West. Surely, understanding that, we could reach some tenable compromise. After all, so the argument ran, the position of power from which he was making his demands was real, not imaginary, and we could not alter it by refusing to face the new situation in the world, that there were now two major nuclear powers.

At Geneva, the pattern was still one step forward and two steps back. At the April 21 meeting Tsarapkin revived a long-buried Soviet proposal that would actually give the U.S.S.R. a two-to-one edge in the personnel that would staff the control posts in China and in other Soviet bloc areas—and added support to the view that fear of having Western observers in her territory was the root of much Soviet suspicion.

On April 25 the French set off another blast in the atmosphere, over the Sahara. Moscow radio condemned this at great length, but Tsarapkin, much to the surprise of Dean and Ormsby-Gore, failed to mention it. At that session Tsarapkin, as it turned out, had something more important to talk about. For the first time since March 21 he actually specified that the troika was "absolutely necessary." At the next meeting Dean again attacked the troika plan as unacceptable. (Even if the West ever did agree to it, the Senate would never ratify any agreement that incorporated it.)

On April 28, after a grand total of 300 meetings, the talks recessed briefly for May Day. At the final meeting before the recess the West noted with great reluctance that in six weeks the U.S.S.R. had made no constructive moves and one destructive one. Dean then returned to Washington to report on "reasonable progress" or lack thereof in Geneva.

This was the time of frantic post-mortems on Cuba. To avenge our setbacks in Cuba and elsewhere by calling off the test-ban talks, resuming United States testing, and giving nuclear weapons out to all our Allies would have been a popular action for the President to take. The Cuban fiasco had increased the conviction of those who favored resuming tests that the President did not know what he was doing, and surely there was the temptation to throw in the towel and have done with the test moratorium.

On May 2 the National Security Council assembled to hear a report from Arthur Dean on Geneva. After hearing it, council members were divided on what to do next. Some contended that since a ban had actually been in effect for thirty months without inspection, the thing to do was just to keep talking and extend the moratorium. There was no evidence that the U.S.S.R. had violated the moratorium, but there was some uneasiness as to how long this could last, and some belief that undetectable tests could have been conducted all along.

The President's press conference of May 5 focused primarily on the test-ban negotiations. Mr. Kennedy began with the statement that "The new United States position represents an earnest and reasonable effort to reach a workable agreement. It constitutes a most significant over-all move in these negotiations." He hoped the U.S.S.R. would consider the United States treaty "in a positive manner," and, in an attempt to avoid inquiry about a cutoff date for the talks, the President volunteered that Dean would report back on the prospects "within a reasonable time." That was also the day of Shepard's successful space flight, the first good news the United States had had in quite a while. (Nixon picked the same date to make a speech gloating over the fact that Khrushchev "has no more intention of coming to a workable agreement [on testing] than he did with the previous Eisenhower Administration.")

Dean left Washington for Geneva that day. And the pressure on Kennedy to resume testing now became intense.

Marquis Childs, columnist of the St. Louis *Post-Dispatch,* was in Geneva in May, soaking up atmosphere for the novel he was writing about life among the diplomats and also covering the arms negotiations. "Recently Arthur Dean got a telephone call from a friend in New York," Childs reported in his strictly nonfiction column of May 24.

The friend, head of a large advertising agency, began by insisting that the nuclear test-ban talks which Dean is conducting for the United States be broken off at once and ended by berating Dean for squandering the tax payers' money in such a wrongheaded endeavor.

It happens that Dean is serving without pay and without an expense allowance, as he has on his Government assignments under both the Eisenhower and Kennedy Administrations. He was disturbed and at first somewhat puzzled by his friend's intense feeling on the subject of nuclear tests. But it developed that along with 200 other advertising executives he had been brought to Washington by the Air Force for an indoctrination in the need to improve America's nuclear weaponry.

Then Childs went on to describe what many reporters knew was going on in Washington but few were reporting.

The Air Force, the munitions industry, certain highly influential scientists, along with other elements in the Pentagon, are pressing President Kennedy to break off the talks or to announce that while they go on the United States will nevertheless start testing again.

Dean and McCloy had continued to stand with the President for continuing negotiations in spite of all the discouragement and pressures against doing so. One of the reasons, Dean explained to Childs, was what he and McCloy had learned about the proposals for new nuclear armaments to be achieved by resumed testing. During a long briefing before McCloy and Dean took on their disarmament jobs, one of the new proposals was unveiled for them. According to Childs, it had lived vividly in Dean's mind as he patiently put the Western case for a controlled test ban up to the Russians.

In oversimplified form the concept, sponsored by physicist Edward Teller, was as follows:

megaton (equivalent to one million tons of TNT) nuclear war-
ad can by testing be reduced from 200 pounds to 35 pounds. Con-
quently, the missile to carry it can be greatly reduced in fire power
d in size.
These small warheads and smaller missiles capable of reaching
rgets in the Soviet Union can be mounted on especially built trucks.
ey can be manned by a lieutenant and a sergeant. Up to 50,000 of
ese missile-equipped trucks would be kept crisscrossing the United
ates night and day on a rotating basis. This would insure that at all
nes a sufficient retaliatory striking power would escape destruction
om a first strike by the Soviets.

The Teller concept was said to have won over a number of the
ilitary proponents of testing. Dean, according to Childs, was im-
essed adversely by the greatly increased danger it would create
 putting nuclear missiles under the control of an ever-larger
imber of individuals who might be erratic enough under certain
rcumstances to set one off. "The chances of an accident—several
ar accidents of catastrophic scale are said to have been kept
om public knowledge—would be increased by a geometric ratio,"
r. Childs added.
Dr. Teller's concept, of course, was but one of many that
dvocates of renewed testing claimed would justify subsequent
orld criticism of the United States. The President personally
ard many of the arguments—and by report asked for a repeat
erformance by at least one group on the case for testing. Even
en he was not persuaded.
On the President's order, Mr. Dean returned to the daily effort
reasoning with the Russians at Geneva—and so keeping the door
en for later discussions. Some new ideas might come out of the
pidly materializing plan for a Kennedy-Khrushchev meeting in
ne.
Meanwhile, Kennedy's thoughts, one assumes, turned to improv-
g the position in which the Chief Executive of the United States
ould stand when he met the Premier of the Soviet Union for the
st time.
Much had already been done to make his role as Commander
Chief more meaningful. Secretary McNamara was being hailed
"a genius" by hard-shelled defense experts of forty years' stand-
g in the Congress, and, at least for a while, his wish would be
eir command.
A task force was at work on a foreign-assistance bill that would
ake American money go further overseas—if it could be ma-

neuvered through Congress. The Peace Corps had been esta
lished and the Food for Peace Program expanded.

Plans for putting the Act of Bogota into operation were w
along—the Alianza para Progreso had been proclaimed. But su
evidence of a vital new America was not dramatic enough to ii
press the Soviet leader. Perhaps space was the answer.

THE RACE INTO SPACE

Scores of times during the Presidential campaign, the Democra
candidate talked of the development of outer space and its ii
portance to the future, psychologically and scientifically. Kenne
chided the Eisenhower Administration for failing to realize "t
impact that being first in outer space would have." "Peo
around the world equate the mission to the moon, the mission
outer space, with productive and scientific superiority." Therefo
at Albuquerque in November 1957, after the Russians successfu
launched Sputnik I, Mr. Kennedy remarked that "the impressi
began to move around the world that the Soviet Union was on t
march, that it had definite goals, that it knew how to accompli
them, that it was moving and that we were standing still. That
what we have to overcome."

Eisenhower had not been alone in failing to foresee what l
than full effort to compete with the Russians would cost. He w
no more shortsighted than many American and also many Sov
space experts. Few if any persons connected with the Vangua
satellite and the United States part in the International Geophy
cal Year anticipated the tremendous political and psychologic
force the launching of the first Soviet Sputnik would exert on t
world.

The Soviet advantage ironically had grown out of United Stat
superiority in weaponry. In the early fifties the United States h
scored a technical breakthrough in learning how to reduce the si
and lighten the weight of nuclear-missile warheads. Small, re
tively inexpensive rocket boosters could launch them. The Sov
Union, which had not perfected a small warhead, was forced
develop large, costly boosters with double the thrust of the Unit
States rockets, in order to launch their intercontinental missil
But when serious efforts to penetrate outer space began, the R
sians found that their big military boosters had a most significa
by-product use. They could hurl large payloads into orbit arou

he earth and beyond the moon, which the United States Atlas and
Titan boosters could not.

Eisenhower and his advisers who had failed to realize the significance of that difference in weight-carrying capability now set
out to match it. The loss of the initial round in the space race,
therefore, came before the U.S.S.R. launched Sputnik I in October
1957. Afterward scientists of the standing of Dr. Lee A. Du-
Bridge, President of California Institute of Technology, told Mr.
Eisenhower that since space had few military uses, it should be
left to civilian scientists to explore gradually.

Kennedy had fully grasped the significance of Sputnik I and
successive prestige losses by the time of the 1960 campaign. And
one of the early task forces he appointed after the election was
assigned to review the space program and report on problems
requiring prompt attention from the new Administration. The
chairman was Dr. Wiesner. In early January the distinguished
group brought in a report that the new President proceeded to
follow more exactly than he followed the advice he received from
most of his task forces.

JOHNSON APPOINTED TO SPACE COUNCIL

The Wiesner report recommended making the Space Council,
established but never used by Eisenhower, manager of all space
activity. Kennedy appointed Vice President Johnson, who was
good at taking charge, as Chairman of the council and let it be
known that he was to do so.

The National Aeronautics and Space Administration command
was weak, the Wiesner report said. In choosing a new director,
Johnson and Kennedy replaced Dr. T. Keith Glennan, a scientist,
with James E. Webb, a forceful administrator, adept at Congressional relations—thus reflecting the general view that NASA's
needs were more administrative than technical.

On the central subject of space exploration, the task-force report
was specific about the priority need for big booster rockets. It
pointed out the danger of placing priority on a man-in-space program when we would continue to lag behind the Russians so long
as we lacked big boosters. And it called for emphasizing instead
the "solid, durable, and worthwhile goals of space activities," such
as an international television relay system, because they were more
likely to produce early success.

Beyond appointing Johnson and Webb to the Space Council and NASA, Kennedy paid little attention to space in the first months of his Administration, which were devoted almost solely to economic-recession problems. In fact, space received the first serious consideration at the White House when the new Administration had to decide whether the 1961–62 budget Eisenhower had requested for NASA was adequate. The agency wanted $308 million more than the budget called for. On March 22, the Vice President and Edward Welsh, a former adviser on military affairs to Senator Stuart Symington and now slated to be Executive Secretary of the Space Council, met with the President to thresh out the NASA budget. The next day the three met again with Dr. Wiesner, now the President's science adviser, and Budget Director David Bell. The decision was not to say yes to the whole NASA request, but to approve stepping up work on big booster rockets—the key to catching up with the Russians. The President approved an additional $126 million for that purpose, and for the preparation of a communications satellite that Eisenhower had cut out of the original Aeronautics and Space Agency budget. President Eisenhower had thought this work should be done by private industry. Kennedy decided that for the time being the Government should control research and development in communications satellites.

President Kennedy then asked Vice President Johnson's Space Council to study all space programs and recommend a future course for the United States. On May 8 the council delivered its report to the President. And on May 25, by which time the plan was firm for meeting Khrushchev in Vienna, the President asked Congress to approve a ten-year undertaking, which might cost $40 billion, to land a man on the moon and return him safely to earth.

PUT A MAN ON THE MOON

What line of thinking carried Mr. Kennedy so far so fast?

The decision to divert from other essential work billions in scarce funds and millions of skilled professional man-hours of time was not a matter of rubber-stamping unanimous advice. There was a division of opinion on a manned moon exploration within the President's Science Advisory Committee as well as among White House staff. Many influential scientists argued that so vastly expanded a space program was not worth the price. Those funds, they said, could far more profitably be spent on education and on research pertaining to earth.

Kennedy at first appeared to be following that opinion. In making his March decision to recommend more funds for developing big boosters, the President had passed over more than $180 million in NASA requests for projects related to putting a man in space. And, in April, after Yuri Gagarin orbited the earth in the first space flight by man, the President told a press conference that perhaps our money would be better spent in other areas "where we can be first and which will bring perhaps more long-range benefits to mankind." NASA Administrator Webb, appearing before the House Science and Aeronautics Committee at the time of the Gagarin flight, continued to take the line that the United States space program was aimed at scientific attainment, not at matching the Soviets—leading Hanson Baldwin to remark in the New York *Times* that "This testimony, given after the first three months of President Kennedy's Administration, sounds almost like a phonograph record of testimony given during the Eisenhower Administration."

In Baldwin's opinion it was "high time to discard this policy." "In fact," the military expert of the *Times* declared, "if the United States is to compete in space, we must decide to do so on a top priority basis immediately, or we face a bleak future of more Soviet triumphs."

Orbiting a space station or sending a man to the moon and bringing him back were, Baldwin thought, "probably years away" for the United States, since "either of them will require engines of immense thrust." Speeding up work on Project Saturn, to produce a booster rocket with a 1.5 million-pound thrust, was the first step. But, as Baldwin noted, funds had not been provided for a "crash" effort on Saturn and other more powerful boosters, much less for a "crash" program to achieve some space objective in advance of the Russians.

Should the United States do that now? The President's personal science adviser, Dr. Wiesner, was not opposed to a greatly expanded program, including manned exploration of the moon, but Dr. Vannevar Bush and others were. The United States, it was certain, could not overtake the Russians in certain endeavors. Our space scientists conceded that the Soviet Union would accomplish the first manned orbiting of the moon. But in setting out to land a man or men on the moon and return them safely to earth, most experts believed we would be starting more nearly even. Some insisted that that race, too, was already lost, but just as many voices were raised on the other side of the argument.

To our knowledge, present Soviet rockets were incapable of

sending a manned expedition to the moon and back. Mr. Webb
was saying in April that there could be "no reliable prediction" as
to when the Russians would be ready to try it until there was evidence that they had developed a more powerful rocket. Because of
the longer-range nature of the manned moon expedition, Webb
and Defense Secretary McNamara both believed that there was "a
chance" that the United States could win the moon race if we
entered it.

"A chance" looked like very good odds to John F. Kennedy in
the not very merry month of May. Instead of swiftly "reversing
the deterioration" and "regaining the initiative" as he had confidently set out to do, the President had seen the Russians, without
study, disdain his offer of new terms on a nuclear-weapons test-ban
agreement by which he laid much store. After that had come Cuba.
And then Gagarin. And now he was preparing to face Khrushchev
at Vienna. A bold new undertaking that would demonstrate national self-confidence had definite appeal at that moment. Especially since it "had a chance." Kennedys had been known to back
longer shots. Khrushchev was to add strength to Webb and Mc-
Namara's opinion when he later conceded, in an interview with an
American reporter, that the U.S.S.R. was capable of sending men
to and around the moon but had not yet solved the problem of
bringing them back.

If Mr. Kennedy stuck to the evaluation of space exploration he
had expressed in his campaign, he could not stick to the rate of activity Eisenhower had considered adequate. As in other areas, he
could increase the space effort only by token acceleration in his
first year, if he was to escape criticism as a "big spender" and a
"fiscal irresponsible." The need for something positive to show
Khrushchev was undoubtedly persuasive in bringing the President
around to a massive early effort in space. But the fact that the
Space Science Board of the National Academy of Sciences (a non-
governmental group) also took that position seems to have exerted
great force, too. After three years of study of the scientific aspect
of space, including the role of man, the Board in February adopted
a view, submitted to the Government at the end of March, that
greatly influenced the report of Johnson's Space Council to the
President and consequently the President's proposals to Congress.

The Board recommended that *"scientific exploration of the
moon and planets should be clearly stated as the ultimate objective
of the U.S. space program for the foreseeable future."* (My italics.)

This objective should be promptly adopted as the official goal of the
United States space program and clearly announced, discussed and

supported. In addition, it should be stressed that the United States will continue to press toward a thorough scientific understanding of space, of solving problems of manned space exploration, and of development of applications of space science for man's welfare.

So many intermediate problems had first to be solved that it was not now possible to decide whether man could accompany early expeditions to the moon and planets. But the Board strongly urged that planning for those explorations proceed on the premise that man would be included—not to do so would inevitably prevent man's inclusion, the Board believed, and "every effort should be made to establish the feasibility of manned space flight at the earliest opportunity."

Experts of the National Academy of Sciences gave their reasons:

There seems little room for dissent that man's participation in the exploration of the moon and planets will be essential if and when it becomes technologically feasible to include him. Man can contribute critical elements of scientific judgment and discrimination in conducting the scientific exploration of these bodies which can never be fully supplied by his instruments, however complex and sophisticated they may become. Thus, carefully planned and executed manned scientific expeditions will inevitably be the more fruitful. Moreover, the very technical problems of control at very great distances, involving substantial time delays in command signal reception, may make perfection of planetary experiments impossible without manned controls on the vehicles.

They had taken into account the nonscientific arguments for a man-in-space program, too, the scientists said in their statement. They pointed to "the sense of national leadership emergent from bold and imaginative U.S. space activity." And they concluded on a note to be repeated by the President later. As individuals, the members of the Space Board said, they regarded "man's exploration of the moon and planets as potentially the greatest inspirational venture of this century and one in which the entire world can share; inherent here are great and fundamental philosophical and spiritual values which find a response in man's questing spirit and his intellectual self-realization." Those factors had parallel importance with the scientific goals, they believed, and "should not be neglected in seeking public appreciation and acceptance of the program."

Composed as it was of leading scientists in various fields from all parts of the country, the Space Board's words carried great weight. (Lloyd Viel Berkner, director of the Graduate Research Center of the Southwest, was its chairman, and among the members were such eminent men as Bruno B. Rossi, Harrison S. Brown, James Alfred Van Allen, and the Nobel Prize winners, Joshua Lederberg and Harold Clayton Urey.) Their findings were carefully read by Dr. Wiesner, Mr. Webb of NASA, Vice President Johnson, and the Space Council. They changed the minds of several members of the President's Science Advisory Committee who had been reluctant to commit the nation to a major space effort. And they provided scientific sanction for the most "far out" action of Kennedy's first year.

"I believe that this nation should commit itself to achieving a goal before this decade is out, of landing a man on the moon and returning him safely to the earth," Mr. Kennedy told Congress on May 25. "No single space project in this period will be more impressive to mankind, or more important for the long-range exploration of space; and none will be so difficult or expensive to accomplish."

A FIRM COMMITMENT

More was involved than sending a man to the moon. Kennedy's ten-year program included speeding up the creation of communications and weather satellite systems; exploration of the moon and planets without man; development of nuclear rockets and ion- or electric-propulsion devices to push spaceships slowly to the distant planets.

His decision had not been taken lightly. And the President did not intend that Congress or the country should approve it lightly either. "Let it be clear," Kennedy said in his message, "that I am asking the Congress and the country to accept a firm commitment to a new course of action"—a course, he pointed out, that would require many years to complete and would cost as many billions of dollars as the entire national defense in 1961. It was important to understand that. For "if we are to go only half way, or reduce our sights in the face of difficulty, in my judgment it would be better not to go at all."

No one could predict with certainty the ultimate yield from mastery of space, the President explained. But in his opinion "we should go to the moon." He and his advisers had weighed the matter for months. Now every citizen and every Congressman should make his own judgment.

There is no sense in agreeing or desiring that the United States take an affirmative position in outer space unless we are prepared o do the work and bear the burdens to make it successful.

This decision demands a major national commitment of scientific and technical manpower, material and facilities, and the possibility of their diversion from other important activities where they are already thinly spread. It means a degree of dedication, organization and discipline which have not always characterized our research and development efforts. It means we cannot afford undue work stoppages, inflated costs of material or talent, wasteful interagency rivalries, or a high turnover of key personnel.

New objectives and new money cannot solve these problems. They could, in fact, aggravate them further—unless every scientist, every engineer, every serviceman, every technician, contractor, and civil servant gives his personal pledge that this nation will move forward, with the full speed of freedom, in the exciting adventure of space.

The response of the country to the President's call for soul-searching was silence. Congress, too, asked few questions, voiced little opposition, quickly voted the funds that the President specified for the first year. The advance into space was begun, but Kennedy and Johnson and Webb and the military men involved understood that it might not always be as simple in the ten years to come when NASA came to Congress to ask for the increasingly larger sums of money it would take each year to sustain the program. For the second fiscal year the request would rise to $2.4 billion. Unless the public and Congress became convinced that heavy investment in space was vital for technological and scientific reasons, the challenge of Soviet successes and the thrill of rocket shots might not be enough to assure appropriations.

Meanwhile NASA reorganized itself to answer persistent criticisms of improper management. In three key steps during September, Webb and his aides selected Cape Canaveral for expansion into a site from which to launch flights to the moon and beyond; selected a Government-owned ordnance plant near New Orleans, Louisiana (home of the late Overton Brooks, Chairman of the House Space Committee), for fabrication of the launching vehicles, and chose Houston, Texas (home of House Space Committee member Albert Thomas and Space Council Chairman Johnson), as location for a new $60-million space-flight command center for manned missions.

The Vice President and Mr. Welsh, acting through the Space Council, were working at the highest level to reconcile the differences between military and civilian agencies as they occurred. The result, in the first year, was basically good rapport between the top rank in NASA and in the Department of Defense, poor at the working level. Many of the military still insisted that space was properly their domain. To the Soviets, they argued, it was all the same. To them both our peaceful Tiros weather satellite (NASA) and our military Midas early-warning and Samos photo satellites are spies in the sky.

One decision contained in the President's May 25 address had great significance for military-civilian relations. It permitted the military to pursue development of a high solid-propellant space booster (they had experience with those, ranging from bazookas to Polaris and Minuteman missiles), while NASA continued to perfect liquid propellants (which they knew best). The race might be halted when it was decided which booster would better serve the moon program—or as it had so often, the costly duplication might continue. It would be up to Johnson and the Council, who had authority to decide.

SHORT CUT TO THE MOON

The Johnson Council introduced a dramatic technological change in objectives late in the year—the decision to back "orbital rendezvous" as a quicker means to get men to the moon. Initially the consensus among experts was that a cluster of giant rockets standing almost as tall as the Washington Monument, would be capable of carrying three men to the moon and returning them directly to earth. The newer rendezvous concept called for sending available smaller rockets and payloads into space, assembling them there, and then dispatching the assembled package to the moon. Smaller Saturn rockets would be used to hurl parts of a space station into orbit, other similar boosters would send up astronauts to join together the orbiting pieces and proceed on the trip to the moon. The rendezvous technique, officials estimated would subtract a year from the United States target date (Kennedy's decision of May 25 had already advanced the date for our probable landing from some time in the 1970's to the mid-1960's) Wernher Von Braun, the German V-2 inventor who now head United States Army space work at the Redstone Arsenal, recently suggested that "rendezvous" could advance the date to 1966.

Both the big Nova booster and the rendezvous techniques would be tested. The remaining decisions would be technical: Would the Nova or the rendezvous technique get men to the moon more quickly, and were large solid propellants more effective than liquids in upper stages of multistage boosters?

The key decision had been Kennedy's—the United States had made a manned lunar landing by 1970 its national goal. The Congress of the United States, which decides things for only two years at a time, had put its temporary seal of approval on the undertaking. The people of the United States would have to be repersuaded at regular intervals that the adventure was worth the continuing pain to the pocketbook. But in five years' time the twelve-year-olds who saw the first Sputnik fly by in 1957 would be United States voters, a new breed of voters familiar with concepts of space and life on other worlds, and presumably more willing than their fathers to pay the high price of going to the stars. In the intervening five years, the President and the scientists would have to burden of educating the older generation to the meaning of space—by easy stages. The Space Board's statement of the broader goals they hope to fulfill in the course of exploring space was not referred to in the President's May 25 message—perhaps for fear that what the scientists see ahead might frighten earth-oriented Congressmen. Scientists, they say, look into space to find "a better understanding of the origins of the solar system and universe, the investigation of the existence of life on other planets and, potentially, an understanding of life itself."

WHERE SPACE LEADS

Sir Bernard Lovell, Director of Britain's Jodrell Bank Experimental Station and one of the world's best-known radio astronomers, has another view of the United States undertaking that perhaps has more tangible appeal for the less theoretically minded. Writing in the New York *Times Magazine* for December 24, 1961, Sir Bernard said: "The announcement last spring by the President that the United States was to engage in a vast program designed to place an American on the moon before a Russian may indeed be recognized in history as one of the fundamental turning-points in the world crisis."

In order to accomplish this feat [he continued] a significant fraction of the nation's science and technology will be diverted to an achievement which, in itself, has no direct military significance, but which will nevertheless use some 10 percent of the resources that might otherwise find a military outlet on earth.

In the Soviet Union it is clear that the same determination exists and the diversion from the direct military machine must be similar. Within two or three decades, when the planets—not the moon—become the targets, the expenditure and effort will be so colossal that it will be hard for the nations to sustain the global military machines in a developing state.

As man's interest and resources "pass rapidly to this extra-terrestrial environment during the next two decades," and global dangers perhaps subside, Sir Bernard sees a new danger ahead. At that point, he warns, "the peoples of the earth must exercise the utmost restraint and vigilance as the major ethical dilemma, which now pervades us on earth, assumes cosmic attributes."

No one, including the President, could imagine the consequences that might flow from Mr. Kennedy's decision to lead the United States into space. But the President could expect that it might lift some hearts at home by space-industry jobs and visions of the future, and improve the sagging appearance of the United States before he set out for Europe.

"WHAT CIVIL DEFENSE CAN AND CANNOT DO"

During the 1950's the Federal Government spent a grand total of $618 million on civil defense, less than President Kennedy finally recommended that Congress appropriate for 1962 alone. This total was the result of Congressional cuts of 74 per cent in Administration requests over the years. It financed the development of a nationwide warning system to be activated by the North American Air Defense Command in Colorado Springs, the preparation of almost 2,000 "packaged hospitals" now in warehouses that could be set up in emergencies, the Conelrad AM radio network of civil-defense information, research on a home-warning system known as NEAR, and training of more than a million Government employees for emergency duties. Not until 1958 was the Office of Civil Defense Mobilization established, merging the Office of Defense Mobilization and the Federal Civil Defense Administration.

Plans had been submitted to Eisenhower, most notably one included in the Gaither Report of 1957, that urged a $20-billion shelter program, but the Budget Bureau vetoed all large-scale civil-defense plans as too expensive. Representative Chet Holifield of California had also advocated a program on that scale in a report of the Joint Atomic Energy Committee.

Kennedy retained for his first year the Eisenhower Adminisration's request for $104 million for civil defense. For director of he OCDM, the President chose Frank Burton Ellis, a New Orleans lawyer who had headed Kennedy's campaign for delegates n Louisiana in 1960. With the enthusiasm of a newcomer to Washington, Ellis had plunged into his new job with a spirit of urgency strange to that backwater agency. OCDM, like the International Cooperation Agency in the final years of the Eisenhower Administration, had become a kind of patronage dumping ground. Ellis, unexpectedly, set out to place OCDM in the vanguard of the New Frontier. Instead of the $104 million for civil defense that Eisenhower had requested and that the Kennedy budget bureau had approved, Mr. Ellis urged a $300-million program. Nevertheless, Budget Director David Bell and McGeorge Bundy of the White House staff were strongly opposed, the latter especially because he felt this was too much money for a low-priority item. Ellis continued to urge it, and to seek allies in his new-found crusade, particularly in the Pentagon, to which Ellis urged moving all OCDM activities. As a politician he could see how much easier it was to persuade Congress to approve appropriations for activities headquartered under the Pentagon roof.

The President liked the idea of centralizing defense activities in the Pentagon for some of the same reasons that motivated the shift of many CIA activities to the Department of Defense. It was argued that such formerly subsidiary forms of warfare as civil defense and subversion had become central to the conduct of war.

By mid-May Ellis had persuaded the White House to his position, although Bell and Bundy were still opposed. Ellis then argued for funds. He quoted a Rand Corporation study, later discredited, as stating that the U.S.S.R. had spent $.5 billion to $1.5 billion for fallout shelters the previous year. And when the President on May 25 sent Congress a special message on space and defense, it included a section on the need for civilian fallout shelters, asking Congress to triple the present allocation for civil defense.

The statement justifying the request was a model of clarity.

This administration has been looking very hard at exactly what Civil Defense can and cannot do. It cannot be obtained cheaply, it cannot give an assurance of blast protection that will be foolproof. . . . and it cannot deter a nuclear attack.

We will deter an enemy from making a nuclear attack only if our retaliatory power is so strong and so invulnerable that he knows he would be destroyed by our response. If we have that strength, Civil Defense is not needed to deter an attack. If we should ever lack it, Civil Defense would not be an adequate substitute.

But this *deterrent concept assumes rational calculations by rational men*. And the history of this planet is sufficient to remind us of the possibilities of an irrational attack, a miscalculation, an accidental war which cannot be either foreseen or deterred. The nature of modern warfare heightens these possibilities. It is on this basis that Civil Defense can readily be justified—as insurance for the civilian population in the event of such a miscalculation. It is insurance we trust will never be needed—but insurance which we could never forgive ourselves for foregoing in the event of catastrophe.

Once the validity of this concept is recognized, there is no point in delaying the initiation of a nationwide long-range program of identifying present fallout shelter capacity and providing shelter in new and existing structures. Such a program would protect millions of people against the hazards of radioactive fallout in the event of a large-scale nuclear attack. To assure effective use of these shelters, additional measures will be required for warning, training, radiological monitoring and stock-piling of food and medicines. And effective performance of the entire program requires not only new legislative authority and more funds, but also sound organizational arrangements.

Kennedy stirred no rush of public sentiment for shelters. But his message did have impact in Congress. One week later the House Appropriations Committee cut only 25 per cent from the requested $104 billion, instead of the customary 50 per cent, and noted that it would consider the new programs separately. The Senate approved the entire $104 million, and the Administration finally got $86.5 million of the $104-million request.

It was at this point that Mr. Kennedy departed for Europe, had his traumatic meeting with Mr. Khrushchev, and experienced a sudden awareness of civil defense.

THE CONFERENCE AT VIENNA

In early January, before Kennedy was even inaugurated, Nikita Khrushchev was dropping remarks about how much he wanted to get to know the new President. In early March, after Ambassador Thompson had sounded out Soviet officials on the subject, Mr. Kennedy indicated that he was willing. But it was not until May 20, when the crises in Cuba and Laos had greatly diminished United States prestige abroad, that Khrushchev took Kennedy up on the offer.

The President's advisers were divided on whether he should accept under the circumstances that prevailed. Former Ambassador to Russia Charles Bohlen believed that Khrushchev was the man to see if you wanted to deal with the Russians, whereas Secretary Rusk remained dubious of such face-to-face encounters. Others feared that Kennedy's trip to Vienna at a time of weakness in United States posture would itself be interpreted as another sign of weakness. They were also concerned that since there was no agenda, Khrushchev might bring up questions about areas in which the United States had not yet decided on a policy, or on which the Western allies had not yet reached agreement. The military troubles in Laos had put Western discord in the spotlight. Kennedy was going to tell Khrushchev of the great strength and determination of the North Atlantic Treaty Organization, although he was stopping in Paris on the way to urge President de Gaulle to play a greater part in it.

Kennedy's prompt decision for an early meeting, preventing careful preparation for the talks, indicated both confidence and need.

Khrushchev, on the surface, had an obvious momentary advantage. The events of April had deflated Europe's initial, and unrealistic, expectations of the effect of Kennedy's assumption of power. The Western alliance had still to be cemented as solidly as Stevenson's November report said it had to be before the United States could achieve a really strong position vis-à-vis the Soviet Union. Latin American nations and neutrals everywhere were disillusioned and estranged by the Cuban affair. The United States had only begun to rebuild the nonnuclear military strength with which to support nations faced with wars of "liberation."

But Kennedy knew that his disadvantage, though real, was temporary. Action was under way to restore the military balance in conventional and guerrilla forces as well as in nuclear forces. He had confidence in the revisions that were being planned in the foreign-aid program. He believed that the Alliance for Progress would become more important to Latin Americans than Castro. And he had faith in Food for Peace and the Peace Corps as powerful new ambassadors.

And at this point Kennedy needed two things that only Khrushchev could give—a nuclear test-ban agreement, and a settlement in Laos. Without them it would be hard to resist demands in the United States for the resumption of nuclear testing and for military intervention to keep Laos from falling to the Communists. It would be reassuring, too, to hear from Khrushchev a definition of "wars of liberation" that meant more than thinly disguised Soviet aggression.

Khrushchev also had need of Kennedy. Coexistence was a fighting word in the Communist world. And Khrushchev, looking toward the showdown that would come at the Party Congress in October, had to make ready his case in defense of the doctrine. He would have to offer evidence that following the policy of peaceful coexistence had produced results. Members of the Kennedy circle had assured Khrushchev's ambassador in Washington and others as well that if the Russians gave him time, Kennedy would prove his wish to settle disagreements peaceably. Studies of the trouble spots were being made, the Russians had been assured; proposals would be forthcoming.

More than four months after Kennedy's Inauguration, a few compromises on technical points relating to a test ban were all that had materialized. Khrushchev had to be sure the Kennedy Administration understood that he couldn't wait forever for something that was more important to the Eastern European satellite countries (on whom he would have to rely for support against the Chinese at the October Congress), something like a Berlin settlement.

Would the similarity of Kennedy and Khrushchev's problems override the differences in their natures and their backgrounds? Was either man capable of understanding the other's situation along with his own?

Perhaps it would have helped, as Kennedy and Khrushchev traveled toward Vienna, if each had had a copy of an editorial that appeared in the independent newspaper *Die Welt* of Hamburg two weeks after President Kennedy's Inauguration. It was written by Editor in Chief Hans Zehrer and, as translated in *Atlas*, ran as follows:

Kennedy has it tougher than Churchill. Twenty-one years ago, when the latter told the House of Commons: "The Battle of France is over; now I await the Battle of Britain," everyone knew it was so. The Battle of Dunkirk had shaken the citizens of Britain into an awareness of reality. If their leaders could dare to speak of blood, sweat, and tears, it was because everyone in England knew that capitulation was the only alternative. Four weeks later, enemy fliers began the Blitz on London.

Kennedy must describe things as they are. That, according to Lasalle, is the only way to overcome an impossible situation. But he is speaking to his prosperous fellow citizens who, like the peoples of other Western countries, have not had the real facts of the situation spelled out to them. They do not yet understand that the world has become one, that its population will double in the next forty years, that it is wracked by hunger, fear of atomic weapons, and the need for more living space. He, too, must talk about a Dunkirk, but a Dunkirk that has not yet happened. For if it had happened, it would already be too late. A difficult and thankless assignment.

Perhaps Kennedy himself has no conception of the realities of the world we live in. But certain passages in his Inaugural Address point out that the crisis deepens daily; every day makes a solution more difficult. As more hostile powers acquire more new weapons, the hour of maximum danger draws nearer.

The people to whom he speaks know little of these things. They live in another world, where everything is nicely arranged and a secure future stretches out before them for the next seventy years. Fundamentally they think no differently than do the people in the East, who also believe they have everything arranged to meet every contingency. All they want is more comforts like those the Western peoples enjoy. Khrushchev cannot talk to them about sacrifices any more; in order to hold their support, he must talk about well-being. So he promises to catch up with America by 1970, but the appointed hour always lies at least five years in the future. After forty-three years of sacrifice, they have had enough ideas and utopias. Now they want something on which they can put their hands. "Nobody here speaks of overtime pay," said Khrushchev before the Plenum of the Central Committee. "Do you think we can win through to Communism with morality alone? Morality is a good thing, but it must rest on a material foundation." The Chinese, on the other hand, will make sacrifices, but now they are going hungry and something has gone wrong with their great forward leap.

Kennedy and Khrushchev both find themselves in similar situations. They know what kind of reality surrounds them. But this knowledge is confined to themselves and to a small circle. They know that they can hold their own only if they succeed in mobilizing the masses and give the masses some idea of the new world in which they live. That is why Kennedy relentlessly explains what has to be done to end the 1961 recession so that the entire power of the United States can be harnessed during the next two years. That is why Khrushchev no less relentlessly reveals the plight of Soviet agriculture, purges officials, and organizes mass meetings all over the country to arouse the people. They also know that if any war comes, it will destroy them both and set humanity back many centuries. That is why Kennedy increases armament. He wants to restore the balance of world power as well as the balance of rocket power. At the same time Khrushchev fights against those forces in his own camp who want to take advantage of their temporary advantage by resorting to war. But both are also interested in reaching agreement with each other and in preventing any new power from arising to bring everything down in ruins. . . ."

FIRST, DE GAULLE

But before Vienna was to come Paris. Months earlier it had been arranged that President de Gaulle be honored by being the first foreign host to the new President. (Kennedy's earlier visit to Prime Minister John G. Diefenbaker of Canada apparently didn't count.) There was fear that the proud General might be piqued by being made to figure as a preface to Khrushchev, but it was worth the chance, for a successful Kennedy-De Gaulle accord could make Kennedy's claim of Western unity far more convincing in Vienna.

After a minimum of hue and cry at home, Kennedy set out to seek his international fortune. The GOP, somewhat dubiously, wished him well, as did his own party. At a $100-a-plate Democratic birthday dinner the President spoke in a nonpartisan tone about the accomplishments of his Administration and his hopes for the Vienna conference. In going to meet Khrushchev, he said, he was seeking "insight," not "solutions."

Along with the pomp and circumstance, and Jacqueline Kennedy's conquest of Paris, the Kennedy-De Gaulle talks, according to report, went very well. The two statesmen first considered Berlin, and, after less than half an hour of discussion, including interpreting, announced complete accord that it should be defended. At several points during his stay in Paris, Kennedy emphasized United States commitments to Europe and our willingness to use all forms of force necessary to resist aggression, but De Gaulle remained unconvinced that the United States would actually use nuclear weapons on behalf of Europe and therefore insisted that France must continue testing. There was talk of Kennedy's gaining Congressional approval for conveying the same nuclear data to France that he is empowered to give Britain. The talks generally increased Kennedy's confidence, and reinforced the appearance if not the substance of Western unity.

KENNEDY MEETS KHRUSHCHEV

Thus Kennedy probably went on to Vienna exhilarated—but also exhausted. He, as well as his wife, was met with wild enthusiasm by the crowds in Vienna and in Paris. Kennedy greeted Khrushchev warmly but with deference, a gesture that Moscow reporters felt was misunderstood as personal awe rather than mere courtesy for an older man.

Laos was the first item on the informal agenda. Two days of talks brought only limited agreement on seeking a solution there, and no agreement at all on anything else.

On Berlin, Khrushchev renewed his advocacy of a German peace treaty, set another six-month deadline, and then, presumably, settled back to listen to what new alternative the new President of the United States would present. The new President made only the old, legalistic argument. His new Secretary of State had not supplied him with any fresh thinking on the subject of a *détente* on Berlin. Bonn still carried more weight in regular State Department channels than the new men Kennedy had brought in. The chief of the European Division, Foy David Kohler, an Acheson protégé schooled in Dulles' policies toward Germany, was not even faintly interested in proposals in the early weeks of the new Administration for an overture toward negotiating a new status for Berlin. And the suggestion seemingly was lost in the shuffle in the White House as wars of liberation began to crowd the stage.

Khrushchev's disappointment must have been as great as Kennedy's when the two discovered they had nothing new to say to each other. To Khrushchev, whether Kennedy had yet faced the fact or not, a test ban without a general disarmament agreement was already a closed book. To Kennedy Berlin was a book he had scarcely opened—the assumption had been that Khrushchev would give the new men in Washington considerable time before forcing the Berlin issue. And neither Kennedy nor his Department of State had done enough homework in finding a way out of the Berlin dilemma.

At Kennedy's request, however, former Secretary of State Dean Acheson had been doing his. A proposal he had developed was the closest thing to a plan for Berlin the United States possessed. Acheson proposed that the United States, Britain, and France agree in advance to an all-inclusive program for action so that each time the Russians acted, the Allies would not have to discuss all the possible reactions. It appealed to Kennedy as a way of freeing himself from the cumbersome diplomatic processes of the Cold War. But the British were critical of wholesale agreement on the ground that it would limit the flexibility of allied responses and could lead to war before the parties realized what was happening. France and Germany were likelier to favor this rigid no-nonsense approach. Shortly before Kennedy's visit, Acheson had visited De Gaulle to outline his proposal with regard to Berlin: if East

Germany or the Soviet Union cut off supplies to West Berlin, the West would respond to the blockade by putting NATO members on an emergency alert, and by using British, French, and United States troops for interim convoys to show defiance of the Communist move. But all this was still in the talking stage—and something the President of the United States would hardly talk over with the Chairman of the Soviet Central Committee even if it were policy.

Kennedy had come to Vienna seeking "insights," not "solutions." Khrushchev, it seems, was seeking evidence that the new regime in Washington had his problem in mind and was working on ways out of the impasse on Berlin. What he got was evidence that this was not the case. Kennedy, according to report, confined his discussion to Allied legal rights in Berlin and technical aspects of maintaining the status quo with respect to access to the city.

At this point Khrushchev apparently misjudged his man and the situation. He turned to blustering and threatening, methods not notably effective with Kennedys. And he seems to have assumed that Kennedy would respond to challenge with a chess player's logic.

CHESS PLAYER'S LOGIC?

The most satisfactory theory of Khrushchev's thinking at Vienna that I have encountered is one advanced in a *New Republic* article by Louis Halle, a former member of the United States State Department's Policy Planning Staff, now on the faculty of the Institute of International Studies in Geneva. Russian theoretical thinking, Mr. Halle says, has always followed the principle that international relations must promptly adjust to "the changing realities of power."

According to the principle [he explains] if one party to a chess game succeeds in developing his strength so that he at last has the means to capture his opponent's queen, then his opponent might as well accept the logic of power and concede the queen forthwith. If one party gains a decisive advantage over the whole board, then the other might as well accept the loss of the game without bothering to play it out.

Mr. Halle believes that, at the time of Vienna, this was the view taken by Mr. Khrushchev and Marshal Malinowski of the situation at Berlin. Since they had neutralized our nuclear capability by the development of their own, so that their superior conven-

ional forces gave them a net advantage, it was clear that they had
he power to take Berlin.

)ne need only look over the board, at the geography and the dis-
ribution of the forces, to see that this is so. Consequently, the Rus-
ian leaders expect us to recognize the reality and adjust to it by
;iving up what we no longer have the means to retain. That is what
hey have meant all along by negotiation over Berlin. No need to
•lay the game out, especially since to do so might involve all con-
erned in such catastrophic destruction. Instead, let us have a negotia-
ion in which we all adjust to the new power realities without actual
ighting.

That would seem only logical to a nation of chess players.

n fact, however, countries in which popular opinion is supreme are
inable to play chess. The American people are not chess players, they
lo not understand that we have been outmatched at Berlin, and it
vould not do for the President to tell them that we must proceed to
;ive up the piece. If the President were in the position of Machiavelli's
Prince, if he were Louis XIV, if he were Bismark, or if he were Mr.
Khrushchev himself, he might now negotiate a bloodless surrender
•f Berlin. But his situation is quite different. In terms of the domestic
cene, he would find it politically disastrous if not impossible to re-
reat. If pressed too hard by Moscow, he would probably find him-
elf compelled to fight, even though it was against all the logic of the
;ame. Moscow ought to recall that, if the British had been chess
•layers, they would have negotiated a settlement with Hitler on his
•wn terms (which would probably have been generous) in 1940.

Khrushchev must have been baffled, therefore, when Kennedy
howed no sign of conceding the game when it was so clear to
Khrushchev the West had lost.

Later events suggest that the burst of anger, or simulated anger,
hat followed was more convincing than Khrushchev intended it
o be. Instead of taking Khrushchev's arrogant manner and bully-
ng words as an extreme form of bargaining, Kennedy took them
is evidence of a firm resolve by Khrushchev to dictate a Berlin
ettlement on his own terms on a day of his choosing—and has-
ened to prepare for the worst.

There appears to have been no meeting of the minds at Vienna.
Kennedy headed for London and a meeting for which he was
)etter prepared. There he tried to interest Prime Minister Harold
Macmillan in Acheson's automatic-reaction proposal as one quick
way of speeding up the time required for Allied action. The Prime
Minister felt it wiser for the West not to draw a line. (One Presi-
lential adviser later criticized Acheson's plan as analogous to pil-

ing a wagon high with nuclear weapons, releasing the brake, and heading it downhill toward another similarly laden wagon carrying a notoriously "irresponsible" driver whose responsibility it would be to get out of the way in time to prevent a collision.) But Kennedy and Macmillan did agree that Russian behavior in negotiations on Laos, discussed at Vienna, would be taken as an acid test of their good faith. And the two reached complete agreement on the next steps to be taken by the West in the Laos talks, the test-ban talks, and plans for the proposed July 31 disarmament conference.

AFTER VIENNA

After Vienna, Secretary Rusk went back to Paris to give President de Gaulle a detailed account of the talks. Ambassador James Gavin and Charles Bohlen went with him. This was viewed by the French as the first step toward implementing Kennedy's promise to treat France as an equal and an ally. Kohler and the United States Ambassador to West Germany, Walter C. Dowling, went to Bonn to give Chancellor Adenauer a similar but perhaps less detailed account.

Khrushchev returned home to brazen out the failure at Vienna. Since China had objected to the meeting beforehand as a sign of accommodation to the West, Khrushchev needed to buttress his position for the forthcoming Party Congress. The Communist press, therefore, hailed Vienna as "a good beginning," and expressed great optimism about its fruitfulness.

Kennedy came home in a mood that must have been darkened as much by his fear that an opportunity might have been missed as by his vision of the consequences. There was no margin for failure in the nuclear age. If the thought arose that lack of preparation for the encounter with Khrushchev had contributed in any way to its failure, it would have been hard to bear—especially with a bad back. His old spinal difficulty had recurred at the critical time of his talks with Khrushchev, and continued to pain Mr. Kennedy in the days after his return from Europe when he was trying to explain to the American people and to himself what had gone wrong.

On the evening of June 8, the President gave a television report to the nation on his meeting with Khrushchev. Its message was grim. Hopes for a nuclear test-ban agreement and a disarmament agreement had been considerably lessened. "The gap between

us," he reported, "has not been materially reduced." Only on Laos
was the situation "hopeful" and "our most somber talks were . . .
on Germany and Berlin" where the stress was on "our presence
and our access rights . . . based on law, not on sufferance. . . .
We are determined to maintain those rights at any risk." Kennedy
said he felt the talks had lessened the chances of a "dangerous mis-
judgment" which was after all the major reason he gave for holding them, but observed that "The Soviets and ourselves give wholly
different meanings to the same words: war, peace, democracy, and
popular will." This "somber mood is not cause for elation or re-
laxation, nor . . . for undue pessimism or fear," he said, but
he was clearly pessimistic. He reported that "Khrushchev did not
talk in terms of war. He believes the world will move his way
without force."

Then the President settled down, aching back and all, to decide
what to do about Berlin.

"DO-IT-YOURSELF" SHELTERS

High in the air above France, en route to London from his Vienna
meeting with Nikita S. Khrushchev, [Joseph Alsop reported a month
after the event] John Fitzgerald Kennedy first addressed himself to
the . . . hardest question of our time . . . the question whether it
is better to risk a war with modern weapons in order to avoid surrender.

The Vienna meeting had just ended on a note of grimmest irony.
At the farewell conference, Khrushchev vowed he would grab Berlin
before December ended. He vowed, too, he would fight anyone who
tried to stop him. Kennedy heard Khrushchev's threats in stony silence,
then replied in six short words.

"It will be a cold winter," he said.

In the plane to London, therefore, the President was forced to
think about the terrible choice involved with any risk of war with
modern weapons in order to avoid surrender. . . . So he mused
about the problem for a while, unburdening his mind almost at
random for his closest staff members.

If one could think only of oneself, he remarked, it would be an
easy problem. He was forty-four. He had had a full, rich, lucky life.
He had never, in any case, been troubled by the deep, anxious fear
of dying that afflicts some men. In that way, too, he supposed
he had been lucky. For the individual, in any case, the duty to make
any sacrifice to avert a great national defeat was crystal clear. "If you
could think only of yourself," he remarked, "it would be easy to say
you'd press the button, and easy to press it, too."

Yet as President, he went on, he could not think only of himself. He had also to think of the next generation and of those who would come after. "That makes it damned hard," he said. He concluded bluntly that it was a choice, none the less, which might have to be made. Then he dismissed the subject and briskly began his preparations for his London meeting with Prime Minister Macmillan. . . .

Back in Washington, "Almost as soon as he reached the White House," Alsop tells us, the President "got out Eisenhower-ordered studies of the potential American casualties in a nuclear exchange. These studies had been filed and forgotten, under pressure from the Eisenhower Budget Bureau, because they recommended a costly civil defense program to reduce the casualty lists to acceptable figures." That was on June 5.

THE NIGHT OF JULY 25

On the night of July 25, President Kennedy answered Premier Khrushchev's challenge in a television address to the nation on the Berlin crisis. He was firmly rejecting the Soviet leader's ultimatum, Mr. Kennedy told the American people. This meant that thermonuclear war was possible by the December deadline Khrushchev had given. And among the emergency measures he was advocating for meeting the crisis was a program of fallout shelters. "In the event of an attack," he advised, "the lives of those families which are not hit in a nuclear blast and fire can still be saved—if they can be warned to take shelter and if that shelter is available. We owe that kind of insurance to our families —and to our country. . . . The time to start is now." "In the coming months," the President promised, he would "let every citizen know what steps he can take without delay to protect his family in case of attack. I know that you will want to do no less," he concluded.

Again, as in the case of Cuba, the President had acted without having all the facts and without properly reckoning on the reaction. Evidence shows that the White House gave serious thought to the subject of shelters only after the President had, in his July 25 speech, called on citizens to protect themselves from the effects of nuclear attack without telling them how to do it. It took five months—from the time of the President's warning—for the Government to produce a simple booklet on "Fallout Protection"— and even this proved of little value.

On June 29, three weeks after his return, the President called a
ational Security Council meeting to discuss how to deal with the
nticipated six to ten months of heightened tension in U.S.-U.S.S.R.
lations. As was his custom, the President reportedly asked for
dvice and reserved his decisions. The two-hour forty-minute ses-
on was devoted to consideration of major, dramatic steps to con-
nce everyone, including the American people, that Washington
as really taking the Berlin crisis seriously. Among the matters
nder consideration were a $3-billion bomb-shelter and fallout-
elter program, an appeal to the public to prepare a supply of
od for two weeks, reinforcement of regular civil-defense medical
cilities, and the distribution of little Geiger counters to measure
llout.
A week later Kennedy held a ninety-minute civil-defense con-
rence with White House aides. Ellis and McNamara were not
reed on how and how much of OCDM's responsibilities should
 transferred to the Pentagon. Nelson A. Rockefeller, as head of
e Governors' Conference Civil Defense Committee, had urged
nphasis on civilian control, but the political advice the President
ceived favored giving the Pentagon a larger role in order to
rry Congressional favor for new funds. McKinsey and Company,
e management consultants who had helped Eisenhower pick ap-
intees, was making a still uncompleted study for the Department
 Defense that was expected to carry considerable weight.

SHELTERS?

But by July 20 Kennedy had made up his mind. On that day an
xecutive Order put the Pentagon in charge of an expanded pro-
am of protection against nuclear attack, a "greatly accelerated
vil defense effort, including a nation-wide fallout shelter pro-
am." It also included warning systems and postattack plans.
llis was made head of the Office of Emergency Planning, remain-
g part of the White House staff and serving as adviser to the
esident. He would ask Congress for $300 million for a program
 utilizing public and quasi-public building areas as shelters for
rge numbers of people, the President announced. Ellis had been
guing that for an additional $200 million, another 30 million
es could be saved.
There was no desire to seek funds for home shelters; according
 a Pentagon official, "It will not have much impact on the home-

owner as such, but we hope it will have considerable effect on th
average citizen."

It did. What the President said about fallout shelters on July 2
started a wave of concern that occasioned a raised-eyebrow speec
from Senate Democratic Leader Mike Mansfield—wouldn't bu
rowing in the ground distract Americans from the real issues
war and peace?—and a field day for fly-by-night shelter man
facturers and suppliers.

"The crucial difference," Walter Lippmann wrote, "betwee
May 25 and July 25 is this. Before his encounter with Khrushche
in Vienna, the President saw clearly and said clearly that a serio
shelter policy would have to be 'a long-range program,' that
could not be cheap, and that it would require new planning ar
new organization. On July 25 he gave the impression, though h
exact words do not say so, that a shelter program could be carri
out as an emergency measure against the six months' ultimatum

Exactly two months after his advocacy of a "long range" pr
gram in May, Kennedy proclaimed in July "immediate objective
for civil defense. In the TV speech to the nation in which
promised "in the coming months . . . to let every citizen kno
what steps he can take without delay to protect his family in ca
of attack," he announced that he was going to ask Congress f
$207 million for shelters and an improved warning system, f
food and medicine stockpiles, for perfection of NEAR, a hom
warning device, and for improvement of fallout-detection facilitie
"While we will not let panic shape our policy, neither will we pe
mit timidity to direct our program," he said. "We seek peace—b
we shall not surrender." He spoke gravely as he expressed conce
about international affairs.

The following day the President sent those requests to Congres
During the first two weeks of August they were scrutinized by t
House Appropriations Committee's Military Appropriations Su
committee in hearings conducted by its chairman, Chet Holifiel
Holifield had been extremely critical of the inadequacy of previo
programs, which he called "very rudimentary, decentralized, u
even." On the first day of these hearings Secretary McNama
conceded to the committee that the Pentagon had not yet made
decision about "do-it-yourself" home shelters, which interest
Congressmen because the letters piling in from their constituer
were asking about them. The following day Mr. Ellis told t
committee he hoped the Federally financed group shelter progra
would be coupled with a drive to get Americans to build hom
shelters, but he had little to say about the latter. Representati

Iolifield observed that if the Government wanted home shelters, he Government would have to build them, because private individuals would not. Representative Kilgore cautioned against rousing the country and then not following through.

The President had stirred the interest of the public, and hence Congress, in civil defense.

"The speech, delivered under the deepest shadow of the crisis in Berlin, set off an incredible surge of interest in civil defense—a ubject previously scorned or ignored," *Time* magazine noted. A ational survey led the *U.S. News & World Report* to conclude 1at "Almost everybody in this country, it seems, is thinking or alking about what to do in case war starts and nuclear bombs all on the US." Inquiries at the Los Angeles and Atlanta offices f OCDM rose 800 per cent; great increases in interest were also eported in Boston and most other regional offices. In Washington 1e demand for literature about shelters rose from 10,000 requests 1 the whole of 1960 to approximately 5,000 a month after the 'resident's July 25 speech. More than a million unfilled requests or a Government pamphlet on stockpiling food for family shelters ad accumulated by the end of November, it was reported. After 1e President's speech there were more requests for information at)CDM headquarters in a day than there had been in a month arlier in the year.

The President had aroused national concern. But he had not repared the Government to cope with it. Steuart L. Pittman, the Vashington attorney Kennedy named on August 30 to be Assistant ecretary of Defense in charge of the Office of Civil Defense, explained that it had been necessary to rouse the country before 1ere could be a plan.

"THE FAMILY FALLOUT SHELTER"
AND CONFUSION

Early in September it became known that the Government was reparing a booklet on how to build a shelter and protect one's amily from radiation; this was scheduled for release before the nd of the month. Ellis said the purpose was not to instill panic, ut to alert the cynics and help those already interested. Pending elease of the new publication, those requesting information received copies of a 1959 Government booklet, "The Family Fallout helter." By September 2 the supply of three million copies was almost exhausted, and an additional press run of two million copies was ordered. (No release date was announced for the new publication.) Ellis said he hoped it would encourage construction of home shelters.

By September the family-shelter business was reported to be booming. The FHA had announced that a new financing arrangement had been devised for shelter construction. A House Government Operations Subcommittee warned homeowners against sleazy shelters that were being sold by "fly by night" firms.

The President's July speech had endorsed individual family shelters only by implication. But on October 6 he made it specific. Appropriately, this was done in a letter to the Governors' Conference Civil Defense Committee, the group that had been urging private-shelter construction in meetings with White House and Pentagon representatives. Kennedy set the country's civil-defense goal as "a fallout shelter for every American as rapidly as possible" and stressed the "do-it-yourself" home shelter. He had reportedly told a luncheon meeting of New Jersey publishers that the Administration would show plans within a month for a family shelter that could be built for $100 to $150, and Pentagon officials admitted that consideration was being given to minimal "dugouts" and similar personal accommodations.

Interest in family shelters and individual action for self-protection grew, as did confusion. Theological debates arose—should you shoot your neighbor if he tries to get into your shelter? And scientific ones—James Van Allen and other University of Iowa scientists condemned articles by former AEC Chairman Willard F. Libby supporting the merit of shelters. The Committee on Science in the Promotion of Human Welfare of the American Association for the Advancement of Science, the foremost scientific body in the United States, at the end of the year gave the opinion that shelters have little worth. "In general, the development of a shelter program cannot greatly influence the conclusion that massive nuclear attack would have the immediate effect of destroying the social structure." In the first place, "A particular shelter system is designed to resist a certain assumed intensity of attack and its success depends on the validity of this asumption." In the second place it would invite more powerful weapons: "Any shelter system short of one that places the nation's entire population and industry permanently underground can be negated by a corresponding increase in the attacker's power."

Dr. John N. Wolfe, Chief of the Environmental Sciences Branch of the AEC, spoke of the totally new problem of survival that nuclear fission had created. "The effects of nuclear war on man and his environment are awesome to contemplate," Dr. Wolfe said in a symposium at Colorado State University. "Thermal and blast effects, and concomitant radiation, would create vast areas that would be useless to the survival of man.

"Fallout shelters in many areas seem only a means of delaying death and represent only a part of a survival plan. With an environment so completely modified, the question is where does man go after his sojourn in shelters. What does he do upon emergence."

The President himself added to the confusion about the value of a shelter program when he told the United Nations on September 25 that "nuclear war would make a flaming funeral pyre" of the world.

REPAIRING THE DAMAGE

Recognizing the mounting crisis in confidence, Kennedy called a conference at his Hyannis Port home during Thanksgiving weekend. Four months after the President had called on citizens to build shelters against the emergency created by Khrushchev's six-month deadline, it was decided to emphasize community rather than individual shelters, and to give the program long-range rather than immediate goals. This meeting also reviewed the long-awaited booklet and, according to Press Secretary Pierre Salinger, "went a long way" toward giving a sense of direction to the civil-defense program. He said the booklet would "definitely" be out in 1961. Secretary McNamara reported that the $93-million study of shelter sites would be ready six months early, in June 1962. Computers were speeding access to data, and 700 architectural and engineering consulting firms had been given contracts for the survey.

In his press conference on November 29 the President referred to the Thanksgiving weekend meeting, saying that some major decisions regarding civil defense had been made and some of them would require co-operation from the individual states, so he would again meet with the Governors. He re-emphasized community shelters, saying he "never" thought the Government should build a shelter in each home. He stressed that information would be made available to homeowners wanting their own shelters, but the "central responsibility" would be to provide for "community shelters." The Hyannis Port meeting, apparently, had finally considered the political and psychological faults in the policy of individual shelters the President had allowed to prevail for four tense and critical months.

"The home shelter system favored the rich over the poor, the single-house dweller over the apartment dweller, the home owner over the renter. It was unequal, unfair, divisive, and therefore politically dangerous," James Reston wrote in the New York *Times* when the policy was changed.

"Moreover, once the President and his aides in the White House belatedly put their minds to the problem of civil defense they began to see other objections to urgent appeals for an immediate home shelter program.

"It helped create a war psychology in the country. It encouraged all kinds of commercial exploitation by shelter builders who were going around door to door showing movies of atomic explosions and scaring people into buying shelters and stocking food they often couldn't afford.

"Also, the shelter scare in America weakened the confidence abroad in Kennedy's judgment," Mr. Reston concluded. In its first issue following the President's July 25 message, the London *Observer* made that clear: "Was not the President defeating his own negotiating ends by rousing his countrymen to such a pitch of alarm and frenzy that any subsequent deals with the Communists would seem a sell-out?" the *Observer* asked. Berlin may yet be "a great testing place of Western courage and will," the *Observer* declared. But "at present it is a much greater testing place of Western diplomacy and vision: these will be the qualities we shall need to avert the intolerable dilemma of surrender or war."

An Administration statement on December 14 made the change of policy official, placing the Federal Government firmly behind the community-shelter program, although it continued to allow for the preference of some for individual shelters. The statement did not say which was likely to be safer.

SHELTER BOOKLET "A HOAX"

Finally, on the last day of 1961, the long-heralded shelter booklet, periodically reported to be forthcoming since September, was released to the public. Both the publisher of the *Scientific American,* Gerard Piel, and one of its editors, James R. Newman, promptly characterized it as a hoax on public opinion. "It is designed to make you think you have a chance when, in fact, you have none," Mr. Newman said. The nuclear scientist Ralph E. Lapp called the booklet "fairly innocuous" and of "limited value." "It could have been written by one man in two days," Lapp said of the work that had taken many men five months to produce. (One of the authors was more disturbed by the Washington *Post*'s editorial comment that the booklet "is not a literary triumph" than by the further criticism that "it does not make a major contribution to the facts of life in a thermonuclear age.")

Dr. Lapp pointed out that basement fallout shelters recommended in the booklet could be dangerous spots up to miles from the blast. A 20-megaton blast could destroy buildings and set fires eleven miles from the blast center, he said. And even a 5-megaton bomb (the example used in the booklet) would destroy most buildings and set fires within two miles of the explosion point. "If the buildings should collapse or burn, people would be trapped in the basement shelters. They would be safe from fallout, but they would die nonetheless," Dr. Lapp stated.

A Pentagon spokesman was asked why the Government booklet had chosen a 5-megaton bomb as the example of what would be used in an attack in view of the fact that the Russians, in their most recent test series, had exploded bombs in the 20–55 megaton range and were talking of a possible 100-megaton weapon. He told the authors of a special study, "Shelters and Survival," which appeared in the *New Republic,* that "the size was merely for illustration." "The implications are strong, however," the authors commented, "that bombs over 20 megatons would make any civil defense appear impractical to impossible, even to the citizen of eighth grade education for whose comprehension the booklet was written."

The booklet assumes that two weeks would be sufficient time to remain under shelter from fallout. At the time of its release, however, scientists were arriving at new estimates. Those who were studying recent evaluations by the National Academy of Sciences were saying that two months in shelters might be necessary following nuclear attack. Dr. Tom T. Stonier, a biologist at the Rockefeller Institute and spokesman for the Scientists' Committee for Radiation Information, stated in early January 1962 that "it is clear from the new radiological data that there would be a serious radiological problem after two weeks." Any person who left his shelter after two weeks would collect 670 roentgens of radiation in the next six weeks, the new estimates indicated. While this might not kill hardy persons, Stonier said, it would weaken them, shorten their lives by thirty years, and probably sterilize the surviving male and much of the female population for many years.

The Administration's policy had straightened out. The facts still had not. Toward the end of the year the research chief for the Deputy Assistant Secretary for Civil Defense, Walmer E. Strope, said, "We know far less than we would like to about fallout from a major weapon. The statement that we need shelters, and we need good shelters, is about the best information we have."

California, the harbinger of America's emotions, moved from confusion toward panic during January 1962 on the subject of shelters. Politicians began seriously to consider how to handle the issue in the critical election campaign of 1962. Scientists affiliated with the Democratic Party prepared private memoranda for Governor Pat Brown and other Democratic candidates, trying to separate fact from fiction. Within the Democratic Party there developed violent opposition to the Administration's shelter proposals. At the state-wide meeting of the California Democratic Council, according to the New York *Times,* "Boos and shouts of 'fraud' swept the auditorium during debate over the issue." A majority of the Resolutions Committee recommended putting the council on record as opposing any Federal, state, or local expenditures for shelters. The majority resolution called on all persons contemplating the building of private shelters to give their time, money, and effort instead to organizations promoting world peace.

"It was a very bad mistake to tie together the six months' deadline about Berlin with a call for immediate action to each citizen to save his family," Walter Lippmann wrote in the autumn, when the initial error had been compounded and the shelter controversy had begun to corrupt morale. A succession of European journalists, stopping in Washington in late summer after touring the United States, reported a growing war psychosis among Americans —a "let's get it over with" psychology that some said the uncertainty over shelters seemed to feed.

The Gallup Poll corroborated what the foreign reporters found. In October 1961, the per cent of Americans who believed the United States was likely to be at war in five years was almost as high as during the Korean War. The number increased from 32 per cent in March to 53 per cent in October.

The President's summons to the American people to save themselves should "irrational attack" occur did not create the fear of nuclear war at any hour that manifested itself in shelter hysteria after the July 25 statement. This fear was born long before the Kennedy Administration. But the President's support of a "do-it-

ourself" shelter program, coupled with a negative report on the
.hrushchev Vienna meeting did not help public understanding of
·hat nuclear war would mean. Mr. Kennedy had yet to learn the
rt of informing without unduly alarming. In effect he confused an
lready bewildered public whom he had asked "to bear the burden
f a long twilight struggle, year in and year out."

BERLIN

In the early spring of 1959, Dag Hammarskjold visited Nikita S.
.hrushchev at Sochi on the Black Sea. On his return to New York,
Iammarskjold told several diplomats and reporters that he be-
eved Khrushchev was ready to negotiate seriously for a peaceful
ettlement on Berlin if the West was prepared to propose some
olution other than the one of German reunification through free
lections. Hammarskjold felt that it was extremely important for
ae West to take the initiative in seeking such negotiations. From
me to time there was desultory talk of the United States doing
o. But Western leaders were reluctant to attack a sacred tenet of
·hancellor Adenauer, on whom we relied so heavily in NATO.
Kennedy habitually circled that forest in his election campaign.
.nd in the White House he did not heed an early suggestion that
e reopen the Berlin question with the Russians. After Vienna,
aerefore, with no United States policy on Berlin, with Adenauer
ampaigning for re-election on a status quo platform, and with
·e Gaulle opposing any negotiations with the Russians on Berlin,
.ennedy was hard-pressed diplomatically. And after the Presi-
ent's report to the country on his meeting with Khrushchev, con-
.deration of a new status for Berlin began to seem politically un-
:asible at home. The President's June 8 television speech and the
nsuing seven weeks of alarms and rumors before a program on
erlin was announced on July 25 created a mood of unrest in the
Inited States that seemed to harden into belligerency.
During the month of July, a representative of a bipartisan citi-
:ns' organization known as the National Committee for an Effec-
ve Congress prepared a report on public and Washington opinion
ased on a trip across the country and talks with thirty members
f the House and Senate of both parties. " 'Even if Berlin means
ar it's worth it. We've got to stand firm there and put every-
aing into it,' " his report read. "These words I heard repeated
ver and over as I traveled in California and Nevada during the
rst days in July." Congressmen were returning at that time from

the July 4 holiday recess. The first member of whom the inquiring
reporter asked what he had found back home replied, "Well, there
isn't much agreement at home about anything. Cuba, parochial
schools, unemployment, etc. But there is one thing everybody, and
I mean everybody, agrees on. That is Berlin. 'Stand firm,' they all
say." They didn't know what they meant, the Congressman said,
whether they were ready for nuclear war, national mobilization,
more taxes, but everybody wanted a "firm stand."

All the other members I talked with report the same thing [the Committee representative wrote to his board]. I found Congressional reaction
to the grass roots "firmness" attitude one of dismay. Members felt that
the public is jumping to a final "war is inevitable" conclusion without
examining any of the preliminary or ultimate steps. Members felt a sort
of military fatalism setting in. . . .

Congressmen worried lest American public opinion "lock in" our
national policy; if things are too cemented, it would be "political suicide at home" to talk negotiation to resolve the Berlin crisis just as it
would be physical suicide to engage in nuclear war. . . . The danger
as one Senator put it, is not that we will be frozen in Berlin but that
we will be frozen in the precincts. . . .

The more senior and experienced members of Congress felt most
apprehensive lest the United States be trapped in an "appeasement or
war" dilemma. They felt that the Russians were setting the stage for
this kind of choice, and that we were not developing a way out. Nobody I talked to argued against the necessity for a military build-up,
but there was a strong feeling that this might readily be taken as a
substitute for an imaginative political-diplomatic offensive prior to
negotiations.

The military necessities were occupying the President—and his
political opponents. Since his Vienna report, Republican spokesmen had been calling on the President to mobilize, to resume
nuclear testing, and in general to prepare to meet force with force.
A television program on July 19, "The Loyal Opposition," gave
the keynote for the GOP demand for action. Senators Goldwater
and Dirksen, and Senator Keating—three different shades in
the party spectrum—joined in denouncing the lack of action or
direction demonstrated by the Administration in foreign affairs.
Nixon echoed this theme the following week, urging support of the
President's request for more funds for conventional weapons, but
demanding that Kennedy stand firm on Berlin and on keeping Red
China out of the United Nations. The Governors' Conference,
meeting in Honolulu during the last days of June, also urged a
firm stand on Berlin and no concessions.

"STAND FIRM"

Others could call for a "firm stand." The President had to determine how firmly to stand where, and what force it would require to do so. He began by turning for advice to those who had experienced the Soviet blockade of West Berlin in 1948. Dean Acheson, Truman's Secretary of State, was asked to study all existing "contingency plans," and recommend a plan of action. Partly in recognition of organizational weakness at the time of Cuba, the Berlin crisis was well staffed out. Acheson's former Policy Planning Chief, Paul Nitze, now Assistant Secretary under McNamara, was assigned to co-ordinate Department of Defense planning on Berlin. And Assistant Secretary of State Foy Kohler, who had served under both Acheson and Dulles, was given the same responsibility in the Department of State. Kohler had the added job of serving as director of a "co-ordinating group" consisting of Rusk, McNamara, Bundy, and Allen Dulles, to sift out all information pertaining to Berlin.

Backing up Kohler at the next level was Martin J. Hillenbrand, director of the Department of State Office of German Affairs. And also involved at high levels were Alexis Johnson, Undersecretary for Political Affairs, George McGhee and Henry Owen of the Policy Planning Staff, and State Department Counsellor Abram Chayes—plus Acheson and Henry A. Kissinger, the MIT expert on nuclear warfare, and General Maxwell D. Taylor, the President's personal military adviser since Cuba.

So far as could be determined from the sidelines in so complicated an operation, many other members of the Kennedy team with experience of the 1948 encounter—veterans like John McCloy, David Bruce, George F. Kennan, Charles Bohlen, and Robert Lovett—were consulted to a much lesser extent. Inventive men like Adlai Stevenson and Chester Bowles, who were both out of the country during much of July, did not take part. The most important roles in the advance planning for another Berlin showdown fell to Mr. Acheson and General Taylor.

There was more discussion of what to do in Berlin than there had been in the case of Cuba—and more disagreement. But the "hard-line" vs. "soft-line" division in the Administration was not the wide chasm some members of the press presented it to be. There was broad agreement that the West could not yield its position in Berlin on Khrushchev's terms; it had to back its firm stand with acts to ensure credibility, and it had to leave the door open for negotiation. The differences of opinion were about degree and timing.

Immediately preceding the Fourth of July weekend the Security Council heard Dean Acheson present his recommendations. The report from the closed meeting was that Acheson repeated his well-known quasi-ultimatum position on Berlin with great force. The Acheson report was widely believed to advocate immediate military mobilization and the calling up of as many as a million reserves and members of the National Guard; the Department of Defense position, by report, favored a build-up one-third that size. Others present urged greater effort to produce, for discussion with the Russians, alternative plans for guaranteed access to West Berlin. The President departed for Hyannis Port, presumably to consider the alternatives during the July 4 weekend.

Kennedy's decision, characteristic in his first year, was to combine various counsels and be prepared to shift course as the situation unfolded. On July 25, the President called for partial mobilization; 153,000 reserves and National Guardsmen would return to active duty, as compared to the one million build-up Acheson was believed to have recommended. McNamara and Roswell L. Gilpatric favored calling out reserves rather than increasing the regular military forces. They would meet the immediate need for more airlift by delaying retirement of old troop-carrier aircraft and by calling to active duty National Guard troop-carrier squadrons and protector aircraft.

THE TEAM IN THE PENTAGON

There was little need for the President to give personal attention to the military build-up at home. It was generally recognized that Mr. Kennedy had the ablest team in charge in the Pentagon in the history of the Department of Defense. Ford Motors President Robert McNamara and Wall Street lawyer Roswell Gilpatric, who as a former Undersecretary of the Air Force knew the Pentagon proved so effective a combination that it was hard to tell which one of them was responsible for any specific project. Together they made use of the authority granted the Secretary of Defense to improve departmental organization, decision making, and comparative analysis of weapons systems—for which the necessity had been evident for years.

To make necessary improvements quickly, McNamara and Gilpatric had earlier ordered a number of "quick fixes," as the military analyst for the St. Louis *Post-Dispatch,* Brigadier General Thomas R. Phillips (Ret.), described them.

The missile gap was tackled by increasing the number of Polaris submarines from 19 to 29, an addition of 160 missiles to a total of 464, and the production rate was stepped up so that the 29 submarines and their missiles will be ready before the time that had been planned.

Provision was made to double the production capacity of the Minuteman missile in case it was decided eventually that an increase was necessary. The Minuteman is not operational; further proving is necessary, and consequently no additional production of the Minuteman was ordered beyond the 600 already appropriated for.

For the interim, to maintain the strategic bomber deterrent, the projected phase-out of the B-47 medium bomber was delayed and a 50 percent increase of bombers on 15-minute alert was provided for.

The provision of badly needed airlift was another ingenious quick fix. Production of jet cargo and troop carrier planes was started at once by splitting the Boeing capacity, formerly devoted to jet tankers, between the tankers and cargo of troop carrier aircraft.

At the same time the production of the C-130 troop carrier was increased greatly so that a large number of these vital aircraft for troop movement will be provided at a greatly increased rate.

Sea-lift was increased one-third by withdrawing from storage the lift capacity for half a division, giving an existing sea-lift for two divisions.

In President Kennedy's report to the nation on Berlin on July 25, he declared, "I shall not hesitate to ask the Congress for additional measures, or exercise any of the executive powers that I possess to meet this threat to peace. Everything essential to the security of freedom must be done; and if that should require more men, or more taxes, or more controls, or other new powers, I shall not hesitate to ask them. The measures proposed today will be constantly studied, and altered as necessary. But while we will not let panic shape our policy, neither will we permit timidity to direct our program."

The President explained that the Administration's military planning was designed to provide "the capability of placing in any critical area at the appropriate time a force which, combined with those of our allies, is large enough to make clear our determination and our ability to defend our rights at all costs—and to meet all levels of aggressor pressure with whatever levels of force are required. *We intend to have a wider choice than humiliation or all-out nuclear action.*"

Read today, the President's address to the nation in July is not alarmist or dominantly militaristic in tone. But had he understood the state of nerves in the country that evening in July, the President could have made a greater effort to communicate his long-range hopes for peace as strongly as he communicated our national dedication to the defense of Berlin.

Mr. Kennedy could give legitimate reassurance that he was not neglecting his responsibility to seek peaceful solutions. Headlines the next day featured "reserve call-ups" and "fallout shelters," but the address itself contained meaningful words on the possibilities of negotiation. "While we are ready to defend our interests," the President declared, "we shall also be ready to search for peace— in quiet exploratory talks—in formal or informal meetings. . . . The choice is not merely between resistance and retreat, between atomic holocaust and surrender. Our peacetime military posture is traditionally defensive; but our diplomatic posture need not be. Our response to the Berlin crisis will not be merely military or negative. It will be more than merely standing firm."

THE WESTERN TROIKA

And having armed, the President set out to "parley," only to run squarely into the West's own troika. If more evidence of the unwieldiness of Khrushchev's formula for divided authority was needed, events of the summer and autumn of 1962 in Western Europe supplied it in abundance. It took six weeks for the Big Three and the NATO ministers to agree on the wording of a reply to Khrushchev's aide memoirs delivered to President Kennedy promptly after their Vienna meeting. The machinery of Allied cooperation was cumbersome. But the main delaying force was De Gaulle. Dedicated to the goal of making France as dominant in Europe as he was in France, the General could not lead the Western Alliance, but he could hold it back and make Allied initiative toward a peaceful Berlin settlement impossible in July.

Khrushchev did his part to make Allied overtures difficult. After Kennedy's July 25 speech, Soviet behavior became more aggressive and the threats to the Western position more specific. In early August, Khrushchev launched Cosmonaut Gherman S. Titov into orbit—around the earth in 89 minutes, 17 times in 25 hours, for the whole world to see on television and wonder at. He could build a 100-megaton bomb, the Soviet leader boasted, and the Titov rocket could launch it.

Meanwhile, refugees from East Germany were pouring into West Berlin at the rate of 2,500 per day. And the greatest fear of the Western foreign ministers, then meeting in Paris, was that tensions at the Berlin border might spark revolt in East Germany —the last thing the West wished to encourage at the moment. The West would wait out the September German elections and the October Communist Congress, which seemed to be leading Khrushchev to undertake so many acts of derring-do. Then they would make quiet contact with Soviet Ambassador Gromyko at the autumn meeting of the United Nations in New York and work toward negotiating a peaceful settlement on Berlin—first at the foreign-minister level and finally at the Summit, perhaps in January 1962. But Khrushchev had different plans. The following Sunday The Wall went up in Berlin.

On Saturday, August 12, the French and English had left the cities for the long midsummer weekend. London and Paris were closed down. President De Gaulle and French Foreign Minister Maurice Couve de Murville were in the country. So were Prime Minister Macmillan and Lord Home. President Kennedy was resting at Hyannis Port.

At 2 A.M. Sunday, East German police appeared at the Brandenburg Gate and proceeded to erect barbed-wire barricades across the East Berlin border. Kennedy conferred by phone with Secretary Rusk—the provocation did not demand immediate action, they agreed. No contrary advice from Western military commanders in Berlin reached the President.

It took two days for the Allies to agree on the statement on the Communist action—and much longer for Washington to realize the consequences. The sealing-off of East Berlin had left the United States without a policy. The President and his advisers erred in supposing the Communists would return to the 1948 strategy of blockade. That miscalculation, Walter Lippmann pointed out on September 7, "led the Administration to concentrate its energy on convincing Khrushchev that the West would fight if he interfered with physical access to West Berlin." This was true, and "it was a prudent precaution to make this plain to Khrushchev. But it should not have been sold to the American people and to the world as a policy. . . . On August 13 we had no policy, and there is reason to ask whether we are on the way to having one now."

The veterans of Stalin's blockade, Mr. Lippmann remarked in assessing the blame, had told the President that "Khrushchev was bluffing, and if the President did not flinch first, Khrushchev would flinch first and once more retreat, as he did in 1958, leaving

everything as it was. Until it was swept away by events," Lippmann declared, "this pipe dream clouded the vision and narcotized
the will to face the realities of the German situation."

STRATEGY FOR PEACE—AND THE PRICE

For the time being the President had gone as far as he could in
meeting the Berlin crisis. While waiting for Allied readiness and
willingness to negotiate with Mr. Khrushchev on an agreed-upon
position, he turned his full attention to what could be accomplished.

Three main courses of action were vigorously pursued: strengthening the Western Alliance politically, economically, and militarily; pushing a reoriented aid program through a reluctant Congress; training local military forces in the art of guerrilla warfare.
To the country and to many Congressmen, there was nothing new
in the Kennedy plans for national security and the strengthening of
the free world. They were wrong. Policies and program were being
designed to meet the realities of a changing world. The President
sought to correct what he believed was the weakness of the Eisenhower Administration, when he said, "We move from crisis to crisis
for two reasons: First, because we have not yet developed a strategy for peace that is relevant to the new world in which we live;
and secondly because we have not been paying the price that that
strategy demands."

President Kennedy and his Administration were trying to develop a positive strategy for peace—long-range in the goals sought,
flexible enough to recognize and quickly meet day-to-day developments without losing the momentum of the master plan.

The President turned now to the Congress to seek their understanding co-operation. He did not spare himself, his staff, or his
Administration in his efforts to convince Congress of the soundness
and urgency of his purpose.

STRENGTHENING THE WESTERN ALLIANCE

Emphasis on the importance of the Western Alliance to the United
States and the importance of the United States to the Western
World was not a Kennedy innovation. Postwar relief, Greek-Turk-
ish Aid, the Marshall Plan, NATO, U.S. assistance in promoting
the economic integration of Western Europe, all reflected the im-

portance the United States attached to the strength and unity of Western Europe.

The Kennedy Administration recognized that Western Europe in 1961–62 was not the Europe of 1947 or 1950 or 1955. The President, as partner of the Western Alliance, updated U.S. planning. Western Europe, recovered from the war, was again enjoying vigorous economic health. The future would be even brighter. Western European nations were no longer competing for United States wheat, coal, and cotton. They were, and would be, competing in the future for markets. In recognition of this economic recovery, Kennedy carefully redesigned U.S. relations to convey willingness to treat our allies as equals. Witness the special deference shown to President De Gaulle. In elevating the position accorded De Gaulle, the President gave proof not only that the new Administration was continuing to support the Western Alliance, but evinced his recognition of the contribution Western European nations as allies and equals of the United States were prepared to make in the long search for peace.

With Berlin now under siege, the immediate challenge was to the military unity of the Western Alliance. On the same day that Mr. Nixon commanded Kennedy to stand firm on Berlin, Prime Minister Macmillan indicated that Britain would look favorably upon negotiations, provided that they were conducted from a position of strength—backed up by a more powerful and more unified Western Alliance.

Vienna had reawakened Kennedy also to the long-run importance of NATO. What Khrushchev most feared, it was clear, was that the Western military alliance would evolve into a unified economic and political community. The task for the West was to keep the alliance strong and vigorous until that evolution could take place. Differences over what stand to take on Berlin could jeopardize the larger possibility.

Our Ambassador to NATO, Thomas Finletter, was recalled to Washington to meet with NATO's Secretary General Dirk U. Stikker, who was coming to visit. Finletter's access to the White House pleased NATO members, who viewed this as a sign of the President's confidence in that body. Kennedy's efforts at getting greater French participation in NATO had been unsuccessful, but he had better luck with Italy. When Premier Fanfani visited Washington on June 13, he and President Kennedy reached agreement on expanding NATO politically and militarily. Representatives of the Big Three—Secretary Rusk, Ambassador Hervé Alphand, and Lord Home—had been meeting in Washington since June 11.

There was then a series of meetings (June 15) at the State Department with Rusk, Acheson, McCloy, Kohler, George McGhee, and Lord Home. Kennedy met with Finletter, Rusk, and Kohler on NATO plans. Finletter and Stikker conferred with the policy-planning staff at State, McCloy and Stikker conferred, and then Stikker and Kennedy. The focus of this "ronde" was final accord on increasing NATO's power with conventional (nonnuclear) armament.

FOREIGN AID

In preparation for his message on foreign aid, the President in his report on Berlin reminded the nation and Congress that foreign aid in 1947 met the challenge of chaos in Europe and that the Atlantic Community was the result of meeting that challenge—the Atlantic Community, which the President called the "heartland of human freedom."

He went on to express to the nation, to the Congress, and to our allies what he believed must now be jointly undertaken.

"While all of these efforts go on," President Kennedy said, "we must not be diverted from our total responsibilities. . . . If new threats in Berlin or elsewhere should cause us to weaken our program of assistance to the developing nations who are also under heavy pressure from the same source—or to halt our efforts for realistic disarmament—or to disrupt or slow down our economy—or to neglect the education of our children—then those threats will surely be the most successful and least costly maneuver in Communist history. For we can afford all these efforts, and more—but we cannot afford *not* to meet this challenge.

"And the challenge is not to us alone. It is a challenge to every nation which asserts its sovereignty under a system of liberty. It is a challenge to all who want a world of free choice. . . .

"We in the West must move together in building military strength. We must consult one another more closely than ever before. We must together design our proposals for peace, and labor together as they are pressed at the conference table. And together we must share the burdens and the risks of this effort."

Nowhere was the Kennedy Administration more eager to "share the burdens and the risks" than in foreign aid. The Administration's new conception, as Presidential Adviser Walt Rostow explained to the Advertising Council in the spring of 1961, looked toward the time when "one area after another with which we have dealt on an emergency basis in the past is put under a long-term arrangement, geared to its own development efforts, and in which not only U.S. funds but the funds of other developed nations will play a part." And to make that possible the President fought a fierce battle with a deeply divided Congress.

PASSMAN IS BACK IN TOWN

A month after Congress adjourned, the Director of the newly created AID—the Agency for International Development—answered his telephone to hear a voice say, "Hello, the worst SOB in the country on foreign aid is back in town." "Why, how are you, Congressman Passman?" Fowler Hamilton answered.

The reference was to the struggle President Kennedy had gone through trying to persuade the 87th Congress in its first session to grant him the power to do what he felt needed to be done in the field of foreign aid.

The battle heavily involved much of the White House staff; Secretary Rusk, Undersecretary Bowles, and a host of officials from State; Secretary Dillon from Treasury; the whole of the International Cooperation Agency under Henry R. Labouisse and the Development Loan Fund under Frank M. Coffin; the Senate, the House, and thousands of interested citizens. But at the end it was chiefly a contest of wills and skills between the President and a single member of the House, Representative Otto E. Passman of Louisiana.

Passman's power arises from his position as Chairman of the Subcommittee on Foreign Aid Operations of the House Appropriations Committee. A shrewd and stubborn fighter, he has been as much a foe of foreign aid in previous Administrations as he turned out to be in Kennedy's. He has proved such a stumbling block that the foreign-aid legislation that President Kennedy hopefully presented to the Congress was designed to bypass Representative Passman by permitting the new agency to borrow from the Treasury for part of its needs instead of having to undergo its annual ordeal with the Representative from Louisiana.

It is curious that in Washington, where power is all, little notice is given to the source of Passman's. He exercises his power, it is true, through his chairmanship of a crucial subcommittee. But it was Clarence Cannon of Missouri, the 82-year-old Chairman of the House Appropriations Committee, who appointed Passman.

It was Cannon who saw to it that a strong majority of the other ten members of the subcommittee were amenable to Passman's ideas and leadership. And it is Cannon, also, who, as an ex-officio member of the subcommittee, always turns up at meetings when bills are being marked, the final phase of committee work, and votes right down the line with his protégé. "The voice is Jacob's voice, but the hands are the hands of Esau."

Passman, who is 61, and a native of Monroe, Louisiana, represents a section of his state that is in many ways more akin to neighboring Mississippi than to the Creole country to the south. He identifies himself as a "country boy" and often takes a verbal swipe at "capitalists." An ardent advocate of flood-control programs in his district, he rouses the ire of duck hunters who are fearful of losing wetlands for their sport. To Passman duck hunters have become "capitalists," and no doubt they often are. The other kind of capitalist he opposes is the businessman, often influential and world-minded, who supports the foreign-trade program. One such man from Baton Rouge who sent Passman a sharp telegram during the most recent foreign-trade battle accusing him of "obstructionism," received a return wire saying "You capitalists have lost the foreign aid program fifty votes."

But curiously Passman is by anybody's definition a capitalist himself. His own claims to wealth are rather modest, ranging around three-quarters of a million dollars. In any event he made it himself. A sharecropper's son, born near Franklinton, he left school at thirteen, worked at such jobs as were available to him in Louisiana and, briefly, in Arkansas, and finally went to night school to get his high-school diploma. Eventually Passman's shrewdness in business made him the owner of firms in Monroe that manufacture commercial refrigerators and hotel supplies.

Passman may not be the best dressed member of Congress, but he is quite probably the most dressed. He is reputed to own no fewer than fifty suits and at least twice as many shirts with an appropriately large assortment of other haberdashery and ornaments. He is also credited with knowing precisely where each sartorial item is at any time, down to the last cuff link. His wardrobe contributes to his dramatic effect when he takes to the House floor to manage an attack on an appropriation for the foreign-aid program. The long-faced Passman makes himself highly evident to other members, and to the press and public in the galleries, by wearing a snow-white silk suit. (Foreign aid always comes up in the summer, toward the end of a session.)

Other than clothes, Passman's only admitted extravagance is

good food. He lives quietly and alone in a hotel suite near the Capitol. Mrs. Passman has remained in Monroe. He takes little part in social activities; President Kennedy's one effort to make what he calls "a little public relations gesture" to Passman, an invitation to the storied party at Mount Vernon for President Mohammed Ayub Khan of Pakistan, apparently went for nought. Passman went, enjoyed the party, and remained as adamant as ever.

Passman's success as the chief tormentor of the foreign-aid program is not entirely due to his strong relationship with Clarence Cannon and the fact that few members of the House are willing to tangle openly with the crotchety chairman of a committee to which they must look for favors for their districts. Passman may be low on formal education, but the memory that serves Passman so well in keeping track of his haberdashery is just as sharp when it comes to remembering budget figures. In House debate, which is almost always severely limited, his ability to remember complex figures and use them in off-the-cuff debate has won him respect in some quarters and grudging admiration in others.

Too, he finds himself supremely comfortable in the coalitions arranged from time to time between Representative Howard Smith's conservative Southerners and Representative Charles Halleck's Republicans. Perhaps this cozy relationship had its effect on his behavior in the election of 1960. Passman openly refused to support John F. Kennedy for the Presidency. Some liberals were hopeful that Speaker Rayburn would punish him by taking away his subcommittee chairmanship. But Speakers, who depend on Southern votes to elect them, do not act that way.

A PROGRAM WITHOUT A CONSTITUENCY

Foreign aid, it is said, is a program without a constituency. None of the large and politically potent organized groups—farmer, labor, patriotic, or educational—can be relied on to support it on the basis of inherent or personal interest. It appears to be a bread-and-butter issue for only foreigners. Every Administration that has sponsored a foreign-aid program has had to get it through a reluctant and foot-dragging Congress.

Opposition to extensive foreign-aid programs has increased in recent years, particularly among farmers; it has grown among some, but by no means all, businessmen who are influenced by such books as *The Ugly American* and by occasional exposés in newspapers that have explored some of the program's undoubted failures. It is anathema to such organizations of the radical right as the John Birch Society, which are basically isolationist. Even some persons who under other circumstances would be regarded as liberal are against foreign aid during periods when there is considerable unemployment at home.

With all these forces ranged against foreign aid, it may appear strange that year after year Congress has made appropriations, often smaller than an Administration requested, but nevertheless substantial. The fact is that these programs have had behind them a powerful moral force: American idealism and the American tradition of generosity for the less fortunate. The constituency of the foreign-aid program is made up of the same groups that persuaded the United States to take the leading part in the establishment of the United Nations, that united in helping to feed and clothe a devastated world after World War II, that made the Marshall Plan a reality—thereby laying the foundation for the present unprecedented prosperity of Europe, and likewise made Point Four effective. Without a significant exception the great churches of America support foreign-aid programs. So do women's organizations, which are often capable of exerting more muscle in the nation's political life than the politicians admit. The League of Women Voters, numerically less impressive than many organizations, is intelligent, informed, persistent, and carries great weight on issues such as this.

AID AGENCY IN LOW ESTEEM

When President Kennedy took office it was with the expectation that foreign aid would be a major tool in the carrying out of his foreign policy. But he inherited, in the International Cooperation Administration, an agency held in low esteem by a considerable section of the Congress, by many members of the Washington press corps—including some of the principal opinion makers of the nation—and probably to a degree by some of the governments of nations the ICA was formed to help. It was not altogether the fault of ICA—since Congress is traditionally suspicious of public-relations staffs for agencies with spending programs—that ICA often appeared unable to defend itself effectively when it was attacked. But it was the fault of ICA or of the Eisenhower Administration that the principle of "Executive privilege," so often invoked to avoid giving Congress information on Executive doings, turned against the program a number of members of Congress who otherwise would have supported it.

In any event, President Eisenhower, despite official statements from time to time about the importance of "mutual security," never appeared to be completely sold on the nonmilitary aspects of the foreign-aid program. At least on one occasion he appointed as the head of the ICA a man philosophically opposed to what it was doing. And he did not protest, if indeed he knew, when ICA was used, just as the Civil Defense organization was used, as a convenient place to put people with political pull.

An early Kennedy act was to replace ICA chief James W. Riddleberger, whose enthusiasm for the foreign-aid program was tepid, by Henry Labouisse, a devoted internationalist respected by many members of Congress and much of the press corps. As Director of the Development Loan Fund, Kennedy chose Frank Coffin, a capable Democratic Congressman from Maine who had lost out in the 1960 election. He then created twin task forces, one to be headed by Labouisse and the other by Coffin, to draft new legislation for a foreign-aid program and improved operations for the Development Loan Fund along the lines indicated in Mr. Stevenson's November report.

In a message to Congress in March, Kennedy proposed that "our separate and often confusing aid programs be integrated in a single administration." Such an agency in his view would include the International Cooperation Administration, the Development Loan Fund, the Food for Peace program, the Peace Corps, and some of the activities of the Export-Import Bank. But by May this concept had changed. The legislation developed by the task forces, approved by Kennedy, and submitted to Congress on May 29 to begin "The Decade of Development" fell short of Kennedy's earlier aim. The new agency that the legislation would establish, the Agency for International Development—given the national fondness for acronyms, it would be called AID—was to include only ICA and the Development Loan Fund. The work of the other agencies was to be co-ordinated, but they were to remain legally separate.

What the President called for was a change in emphasis. The aid program—at least in its nonmilitary aspects—was no longer to be sold as a weapon in the cold war; its sole justification was "to help make a historic demonstration that economic growth and political democracy can go hand in hand to the end that an en-

larged community of free, stable, and self-reliant nations can reduce world tensions and insecurity."

The legislation submitted to Congress embodied the President's
intention to reverse the Dulles doctrine that nations not with us
were to be regarded as against. Neutralism, as practiced for instance by India, was to be recognized as respectable and no bar
to participation in the aid program. But under the influence of
events, the President's opinion of some so-called neutrals was to
change and the application of the various aid programs, including
that of AID, was to change accordingly.

What was to be the most controversial part of the proposed
legislation was its authorization of long-term borrowing to permit
the development of projects on more than a year-to-year basis.
President Eisenhower had sought something similar and had failed
to get it. What President Kennedy asked was permission to borrow
funds for development loans from the Treasury, thus making it
unnecessary to go through the annual agony and uncertainty of
getting appropriations from Congress. Most of the agony and uncertainty were caused by Representative Passman. He announced
during a hearing in the spring that he had been told by another
member of Congress that two unnamed officials of ICA had said
that, if Passman would resign from the Subcommittee, the ICA
would withdraw the effort to bypass the Appropriations Committee. The story may be apocryphal, but it has the ring of truth.

The President asked Congress to authorize loans repayable in
United States dollars—and this was a change—"to promote the
economic development of less-developed countries and areas." He
requested authority to borrow $900 million in fiscal 1962 and $1.6
billion in each of the following four years. He also asked for permission to re-lend the approximately $1.5 billion that would be
repaid during the five-year period, on projects undertaken in earlier
programs. In addition, money repaid from loans in the new program would be used to make still more loans. The total amount of
long-term borrowing for which the President requested authority
was $7.3 billion.

There was nothing new in the resort to Treasury borrowing—
except that Passman decided to take this particular proposal as a
personal challenge to himself. Congress has previously granted
such authority more than a score of times to agencies such as the
Commodity Credit Corporation, the Export-Import Bank, the
Farmers Home Administration, the Tennessee Valley Authority,
and the ICA itself. The name of the "hero" who coined the term,
"backdoor spending," to describe and discredit what the President

sought to do is unrecorded. But "backdoor spending" was a great gift to the opponents on foreign aid. With this slogan, and the total amount requested by Kennedy for the whole foreign-aid program, they went into battle.

Including the amount Kennedy asked for development loans, the appropriations he requested for the new AID came to a total of $4.8 billion. He asked for a clear division between the military and the nonmilitary aspects of the program so that sensitive nations like India, which did not participate in the military-aid programs, would have no cause for embarrassment in requesting and accepting nonmilitary aid. He asked for authority to guarantee private investments up to $1 million—the limit had been $500,000. But he requested that guarantees for losses stemming from nonconvertibility, expropriation, wars, or revolution be extended only to investments in the less developed areas. He asked that two new causes of possible losses, "insurrection or civil strife," be added. In addition he asked Congress to grant authority to issue guarantees against loss of "a loan investment due to non-payment for any reason." There was also a request for a $5-million appropriation for surveys of investment opportunities other than in extraactive industries, which, as experience has shown, can command ample private funds. And because of his experience in attempting to deal with unexpected or rapidly developing situations such as those that arose in the Congo, the President asked for a doubling of the discretionary fund (to $500 million) which he could make available for nonmilitary aid when "he determines such use to be important to the national interest."

The total amount of Kennedy's request added up to $4,805,-000,000. This was more than a billion dollars more than the Eisenhower Administration had been allowed by Congress for the same purposes in 1960, and Congress had cut the Eisenhower requests for aid funds by almost half a billion dollars.

After surveying Kennedy's requests, *Congressional Quarterly,* which had a decade of close watch on the Congress behind it, informed its subscribers that "the President was certain to receive less money than requested and by no means certain to get his request for long-term borrowing authority." It was right on both counts.

THE FOREIGN-AID BATTLE

The coming foreign-aid battle divided into two phases: a drive for the passage of an authorization bill that carried with it the fate of the long-term borrowing authority the President had requested; and, once that bill was passed, an appropriation bill that might or might not carry the money to provide for the functions previously authorized by Congress. On this occasion the President, his staff, and his advisers were united; the division of opinion that had adversely affected the Aid to Education Bill was happily absent.

Presidential Assistant Ralph Dungan was assigned to marshal the White House forces in the fight for the foreign-aid program, and because of Kennedy's special concern a lawyer in private practice but with long experience in the Federal Government was appointed to a temporary position as Assistant to the Secretary of State, and directed to run the bills through the Congressional gauntlet. This was Theodore H. Tannewald, Jr., of New York. The White House had previously declined the services of a citizens' organization headed by Eric A. Johnston that had helped with the passage of foreign-aid measures in the previous Administration. But in preparation for the battle ahead, it was decided that such an organization could be useful, particularly in attempting to round up the votes of Republican liberals and moderates. So the Citizens Committee for International Development, headed by Warren Lee Pierson, Chairman of the Executive Committee of Transcontinental and Western Airlines, came into being.

At the very outset of the effort to update the foreign-aid program, Kennedy was put on notice that this time the doubters included not only the perennial objectors from the right, but moderates and liberals from both parties. Following testimony before the Senate Foreign Affairs Committee by Secretary Rusk, Senator George D. Aiken, the leader of the Republican moderates, told him that "without better administration, more money will only make the operation worse." Senator Alexander Wiley, ranking Republican on the Foreign Relations Committee, said gloomily that "Foreign aid will have to be re-sold to the American people." And from the Democratic left, Senator Wayne Morse announced that "Congress has delegated too much authority in this field."

Despite the numerical majority of the Democrats in both House and Senate, it was clear that it would take more than Democratic votes either to put over the plan for long-range financing or to obtain a generous appropriation. This was a reflection of sweeping changes in the South—economic, social, and political—that were making it more protectionist and to a degree more isolationist; and the shift in Southern sentiment showed up most clearly in the Southern House membership, which always reflects heavy favoritism for rural and small-town opinion. Thus a bolt against Kennedy on foreign aid by members of Congress who otherwise would be counted as liberal was a real threat. All of their votes would be needed to offset the Southern defection, and so would the votes of some thirty or more Republicans in the House.

As it turned out, the progress of the legislation was deeply affected by international events—by pressures suddenly applied by Khrushchev on Berlin, by the crisis in the Congo, by the failure of the Cuban adventure and the intensification of the problem of Castro, by aggression in Laos, and lastly by the action of the neutral nations meeting in Belgrade. And, although no one could have foreseen it, Speaker Rayburn's illness and his forced retirement in the last hour of the battle, by weakening the power structure of the House, contributed not a little to the fate of Kennedy's foreign-aid program.

On July 10 the officers and members of the Executive Committee of the newly formed Citizens Committee for International Development met with President Kennedy in his office in the White House. He spoke with the candor that he often uses on such occasions. There were three types of foreign aid, of countries that needed it, the President told them. First, there were such nations as India and Pakistan that had well-developed planning and could use aid most effectively. Second, there were new nations whose planning was less developed but nevertheless promising— and he named Ghana and Nigeria as examples. Then, he said, there are some nations without viable economies, which cannot use aid effectively but whose governments would go under without such support. That aid is political, he said. He pointed to a South American country that has been the recipient of substantial aid. "I don't like to pour $150 million down a hole," Kennedy said. But country X, he pointed out, was next to countries A, B, and C, and if it became the victim of Communism or Castroism, the infection could easily seep over the borders. Congress criticizes aid to such a country, the President said, but it would be much more critical of the Administration if that country went under.

The President took pains to emphasize the importance of foreign aid to the whole problem of foreign policy. He said he recognized that mistakes had been made in the aid program and announced his intention of strengthening, considerably, the aid program's administration. He specifically asked for help in bringing into that administration people trained by business and industry.

An impressed member of the Committee asked the President, "Why don't you tell this sort of thing to members of Congress?"

Kennedy stopped short as if he had been given an idea. He then led his guests into the rose garden where, before the press, he made the brief speech, without notes, in which he laid his case for a long-term foreign-aid program of generous dimensions before the public. Kennedy termed his foreign-aid measure, as he had previously termed the Aid to Education Bill, "probably the most vital legislation of this session of the Congress."

The bill, the President said, "involves the effort by this country for its own security, for its own well-being, to assist other countries in maintaining their security."

All of us have been concerned, rightfully, when one or another country passes behind the Iron Curtain. I can say, as my predecessor President Eisenhower said before me, that if the United States were not engaged in this program, if we fail to meet our responsibilities in this area this year and in the days to come, then other countries must inevitably fall.

The Communists are making a great effort to expand their center of power outward. The thing that stands between them and their objective are these Governments and these people.

I believe we have an opportunity to assist them to maintain their countries' independence. They depend in large degree upon us. This country is a free country. It has great resources, and I think we have to recognize that freedom for ourselves and others is not purchased lightly. It requires an effort by each of us. This is a matter of the greatest national importance. It is a matter which has engaged the attention of the United States since the end of the second world war. We have seen the assistance which we gave Western Europe permit Western Europe to be rebuilt into a strong and vital area upon which our security depends. We see ourselves heavily engaged in Latin America. We see ourselves involved in a great effort to maintain the independence of countries in Africa, in Asia.

It is not an easy matter for our people to again support this kind of assistance abroad, but I want to make it very clear that it is assistance to the United States itself. We cannot live in an isolated world. And I would much rather give our assistance in this way—a large part of it consists of food, defense support as well as long-term loans—than to have to send American boys to do it.

We believe in this program. One of the most important parts of it now is the provision for long-term commitments. That means we will say to a country that if you will do "one, two, three" on taxes and land reform and capital investment, then the United States, along with other prosperous countries of Western Europe, will be prepared to meet responsibilities over a longer period.

Now when we move from year to year, without having any idea what we can do in the future, the country's programming, the country's organization for its advance is bound to be haphazard. And I think that is one of the reasons why the program has not always been successful, and one of the reasons why we have had waste in the past.

We are bringing new people into this organization. We are getting the best talent we can get. I hope we are going to get long-term authorization to permit us to move ahead over a period of time. . . . And I want to ask the American people to support this program as a vital one in the fight for our own security and in the fight for peace.

AID CAMPAIGN IN HIGH GEAR

When the President returned to his office, his campaign to put the AID bill across went into high gear. He almost immediately began making plans to see hundreds of members of Congress in small groups. The Citizens Committee began pouring out material to editors and members of Congress, emphasizing in particular that as much as 60 per cent of the foreign-aid appropriations in the past had actually been spent on goods and services in the United States. The legislative representatives of the White House, the State Department, the AFL-CIO and many of its constituent unions, and those of many private organizations descended on Capitol Hill.

General Eisenhower, it was reported, had warned President Kennedy of the troubles he was likely to have with Representative Passman. And when, the day after the rose garden speech, the two Republican leaders, Senator Everett Dirksen and Representative Charles Halleck, received an invitation to Gettysburg, it was assumed that General Eisenhower would, as the New York *Herald Tribune* put it, "use his influence and prestige with his own party to assist the foreign aid bill through Congress." If any persuasion on the foreign-aid program was undertaken at Gettysburg, it must have worked in reverse. Halleck remained an implacable foe of long-term financing and a partner in Passman's efforts to trim the appropriation. And the only thing General Eisenhower said publicly about foreign aid during President Kennedy's battle was that some people were for it and some people against it.

Yet Kennedy was full of optimism about the chances for his bill. The tactics he ordered to be used in dealing with Congress called for no compromise, no retreat. In the House, while the Foreign Affairs Committee under the Chairmanship of Thomas E. Morgan of Pennsylvania prepared to report out a bill along the lines requested by the President, Representative Passman announced that he was calling off hearings on foreign-aid appropriations on the grounds that he didn't know what the authorization bill would be like and that until he did, hearings would be a waste of time. Whether Passman knew it or not, delaying appropriation hearings greatly increased the possibility that final action on the foreign-aid appropriation would be one of the last measures to be studied at the end of the session—by a tired, hot Congress, impatient to go home; a danger to any measure. Passman certainly could not have known that, by the time Congress was ready for final action on the appropriation, the strong hand of Sam Rayburn would have relaxed its grip on the House.

The President's optimism about the chances for his bill was increased by an odd event: the head of a foreign state, on a visit to Washington, made a direct plea, near to a demand, to Congress that it act favorably on foreign aid. It was the President of Pakistan, Ayub Khan, who had come to Washington on an official visit at the invitation of Vice President Johnson and who, as formal honors require, was invited to address a joint session of Congress. It was widely thought that either the Vice President or Kennedy himself suggested to Ayub Khan that he make the blunt appeal he did make. It was not true. Ayub did inform the President that he intended to make a strong and direct statement to Congress on the subject of aid, and the President attempted strongly but tactfully to dissuade him. But the visitor, a man of remarkable independence of mind, was not dissuaded.

"We are pressing against you today as friends," Ayub told the Congress. "If we make good I think you will in some fashion get your money back. If we do not make good and if, heaven forbid, we go under Communism, then we shall press against you, but not as friends."

As for aid, he said, "the affluent United States has no choice. You have to give it to us because so much is involved."

The Congress, much to its own surprise, applauded. A pleased President Kennedy and his wife gave a famous and splendid party for the Pakistan President at Mount Vernon. Hopefully, the President included Representative Passman among the guests, but that gracious gesture changed him not a whit.

Even stronger pressures affecting the aid bill were building up in Moscow. The Berlin problem was again being blown up to the crisis stage. "Every year," said an observer on Capitol Hill, "they pull the same stuff and get this bill passed." Meanwhile Representative Walter H. Judd of Minnesota, a leading Republican member of the House Foreign Affairs Committee, sought to arrange a compromise on the long-term feature of the President's bill that both the President and the Republican leadership would accept. An optimistic President turned him down.

In the Senate the Foreign Relations Committee under the leadership of Senator Fulbright reported out a bill exactly to the President's liking. Senator Byrd of Virginia sought to amend the bill so that while a five-year development-loan program would be authorized, the Administration would have to come to Congress for appropriations on an annual basis. "Wholly unacceptable," announced the White House, and the Byrd amendment was overwhelmingly defeated. The Senate then voted, again by a large majority, for nearly everything that Kennedy wanted.

The House remained the greatest threat to the President's bill, and it was there, on August 16, that a blow fell from an astonishing source. A favorable bill had been reported from the Foreign Affairs Committee. It was on the floor and subject to amendment. The first amendment offered was by Representative D. S. Saund, the Indian-born liberal Democrat from California whose first election had so surprised and delighted Democrats that Speaker Rayburn moved to put him on the Foreign Affairs Committee. Representative Saund's amendment reduced the term of development loans from five years to one and authorized an expenditure of $1.2 billion for the fund for that year.

Whatever amendments the Republicans had to offer they quickly put in their pockets. Minority Leader Halleck, astonished at his luck in having the heart taken out of the President's bill by a Democrat, and a liberal Democrat at that, gave the signal to the Republicans to vote for Saund's amendment. On a standing vote the House passed it, 197 to 185. President Kennedy immediately called for the House to reverse itself, but the amendment stayed in the bill. Representative Saund declared that he had taken his action in behalf of the little man. "We must stop coddling kings and dictators and protecting the status quo," he said.

Supporters of the foreign-aid program, acutely aware by now of the perilously thin Republican support for a long-term program, sought, and thought they would receive, help from Governor Nelson Rockefeller of New York. He was persuaded to send each Republican member of the House a telegram that on its face appeared to be favorable to the program.

The White House hoped that the Rockefeller telegram would turn the tide. It was a short-lived hope. Cries of outrage rose from the more conservative House Republicans who fired back at Rockefeller telegrams of complaint, some reportedly collect. The most persuasive telegram was sent by Minority Leader Halleck. It brought a reply from Rockefeller saying that his earlier telegram had been misinterpreted and that he really supported annual appropriations for aid programs. Then Richard Nixon came up with a newspaper article in which he too came out in favor of yearly trips to the appropriations committees.

That was that and, when it came to a vote, instead of the thirty Republicans the White House had hoped it could persuade, only five could be counted on its side. The conservative coalition had won again, and this time Speaker Rayburn was not there to say it nay. Acting Speaker John W. McCormack, perhaps with an eye on Southern support for the Speakership itself if it should become vacant, insisted that the Administration's best chance would come in the Conference Committee. That committee, he pointed out, would be full of friends of foreign aid. But in the bitter battle that followed in the committee, the House conferees refused to back down, saying the House had proved that it would never accept Treasury borrowing for the development-loan program.

At that point the White House, which had turned its face so sternly against compromise, gave in. Larry O'Brien came back from the Hill with the bad news and recommended to the President that he advise Senator Fulbright that a compromise would be acceptable. Tired and bitter, the Senator agreed. There would be long-term authorization, but the annual agonies before Passman and his committee would continue. When the Senate had voted for the compromise, Fulbright walked across the floor to Senator Byrd. "Congratulations, Harry," he said. "You won." In a way this was true, since the compromise bill was almost exactly what the defeated Byrd amendment would have called for. But the real victor was in the other house, and his name was Passman.

"Wholly satisfactory," the White House said about the bill. Supporters of the bill said, "A moral commitment has been made by Congress to now supply the funds to carry out the Act." Yet doubt remained whether Representative Passman felt himself included in such a "moral commitment."

PUNTA DEL ESTE

In the meantime, the President had been making a large moral commitment for the United States. In August, at the Inter-American Economic and Social Conference at Punta del Este, representatives of the United States and Latin American nations agreed upon the ground rules for the Alliance for Progress, a sort of

Marshall Plan for the southern nations. President Kennedy pledged $20 billion in aid, some of it private, most of it public, for Latin America, if those nations agreed to fiscal, social, and land reforms.

Kennedy made the program his in its scope, its degree of daring, and its nomenclature, but it had had its beginnings in the Eisenhower Administration, when the need for such a program and the opportunities inherent in it had impressed Douglas Dillon, then Undersecretary of State. President Kennedy had hoped to be present at Punta del Este, but pressures on Berlin kept him in Washington. The failure of the Cuban invasion and early attempts to export Castroism to the rest of the hemisphere, along with political crises in Brazil, Ecuador, and elsewhere, had given added point to Kennedy's concern with the Alianza. But the sheer bulk of the problem together with ancient inertia made for slow going for the great program. Just before Christmas, Kennedy made quick trips to Venezuela and Colombia to light some torches. "I have called on all the peoples of the hemisphere to join a new Alliance for Progress—Alianza para Progreso—a vast effort, unparalleled in magnitude and nobility of purpose, to satisfy the basic needs of the American people for homes, work, land, health, and schools," he said. He was warmly received, but it remained to be seen whether his words had started any fires.

MONEY FOR AID

Back in Washington an intense battle began over the appropriation to carry out the new AID Act. It was obvious early that the "moral commitment" of Passman was not as deep as a well. His committee cut the Administration's requests for funds drastically, and the House finally voted for an appropriation of $3.6 billion —a billion dollars less than Kennedy had asked. The Senate countered with an appropriation of $4.2 billion and a conference committee was appointed. It promptly turned into the most bitter wrangle of the session. At one point Passman suggested that the effort to reach a settlement be abandoned and that Congress "take a fresh look" next year. "These people [the Senate conferees] seem to resent my position. They have the attitude that we don't know what we are talking about. Well, we do," he said.

It was a contest of wills and in the end Otto Passman won. The New York Times said that the final "compromise" was "dictated by a fanatical opponent of all foreign aid." The final total arrived at was $3,914,600,000 of which only $3,877,100,000 was new money, the remainder being balances from the previous year. "This was a billion less than originally requested by President Kennedy," said the *Times,* "and $376,400,000 less than Congress had first approved in its silly annual game of first authorizing a program and then denying it the authorized funds."

No doubt the Administration will manage to live within the appropriated total by trimming the program to fit its purse. But the consequences of this procedure in this time of crisis may cost us dearly. The whole Congressional session and the foreign aid cuts in particular provide dramatic illustration not only of the growing domination of Congress by the House but also of the urgent need for a reapportionment of Congressional districts to correct the unfair predominance of Congressmen from rural areas who can frustrate the will of the majority and the needs of the nation to satisfy their own local politicians.

AID AGENCY REFORMED

President Kennedy was too old a hand at the legislative process to cry much over the spilt milk. He began to do what some of his critics had said he never would do, which was sharply to reform the administration of the aid program. He appointed a committee headed by Thomas J. Watson, Jr., to scour the business community for likely appointees to the new Agency for International Development. And here Kennedy came breathlessly close to a hot controversy. The story that leaked from the White House was that the administrator of the new agency would be George David Woods, chairman of the First Boston Corporation, a leading financial enterprise. The newspaper stories had no more than hit the Capitol before a storm began to rise. George Woods and his firm had been intimately involved with the abortive Dixon-Yates contract, and some Senators, veterans of the hearings on Dixon-Yates were convinced that the whole plan had originated with him. They pointed out that it was the conflict of interest involving First Boston which brought the downfall of the Dixon-Yates contract in the courts. For two days the anti-Woods chorus swelled. Finally Kennedy was advised that while Woods would probably be confirmed by the Senate, there would be enough votes against him to embarrass him, especially as the head of a controversial agency. Mr Woods requested to be let out, and the President agreed.

The final choice for an AID head was a surprising but promising one. A New York lawyer, Fowler Hamilton, with considerable government experience behind him, had been brought to Washington and installed at the CIA with the general expectation that he would succeed Allen Dulles as head of that vast and secret agency. There were signs that Hamilton was not satisfied with the CIA assignment, the AID job was open, and as a former law partner of George Ball, the Undersecretary of State for Economic Affairs, he quickly came to mind. He was named to head the agency, and the gentle Henry Labouisse, the retiring head of ICA, was chosen as Ambassador to Greece.

Under the law and the directions of the President, ICA employees were not blanketed into the new AID, and Hamilton's first act was to set up machinery for reviewing the qualifications of each employee before he became permanently attached to the new organization. Hamilton also ordered a review of each of the more than 4,000 aid projects financed by ICA that were still in progress. And he began the critical task of selecting assistant administrators for the geographical regions in which AID would operate. With the approval of President Kennedy, the first of these assistant administrators to be appointed was Teodoro Moscoso, the Puerto Rican-born Ambassador to Venezuela, who was picked to run the Alliance for Progress. For three months the foreign-aid program came almost to a halt while these changes were in progress, but when operations were running again, Hamilton took off around the world to see for himself what his agency was doing.

RESISTING GUERRILLA TACTICS

The June graduating class of the U.S. Army Special Warfare School at Fort Bragg, North Carolina, including military men from nineteen underdeveloped nations, heard the President's deputy for national-security affairs, Walt W. Rostow, explain in his speech at the graduation exercises the new importance Mr. Kennedy attached to training in guerrilla tactics.

When this Administration came to responsibility it faced four major crises: Cuba, the Congo, Laos, and Viet-Nam. Each represented a successful Communist breaching—over the previous two years—of the Cold War truce lines which had emerged from the Second World War and its aftermath. In different ways each had arisen from the efforts of the international Communist movement to exploit the inherent instabilities of the underdeveloped areas of the non-Communist world; and each had a guerrilla warfare component.

Cuba, of course, differed from the other cases [Rostow emphasized]. The Cuban revolution against Batista was a broad-based national insurrection. But that revolution was tragically captured from within by the Communist apparatus; and now Latin America faces the danger of Cuba's being used as the base for training, supply, and direction of guerrilla warfare in the Hemisphere.

More than that, Mr. Khrushchev, in his report to the Moscow conference of Communist parties (published January 6, 1961), had explained at great length that the Communists fully support what he called wars of national liberation and would march in the front rank with the peoples waging such struggles. The military arm of Mr. Khrushchev's January 1961 doctrine is, clearly, guerrilla warfare.

These four crises, Rostow told the Special Warriors, pressed in on the President from day to day as he faced up to the candidly stated position of Mr. Khrushchev.

To understand the problem, he went on, it is necessary to begin with the great revolutionary process that is going forward in the southern half of the world; for the guerrilla-warfare problem in these regions is a product of that revolutionary process and of the Communist effort and intent to exploit it.

What followed was Rostow's explanation, as an historian, of the broader meaning of "guerrilla war":

What is happening throughout Latin America, Africa, the Middle East and Asia is this: old societies are changing their ways in order to create and maintain a national personality on the world scene, and to bring to their peoples the benefits modern technology can offer. This process is truly revolutionary. It touches every aspect of the traditional life: economic, social and political. The introduction of modern technology brings about not merely new methods of production but a new style of family life, new links between the villages and the cities, the beginnings of national politics, and a new relationship to the world outside.

Like all revolutions, the revolution of modernization is disturbing. Individual men are torn between the commitment to the old and familiar way of life and the attractions of a modern way of life. The power of old social groups—notably the landlord who usually dominates the traditional society—is reduced. Power moves towards those who can command the tools of modern technology, including modern weapons. Men and women in the villages and the cities, feeling that the old ways of life are shaken and that new possibilities are open to them, express old resentments and new hopes.

This is the grand arena of revolutionary change which the Communists are exploring with great energy. They believe that their techniques of organization—based on small disciplined cadres of conspirators—are ideally suited to grasp and to hold power in these turbulent settings. The weak transitional governments that one is likely to find during this modernization process are highly vulnerable to subversion and to guerrilla warfare. And whatever Communist doctrines of historical inevitability may be, Communists know that their time to seize power in the underdeveloped areas is limited. As momentum takes hold in an underdeveloped area—and the fundamental social problems inherited from the traditional society are solved—their chances to seize power decline. It is on the weakest nations—facing their most difficult transitional moments—that the Communists concentrate their attention. . . .

The history of this country teaches us that communism is not the long run wave of the future towards which societies are naturally drawn. On the contrary. But it is one particular form of modern society to which a nation may fall prey during the transitional process. Communism is best understood as a disease of the transition to modernization.

What is our reply to this historical conception and strategy? What is the American purpose and the American strategy? We, too, recognize that a revolutionary process is under way. We are dedicated to the proposition that this revolutionary process of modernization shall be permitted to go forward in independence, with increasing degrees of human freedom. We seek two results: first, that truly independent nations shall emerge on the world scene; and, second, that each nation will be permitted to fashion, out of its own culture and its own ambitions, the kind of modern society it wants. . . .

The U.S. has no interest in political satellites. Where we have military pacts we have them because governments feel directly endangered by outside military action, and we are prepared to help protect their independence against such military action. But, to use Mao Tse-tung's famous phrase, we do not seek nations which "lean to one side." We seek nations which shall stand up straight. And we do so for a reason: because we are deeply confident that nations which stand up straight will protect their independence and move in their own ways and in their own time towards human freedom and political democracy.

Thus, our central task in the underdeveloped areas, as we see it, is to protect the independence of the revolutionary process now going forward. This is our mission and it is our ultimate strength. For this is not—and cannot be—the mission of communism. And in time, through the fog of propaganda and the honest confusions of men caught up in the business of making new nations, this fundamental difference will become increasingly clear in the southern half of the world. . . .

I do not need to tell you that the primary responsibility for dealing with guerrilla warfare in the underdeveloped areas cannot be American. There are many ways in which we can help—and we are searching our minds and our imaginations to learn better how to help; but a guerrilla war must be fought primarily by those on the spot. This is so for a quite particular reason. A guerrilla war is an intimate affair, fought not merely with weapons but fought in the minds of the men who live in the villages and in the hills; fought by the spirit and policy of those who run the local government. An outsider cannot, by himself, win a guerrilla war; he can help create conditions in which it can be won; and he can directly assist those prepared to fight for their independence. We are determined to help destroy this international disease; that is, guerrilla war designed, initiated, supplied, and led from outside an independent nation. . . .

I am sometimes lectured that this or that government within the Free World is not popular; they tell me that guerrilla warfare cannot be won unless the peoples are dissatisfied. These are, at best, half truths. The truth is that guerrilla warfare, mounted from external bases—with rights of sanctuary—is a terrible burden to carry for any government in a society making its way towards modernization. As you know, it takes somewhere between ten and twenty soldiers to control one guerrilla in an organized operation. Moreover, the guerrilla force has this advantage: its task is merely to destroy; while the government must build and protect what it is building. A guerrilla war mounted from outside a transitional nation, is a crude act of international vandalism. There will be no peace in the world if the international community accepts the outcome of a guerrilla war, mounted from outside a nation, as tantamount to a free election.

The sending of men and arms across international boundaries and the direction of guerrilla war from outside a sovereign nation is aggression; and this is a fact which the whole international community must confront and whose consequent responsibilities it must accept. Without such international action those against whom aggression is mounted will be driven inevitably to seek out and engage the ultimate source of the aggression they confront. . . .

In facing the problem of guerrilla war, I have one observation to make as an historian. It is now fashionable to read the learned works of Mao Tse-tung and Che Guevara on guerrilla warfare. This is, indeed, proper. One should read with care and without passion into the minds of one's enemies. But it is historically inaccurate and psychologically dangerous to think that these men created the strategy and tactics of guerrilla war to which we are now responding. Guerrilla warfare is not a form of military and psychological magic created by the Communists. There is no rule or parable in the Communist texts which was not known at an earlier time in history. The operation of Marion's men in relation to the Battle of Cowpens in the American Revolution was, for example, governed by rules which Mao merely echoes; Che Guevara knows nothing of this business that T. E. Lawrence did not know or was not practiced, for example, in the Peninsular Campaign during the Napoleonic wars, a century earlier. The orchestration of professional troops, militia, and guerrilla fighters is an old game whose rules can be studied and learned.

We are up against a form of warfare which is powerful and effective only when we do not put our minds clearly to work on how to deal with it. . . .

THE U.S.S.R. RESUMES TESTS

When the wall went up in Berlin, more and louder cries for resuming nuclear testing went up in the United States.

During all the furor over Berlin, test-ban negotiations were still officially under way in Geneva. To call attention to the continued stalemate and to pacify test advocates a trifle, President Kennedy called Ambassador Dean home in late August for consultations. On August 28 Dean returned to Geneva for what Kennedy termed the "decisive" round of the test-ban negotiations. Then, the President said, "I will make the appropriate decision"—the closest he had come to acknowledging that the United States was considering test resumption. The neutral nations were meeting in Belgrade on September 1, and the United States wanted to re-emphasize that we were hopeful, blameless, flexible, and willing in our efforts to achieve a test-ban agreement.

On August 31 the U.S.S.R. announced it would resume nuclear tests at once. And on September 1 Washington announced the first detection of a nuclear blast in the U.S.S.R. since the beginning of November 1958. Khrushchev blamed the West for "fanning up the arms race." He noted that the French had been conducting tests all during the moratorium, and he promised that he would explode a series of bombs in succession of 20, 30, 50, and 100 megatons.

The United Nations General Assembly was now in special session to consider the problem of Tunisia, and the Belgrade conference had opened. In Belgrade, especially, the lack of protest at the Soviet move appalled Washington. Nasser's lukewarm expression of shock received all the American headlines since other participants expressed even less.

The White House immediately condemned the Soviet decision to test as "a hazard to every human being" and "a threat to the entire world." A meeting of the National Security Council the next day with leaders of the Atomic Energy and Foreign Affairs and Foreign Relations Committees resulted in a statement that accused the U.S.S.R. of "atomic blackmail." The United States and Britain at once called on the U.S.S.R. to agree to test underground only. The first Soviet blast, detected on Friday, September 1, was of "intermediate range" in the atmosphere and had obviously been in preparation for weeks, while the Soviets were talking about and urging us to continue the moratorium.

This was the technological scorecard early in September: The Russians were ahead in rocketry, generally, and we were ahead in delivery devices for warheads. Our tactical nuclear arsenal was more varied, and our stockpiles in number of bombs were larger, but their individual bombs were larger. We might have two to five times as many total megatons stockpiled, but our largest bomb was only twelve or thirteen megatons, and our largest missile warhead was no more than five megatons.

On September 6, the President announced that the U.S.S.R. had set off its third blast in five days, and that the United States felt it necessary to resume tests. There had been some desire to wait until the Soviet reply to the "underground only" request was received, but, it was argued, the continuing Soviet blasts in the atmosphere were themselves the reply. Slightly more than sixteen years after the United States dropped the first atomic bomb, therefore, the nuclear race was resumed.

The *Manchester Guardian* the next day called the President's decision "remarkably inept." "Coming so soon after the Soviet tests, the President's action looks suspiciously like a panic measure; moreover it has made him look over-anxious to get in his blow before indignation with the Kremlin has begun to cool. If he had waited for the United Nations to meet he could have gone before it as the innocent party to present the whole Western case on a test ban."

In mid-September, the regular session of the United Nations General Assembly convened, with disarmament as item #19 on its 95-point agenda.

On September 18 Secretary General Dag Hammarskjold was killed in a plane crash in the Congo, and the UN was thrown into chaos.

"... Before They Abolish Us"

ne week later, against that black background, John Fitzgerald
.ennedy heartened the world with his first speech to the United
(ations. It is presented here in full because of its historic import.

Ir. President, honored delegates, ladies and gentlemen:
  We meet in an hour of grief and challenge. Dag Hammarskjold is
ead. But the United Nations lives. His tragedy is deep in our hearts,
ut the task for which he died is at the top of our agenda. A noble
ervant of peace is gone. But the quest for peace lies before us.
  The problem is not the death of one man—the problem is the life of
is organization. It will either grow to meet the challenge of our age—
r it will be gone with the wind, without influence, without force,
ithout respect. Were we to let it die—to enfeeble its vigor—to cripple
s powers—we would condemn the future.
  For in the development of this organization rests the only true al-
rnative to war—and war appeals no longer as a rational alternative.
nconditional war can no longer lead to unconditional victory. It can
) longer serve to settle disputes. It can no longer concern the great
)wers alone. For a nuclear disaster, spread by winds and waters and
ar, could well engulf the great and the small, the rich and the poor,
e committed and the uncommitted alike. Mankind must put an end
) war—or war will put an end to mankind.
  So let us here resolve that Dag Hammarskjold did not live—or die—
vain. Let us call a truce to terror. Let us invoke the blessings of
ace. And, as we build an international capacity to keep peace, let us
in in dismantling the national capacity to wage war.
  This will require new strength and new roles for the United Nations.
or disarmament without checks is but a shadow—and a community
ithout law is but a shell. Already the United Nations has become
)th the measure and the vehicle of man's most generous impulses.
lready it has provided—in the Middle East, in Asia, in Africa this
ar in the Congo—a means of holding violence within bounds.

But the great question which confronted this body in 1945 is st
before us—whether man's cherished hopes for progress and peace a
to be destroyed by terror and disruption—whether the "foul winds
war" can be tamed in time to free the cooling winds of reason—a
whether the pledges of our Charter are to be fulfilled or defied: pledg
to secure peace, progress, human rights and world law. In this Ha
there are not three forces, but two. One is composed of those who a
trying to build the kind of world described in Articles I and II of t
Charter. The other, seeking a far different world, would undermine th
organization in the process.

Today of all days our dedication to the Charter must be maintaine
It must be strengthened first of all, by the selection of an outstandi
civil servant to carry forward the responsibilities of the Secretary Ge
eral—a man endowed with both the wisdom and the power to ma
meaningful the moral force of the world community. The late Secr
tary General nurtured and sharpened the United Nation's obligation
act. But he did not invent it. It was there in the Charter. It is still the
in the Charter.

However difficult it may be to fill Mr. Hammarskjold's place, it c
better be filled by one man rather than by three. Even the three hors
of the Troika did not have three drivers, all going in different dire
tions. They had only one—and so must the United Nations executi
To install a triumvirate, or any rotating authority, in the United N
tions administrative offices would replace order with anarchy, acti
with paralysis, and confidence with confusion.

The Secretary General, in a very real sense, is the servant of t
General Assembly. Diminish his authority and you diminish the a
thority of the only body where all nations, regardless of power, a
equal and sovereign. Until all the powerful are just, the weak will
secure only in the strength of this Assembly.

Effective and independent executive action is not the same question
balanced representation. In view of the enormous change in membe
ship in this body since its founding, the American delegation will jo
in any effort for the prompt review and revision of the composition
United Nations bodies.

But to give this organization three drivers—to permit each gre
power to decide its own case—would entrench the Cold War in t
headquarters of peace. Whatever advantages such a plan may hold o
to my own country, as one of the great powers, we reject it. For v
far prefer world law, in the age of self-determination, to world war,
the age of mass extermination.

Today, every inhabitant of this planet must contemplate the d
when this planet may no longer be habitable. Every man, woman a
child lives under a nuclear sword of Damocles, hanging by the slende
est of threads, capable of being cut at any moment by accident or mi
calculation or by madness. The weapons of war must be abolished b
fore they abolish us.

Men no longer debate whether armaments are a symptom or a cause of tension. The mere existence of modern weapons—ten million times more powerful than anything the world has ever seen, and only minutes away from any target on Earth—is a source of horror, and discord and distrust. Men no longer maintain that disarmament must wait the settlement of all disputes—for disarmament must be a part of any permanent settlement. And men may no longer pretend that the quest for disarmament is a sign of weakness—for in a spiraling arms race, a nation's security may well be shrinking even as its arms increase.

For 15 years this organization has sought the reduction and destruction of arms. Now that goal is no longer a dream—it is a practical matter of life or death. The risks inherent in disarmament pale in comparison to the risks inherent in an unlimited arms race.

It is in this spirit that the recent Belgrade Conference—recognizing that this is no longer a Soviet problem or an American problem, but a human problem—endorsed a program of "general, complete and strictly an internationally controlled disarmament." It is in this same spirit that we in the United States have labored this year, with a new urgency, and with a new, now-statutory agency fully endorsed by the Congress, to find an approach to disarmament which would be so far-reaching yet realistic, so mutually balanced and beneficial, that it could be accepted by every nation. And it is in this spirit that we have presented with the agreement of the Soviet Union—under the label both nations now accept of "general and complete disarmament"—a new statement of newly-agreed principles for negotiation.

But we are well aware that all issues of principle are not settled—and that principles alone are not enough. It is therefore our intention to challenge the Soviet Union, not to an arms race, but to a peace race—to advance together step by step, stage by stage, until general and complete disarmament has been achieved. We invite them now to go beyond agreement in principle to reach agreement on actual plans.

The program to be presented to this assembly—for general and complete disarmament under effective international control—moves to bridge the gap between those who insist on a gradual approach and those who talk only of the final and total achievement. It would create machinery to keep the peace as it destroys the machines of war. It would proceed through balanced and safeguarded stages designed to give no state a military advantage over another. It would place the final responsibility for verification and control where it belongs—not with the big powers alone, not with one's adversary or one's self—but in an international organization within the framework of the United Nations. It would assure that indispensable condition of disarmament—true inspection—and apply it in stages proportionate to the stage of disarmament. It would cover delivery systems as well as weapons. It would ultimately halt their production as well as their testing, their transfer as well as their possession. It would achieve, under the eye of an international disarmament organization, a steady reduction in forces.

both nuclear and conventional, until it has abolished all armies and all weapons except those needed for internal order and a new United Nations Peace Force. And it starts that process now, today, even as the talks begin.

In short, general and complete disarmament must no longer be a slogan, used to resist the first steps. It is no longer to be a goal without means of achieving it, without means of verifying its progress, without means of keeping the peace. It is now a realistic plan, and a test—a test of those only willing to talk and a test of those willing to act.

Such a plan would not bring the world free from conflict or greed—but it would bring a world free from the terrors of mass destruction. It would not usher in the era of the super state—but it would usher in an era in which no state could annihilate or be annihilated by another.

In 1945, this Nation proposed the Baruch Plan to internationalize the atom before other nations even possessed the bomb or demilitarized their troops. We proposed with our allies the Disarmament Plan of 1951 while still at war in Korea. And we make our proposals today while building up our defenses over Berlin, not because we are inconsistent or insincere or intimidated, but because we know the rights of free men will prevail—because while we are compelled against our will to rearm, we look confidently beyond Berlin to the kind of disarmed world we all prefer.

I therefore propose, on the basis of this Plan, that disarmament negotiations resume promptly, and continue without interruption until an entire program for general and complete disarmament has not only been agreed but has been actually achieved.

The logical place to begin is a treaty assuring the end of nuclear tests of all kinds, in every environment, under workable controls. The United States and the United Kingdom have proposed such a treaty that is both reasonable, effective and ready for signature. We are still prepared to sign that treaty today.

We also proposed a mutual ban on atmospheric testing, without inspection or controls, in order to save the human race from the poison of radioactive fall out. We regret that that offer was not accepted.

For 15 years we have sought to make the atom an instrument of peaceful growth rather than of war. But for 15 years our concessions have been matched by obstruction, our patience by intransigence. And the pleas of mankind for peace have met with disregard.

Finally, as the explosions of others beclouded the skies, my country was left with no alternative but to act in the interests of its own and the Free World's security. We cannot endanger that security by refraining from testing while others improve their arsenals. Nor can we endanger it by another long, uninspected ban on testing. For three years we accepted those risks in our open society while seeking agreement on inspection. But this year, while we were negotiating in good faith at Geneva, others were secretly preparing new experiments in destruction.

Our tests are not polluting the atmosphere. Our deterrent weapons are guarded against accidental explosion or use. Our doctors and scientists stand ready to help any nation measure and meet the hazards to health which inevitably result from the tests in the atmosphere.

But to halt the spread of these terrible weapons, to halt the contamination of the air, to halt the spiralling nuclear arms race, we remain ready to seek new avenues of agreement; our new Disarmament Program thus includes the following proposals:

First, signing the test-ban treaty by all nations. This can be done now. Test-ban negotiations need not and should not await general disarmament.

Second, stopping the production of fissionable materials for use in weapons, and preventing their transfer to any nation now lacking in nuclear weapons.

Third, prohibiting the transfer of control over nuclear weapons to states that do not own them.

Fourth, keeping nuclear weapons from seeding new battlegrounds in outer space.

Fifth, gradually destroying existing nuclear weapons and converting their materials to peaceful uses; and

Finally, halting the unlimited testing and production of strategic nuclear delivery vehicles, and gradually destroying them as well.

To destroy arms, however, is not enough. We must create even as we destroy—creating world-wide law and law enforcement as we outlaw world-wide war and weapons. In the world we seek, the United Nations Emergency Forces which have been hastily assembled, uncertainly supplied and inadequately financed will never be enough.

Therefore, the United States recommends that all member nations earmark special peace-keeping units in their armed forces—to be on call of the United Nations—to be specially trained and quickly available—and with advance provision for financial and logistic support.

In addition, the American delegation will suggest a series of steps to improve the United Nation's machinery for the peaceful settlement of disputes—for on-the-spot fact-finding, mediation and adjudication—or extending the rule of international law. For peace is not solely a matter of military or technical problems—it is primarily a problem of politics and people. And unless man can match his strides in weaponry and technology with equal strides in social and political development, our great strength, like that of the dinosaur, will become incapable of proper control—and like the dinosaur vanish from the earth.

As we extend the rule of law on earth, so must we also extend it to man's new domain: outer space.

All of us salute the brave cosmonauts of the Soviet Union. The new horizons of outer space must not be driven by the old bitter concepts of imperialism and sovereign claims. The cold reaches of the universe must not become the new arena of an even colder war.

To this end, we shall urge proposals extending the United Nations

Charter to the limits of man's exploration in the Universe, reserving outer space for peaceful use, prohibiting weapons of mass destruction in space or on celestial bodies, and opening the mysteries and benefits of space to every nation. We shall further propose cooperative efforts between all nations in weather prediction and eventually in weather control. We shall propose, finally, a global system of communication satellites linking the whole world in telegraph and telephone and radio and television. The day need not be far away when such a system will televise the proceedings of this body to every corner of the world for the benefit of peace.

But the mysteries of outer space must not divert our eyes or our energies from the harsh realities that face our fellow men. Political sovereignty is but a mockery without the means of meeting poverty and illiteracy and disease. Self-determination is but a slogan if the future holds no hope.

That is why my nation—which has freely shared its capital and it technology to help others help themselves—now proposes officially designating this decade of the 1960's as the United Nations Decade of Development. Under the framework of that Resolution, the United Nations' existing efforts in promoting economic growth can be expanded and coordinated. Regional surveys and training institutes can now pool the talents of many. New research, technical assistance and pilot projects can unlock the wealth of less developed lands and un tapped waters. And development can become a cooperative and not a competitive enterprise—to enable all nations, however diverse in their systems and beliefs, to become in fact as well as in law free and equal nations.

My country favors a world of free and equal states. We agree with those who say that colonialism is a key issue in this Assembly. But let the full facts of that issue be discussed in full.

On the one hand is the fact that, since the close of World War II a world-wide declaration of independence has transformed nearly billion people and 9 million square miles into 42 free and independent states. Less than 2 percent of the world's population now lives in "de pendent" territories.

I do not ignore the remaining problems of traditional colonialism which still confront this body. Those problems will be solved, with patience, good will and determination. Within the limits of our re sponsibility in such matters, my country intends to be a participant and not merely an observer, in the peaceful, expeditious movement of na tions from the status of colonies to the partnership of equals. That continuing tide of self-determination, which runs so strong, has our sympathy and our support.

But colonialism in its harshest forms is not only the exploitation of new nations by old, of dark skins by light—or the subjugation of the poor by the rich. My nation was once a colony—and we know what colonialism means; the exploitation and subjugation of the weak by the powerful, of the many by the few, of the governed who have given no consent to be governed, whatever their continent, their class or their color.

And that is why there is no ignoring the fact that the tide of self-determination has not reached the communist empire where a population far larger than that officially termed "dependent" lives under governments installed by foreign troops instead of free institutions—under a system which knows only one party and one belief—which suppresses free debate, and free elections, and free newspapers, and free books and free trade unions—and which builds a wall to keep truth a stranger and its own citizens prisoners. Let us debate colonialism in full—and apply the principle of free choice and the practice of free plebiscites in every corner of the globe.

Finally, as President of the United States, I consider it my duty to report to this Assembly on two threats to the peace which are not on your crowded agenda, but which causes us, and most of you, the deepest concern.

The first threat on which I wish to report is widely misunderstood: the smoldering coals of war in Southeast Asia. South Vietnam is already under attack—sometimes by a single assassin, sometimes by a band of guerrillas, recently by full battalions. The peaceful borders of Burma, Cambodia and India have been repeatedly violated. And the peaceful people of Laos are in danger of losing the independence they gained not so long ago.

No one can call these "wars of liberation." For these are free countries living under governments. Nor are these aggressions any less real because men are knifed in their homes and not shot in the fields of battle.

The very simple question confronting the world community is whether measures can be devised to protect the small and weak from such tactics. For if they are successful in Laos and South Vietnam, the gates will be opened wide.

The United States seeks for itself no base, no territory, no special position in this area of any kind. We support a truly neutral and independent Laos, its people free from outside interference, living at peace with themselves and with their neighbors, assured that their territory will not be used for attacks on others, and under a government comparable (as Mr. Khrushchev and I agreed at Vienna) to Cambodia and Burma.

But now the negotiations over Laos are reaching a crucial stage. The ceasefire is at best precarious. The rainy season is coming to an end. Laotian territory is being used to infiltrate South Vietnam. The world community must recognize—all those who are involved—that this potent threat to Laotian peace and freedom is indivisible from all other threats to their own.

Secondly, I wish to report to you on the crisis over Germany and Berlin. This is not the time or the place for immoderate tones, but the world community is entitled to know the very simple issues as we see them. If there is a crisis it is because an existing peace is under threat—because an existing island of free people is under pressure—because solemn agreements are being treated with indifference. Established international rights are being threatened with unilateral usurpation. Peaceful circulation has been interrupted by barbed wire and concrete blocks. One recalls the order of the Czar in Pushkin's Boris Godunov: "Take steps at this very hour that our frontiers be fenced in by barriers. . . . That not a single soul pass o'er the border, that not a hare be able to run or a crow to fly."

It is absurd to allege that we are threatening a war merely to prevent the Soviet Union and East Germany from signing a so-called "treaty" of peace. The Western Allies are not concerned with any paper arrangement the Soviets may wish to make with a regime of their own creation, on territory occupied by their own troops and governed by their own agents. No such action can affect either our rights or our responsibilities.

If there is a dangerous crisis in Berlin—and there is—it is because of threats against the vital interests and the deep commitments of the Western Powers, and the freedom of West Berlin. We cannot yield these interests. We cannot fail these commitments. We cannot surrender the freedom of these people for whom we are responsible. A "peace treaty" which carried with it the provisions which destroy the peace would be a fraud. A "free city" which was not genuinely free would suffocate freedom and would be an infamy.

For a city or a people to be truly free, they must have the secure right without economic, political or police pressure, to make their own choice and to live their own lives. And as I have said before, if anyone doubts the extent to which our presence is desired by the people of West Berlin, we are ready to have that question submitted to a free vote in all Berlin and, if possible, among all the German people.

The elementary fact about this crisis is that it is unnecessary. The elementary tools for a peaceful settlement are to be found in the charter. Under its law, agreements are to be kept, unless changed by all those who made them. Established rights are to be respected. The political disposition of people should rest upon their own wishes, freely expressed in plebiscites or free elections. If there are legal problems, they can be solved by legal means. If there is a threat of force, it must be rejected. If there is desire for change, it must be a subject for negotiation and if there is negotiation, it must be rooted in mutual respect and concern for the rights of others.

The Western Powers have calmly resolved to defend, by whatever means are forced upon them, their obligations and their access to the free citizens of West Berlin and the self-determination of those citizens. This generation learned from bitter experience that either brandishing or yielding to threats can only lead to war. But firmness and reason can lead to the kind of peaceful solution in which my country profoundly believes.

We are committed to no rigid formula. We see no perfect solution. We recognize that troops and tanks can, for a time, keep a nation divided against its will, however unwise that policy may seem to us. But we believe a peaceful agreement is possible which protects the freedom of West Berlin and allied presence and access, while recognizing the historic and legitimate interests of others in assuring European security.

The possibilities of negotiation are now being explored; it is too early to report what the prospects may be. For our part, we would be glad to report at the appropriate time that a solution has been found. For there is no need for a crisis over Berlin, threatening the peace— and if those who created this crisis desire peace, there will be peace and freedom in Berlin.

The events and decisions of the next ten months may well decide the fate of man for the next ten thousand years. There will be no avoiding those events. There will be no appeal from these decisions. And we in this hall shall be remembered either as part of the generation that turned this planet into a flaming funeral pyre or the generation that met its vow "to save succeeding generations from the scourge of war."

In the endeavor to meet that vow, I pledge you every effort this nation possesses. I pledge you that we shall neither commit nor provoke aggression—that we shall neither flee nor invoke the threat of force—that we shall never negotiate out of fear, we shall never fear to negotiate.

Terror is not a new weapon. Throughout history it has been used by those who could not prevail, either by persuasion or example. But inevitably they fail—either because men are not afraid to die for a life worth living—or because the terrorists themselves came to realize that free men can not be frightened by threats, and that aggression would meet its own response. And it is in the light of that history that every nation today should know, be he friend or foe, that the United States has both the will and the weapons to join free men in standing up to their responsibilities.

But I come here today to look across this world of threats to the world of peace. In that search we cannot expect any final triumph— for new problems will always arise. We cannot expect that all nations will adopt like systems—for conformity is the jailer of freedom, and the enemy of growth. Nor can we expect to reach our goal by contrivance, by fiat or even by the wishes of all.

But however close we sometimes seem to that dark and final abyss, let no man of peace and freedom despair. For he does not stand alone. If we all can preserve—if we can in every land and office look beyond our own shores and ambitions—then surely the age will dawn in which the strong are just and the weak secure and the peace preserved.

Ladies and gentlemen of this assembly—the decision is ours. Never have the nations of the world had so much to lose—or so much to gain. Together we shall save our planet—or together we shall perish in its flames. Save it we can—and save it we must—and then shall we earn the eternal thanks of mankind and, as peace makers, the eternal blessing of God.

DISARMAMENT AND CONTROLS

While he was stubbornly resisting pressure to end the test-ban talks and resume nuclear testing throughout the spring, the President had kept persistent pressure of his own on Disarmament Administrator McCloy to produce a plan for an enlarged and strengthened disarmament agency to propose to Congress.

Senator Humphrey and Science Adviser Wiesner were pushing the President to present legislation. During May, Humphrey became insistent. There was pressure on him to introduce a bill of his own, but he was holding back in order to support an Administration-approved measure.

The big question McCloy had to resolve was whether to recommend an independent agency, responsible only to the White House, or expansion of the small inflective division Eisenhower had established in the Department of State. At interminable meetings representatives of departments other than State unanimously favored an independent organization. It was known that the Senate Foreign Relations Committee, likely to have the last word, favored keeping disarmament activities in State Department hands.

The realistic Senator Humphrey, a member of the committee, was willing to settle on the committee's terms. But Mr. McCloy and his deputy, Adrian Fisher, after four months of working through regular State Department channels even to clear the cost of a cable to Geneva, came out flatly for independence. McCloy knew that he wanted as permanent director in his stead William C. Foster, the former Republican director of foreign aid under Eisenhower and Truman, who had earlier refused the job because it was located in the Department of State.

McCloy recommended an independent agency in spite of Senate opposition. President Kennedy accepted his recommendation. A bill to that effect was sent to Congress.

By parliamentary error the bill was assigned to the Senate Committee on Government Operations, not an internationally inclined group, instead of to the Committee on Foreign Relations. It

took Humphrey and McCloy from June 29, when the bill was introduced, until mid-August to transfer the bill from the Government Operations to the Foreign Relations Committee. A lesser, or
less secure, man than Mr. McCloy might have been discouraged
when it was clear that because of the delay, consideration of his
bill would collide with consideration of the top-priority foreign-aid
bill—on which so much of the long-range strategy of the Kennedy
Administration depended. When the conflict in schedule was clear
to the President, he encouraged McCloy to do his best but not to
expect extraordinary help from the White House. Foreign aid had
to come first.

Mr. McCloy set out to do his best. First he telephoned General
Eisenhower. Mr. Foster called Nixon. They invited such former
Eisenhower Administration men as Christian A. Herter, Navy
Secretary Thomas S. Gates, Jr., Defense Research Chief Herbert
Frank York, and former Defense Secretary Robert Lovett to
testify for their bill. Nixon agreed to be neutral; the rest helped.
Mr. Lovett, trying to be reassuring, volunteered to tell the com-
mittee that the new agency would not be a "home for beatniks"—
with the result that the Disarmament Agency was ordered to subject employees to the highest security clearance in Government.

McCloy was less adept at Congressional than at Republican
Party strategy. Richard Russell, the arbiter of things military in
the Senate, had been overlooked in lining up advance support.
When McCloy finally realized the omission and tried to telephone,
Russell did not answer his calls. When at last they met, Russell
agreed not to work against McCloy's bill, and kept his word.

There was a nervous moment, however. When the subject of
reassigning the bill to Foreign Relations came up, Senator Russell
rose to deliver himself of a few remarks on the subject of human
ingenuity.

He had thought he knew the limits of his fellow man's capacity
to invent new reasons for expanding Federal Government, the
Senator from Georgia said. But he had clearly underestimated it.
This bill took the cake.

Before Russell could take his seat, the presiding officer interrupted to ask if the distinguished Senator would like the bill referred to his Committee on the Armed Services? Perhaps remembering his promise to Mr. McCloy, the Senator muttered, "No."

When the Soviet Union unexpectedly broke the moratorium
and resumed nuclear testing in the atmosphere, both the President
and McCloy grew discouraged about chances of persuading Con-

gress to go ahead with authorization of the disarmament agency. But McCloy and Humphrey persisted.

Congress authorized a new Arms Control and Disarmament Agency only one and one-half days before the session ended; funds were granted at 4 A.M. on the morning of September 26, before Congress adjourned sine die at 6.

Now at last, it was hoped, planning for disarmament could be carried on at a proper level with appropriate staff. No longer would negotiators assigned to the task of seeking agreements on reducing arms be forced to rely for advice and assistance on military and AEC experts opposed to reducing arms or banning arms tests. And now finally there could be co-ordinated effort to draft a comprehensive agreement for presentation when serious discussions resumed in March 1962.

"TRYING EVERYTHING POSSIBLE . . ."

As 1962 opened, the momentous decision that had faced the President throughout most of 1961 was still confronting him. From the day in March when Comrade Tsarapkin adopted a hard stand on a nuclear test ban, pressures on the President to resume nuclear testing had mounted. Ted Sorensen wryly told me once that perhaps Mr. Kennedy's most important decisions are his unannounced refusals to do countless things he is urged to do every day. And presumably the resumption of United States nuclear testing in the air headed that list from early September when the U.S.S.R. again began setting off atmospheric blasts.

After ordering new underground tests at that time, President Kennedy also ordered preparations to permit atmospheric testing in the Pacific by the early spring of 1962. Prime Minister Macmillan made Christmas Island available for that purpose. But Kennedy continued to reserve his decision. From September through January the arguments raged around him.

The Atomic Energy Commissioners (with certain reservations), the Joint Chiefs of Staff, most of the military services, CIA Director John McCone, ranking members of the Congressional Joint Committee on Atomic Energy, and many scientists (including the highly vocal Dr. Edward Teller) urged new tests in the air.

The Council of the Federation of American Scientists, an organization of 2,100 scientists and engineers, officially appealed to the President not to order resumption of tests in the atmosphere.

Political and propaganda losses, the Council said, would far outweigh gains to the United States in nuclear arms. The Federation particularly feared that testing would bring a new round in the arms race.

Since it was not technically necessary to test now, the opposition argument ran, the United States should hold off for two or three years and use the pause in the arms race for a serious attempt at a beginning of disarmament with inspection and control.

In the interest of "trying everything possible before we test," the President surprised Washington by announcing that the United States would agree to combine the talks aimed at a test ban with the eighteen-nation discussions of a general disarmament agreement scheduled for Geneva on March 14—a move the Russians had been demanding throughout the year. In this way France might finally be brought into test-ban negotiations. And if the Soviet Union had thoughts of staging more atmospheric tests at once, perhaps it would be deterred by so large a show of interest in slowing the arms race.

At their December 20 conference in Bermuda, where plans were laid for United States initiative in negotiating a settlement on Berlin, President Kennedy and Prime Minister Macmillan found themselves in spontaneous conversation about the urgent need to try again to end the arms race. Britain clearly would be an enthusiastic partner in a serious effort to reach a staged disarmament agreement. But if the effort was to have a real chance, careful attention had to be given to the position in which the adversary would find himself. Kennedy knew better now than he had at the time of Vienna what would worry Khrushchev. At Vienna Khrushchev had discussed with Kennedy the effect United States weapons-development programs had on Soviet policy and vice versa. The Soviet leader is reported to have said that whenever the United States made a new move in nuclear weaponry, his scientists and military men demanded more support for their work, and he was sure it was the same in the United States.

By his resistance to new atmospheric testing Mr. Kennedy indicated his understanding of how important was the "escalation" dilemma and of the desirability of eliminating it. The clearest statement of the objective, however, came not from the President, but from his Undersecretary of Defense, Roswell Gilpatric. Gilpatric explained to a television audience, soon after the President's decision to combine the disarmament and test-ban talks, that what the United States seeks is to "reach a stage of some stability where neither our adversaries feel they are to be overwhelmed nor do we feel we are exposed to any great risk from them."

We want to get away from the conception of a race, a competition, a struggle always to be ahead. We are not trying to put ourselves in an aggressive posture. Ours is entirely a deterrent posture. But if they feel they are so outnumbered, that they have such an inferiority, it might provoke them to adventurous opportunistic moves that in a more stable situation they would not feel it necessary to take.

And so the President prepared for a new encounter in a new spirit. The defensive belligerence with which he had approached the June meeting in Vienna had given way to a greater sense of accommodation.

United States representatives made ready to go to Geneva in the spirit Ambassador Adlai Stevenson had defined in his speech of November 15, 1961, to the United Nations, when he underlined and made specific the new position on disarmament President Kennedy had announced in that forum two months before. "We are flexible about first steps," Stevenson said as he began his eloquent illumination of the new United States policies; "we are adamant only on the point that we begin at once—immediately— to disarm." The new position had been hammered into a comprehensive program. Though certainly "not perfect," as Stevenson was quick to volunteer, "it can stand up to close scrutiny—for it has been prepared at great pains and in good faith."

The commitment of the United States to general and complete disarmament was finally clear for all who would see. But what of the less inspiring and more immediate question of what to do about following the Soviet lead back into the "grim, unwelcome" business of testing nuclear weapons in the air?

President Kennedy had used the six months between the Soviet resumption of tests in September and the final days before the Geneva Conference to strengthen the United States position in the eyes of the world as a nation that would go "the last mile" to abolish testing and advance the day when the world could begin to disarm. Now he was faced with deciding whether to continue his refusal to accept their challenge to a new round of testing.

On the night of March 2, 1962, Mr. Kennedy told the American people what he had decided to do about nuclear testing and why he had decided to do it. In late April, he announced, the United States would begin a series of atmospheric tests unless the Soviet Union before then agreed to a treaty banning all tests under verifiable conditions.

"No single decision of this Administration has been more thoroughly or more thoughtfully weighed," the President assured the nation. Because of its importance, he told his nationwide television audience, "I want to share with you and all the world, to the fullest extent our security permits, all of the facts and thoughts which have gone into my decision.

"Many of these facts are hard to explain in simple terms," he warned; "many are hard to face in a peaceful world—but these are facts which must be faced and must be understood."

The President then proceeded to explain with great clarity and candor where the country stood in the precariously balanced nuclear-arms race and how he proposed eventually to lead us out of it.

For the first time in the nuclear age an American Chief Executive took the public deeply into his confidence on matters of nuclear policy and trusted in their ability and desire to understand what he had to say. His words, therefore, have lasting import.

Seventeen years ago man unleashed the power of the atom. He thereby took into his mortal hands the power of self-extinction. Throughout the years that have followed, under three successive Presidents, the United States has sought to banish this weapon from the arsenals of individual nations. For of all the awesome responsibilities entrusted to this office, none is more somber to contemplate than the special statutory authority to employ nuclear arms in the defense of our people and freedom.

But until mankind has banished both war and its instruments of destruction, the United States must maintain an effective quantity and quality of nuclear weapons, so deployed and protected as to be capable of surviving any surprise attack and devastating the attacker.

The two-month series of Soviet tests that "represented a major Soviet effort to put nuclear weapons back into the arms race" called for a re-examination of our basic security. And "this week," the President reported, "the National Security Council has completed its review of this subject."

The scope of the Soviet tests has been carefully reviewed by the most competent scientists in the country. The scope and justification of proposed American tests have been carefully reviewed, determining which experiments can be safely deferred, which can be deleted, which can be combined or conducted underground, and which are essential to our military and scientific progress. Careful attention has been given to the limiting of radioactive fall-out, to the future course of arms control diplomacy, and to our obligations to other nations.

Every alternative was examined. Every avenue of obtaining Soviet agreement was explored. We were determined not to rush into imitat-

ing their tests. And we were equally determined to do only what our
security required us to do. . . .

I find it deeply regrettable that any radioactive material must be
added to the atmosphere—that even one additional individual's health
may be risked in the foreseeable future. And however remote and
infinitesimal those hazards are judged to be, I still exceedingly regret
the necessity of balancing these hazards against the hazards to hundreds of millions of lives which would be created by any relative
decline in our nuclear strength.

Last fall's tests, in and by themselves, did not give the Soviet Union
superiority in nuclear power. They did, however, provide the Soviet
laboratories with a mass of data and experience on which, over the
next two or three years, they can base significant analyses, experiments
and extrapolations, preparing for the next test series which would confirm and advance their findings.

And I must report to you in all candor that further Soviet series, in
the absence of further Western progress, could well provide the Soviet
Union with a nuclear attack and defense capability so powerful as to
encourage aggressive designs. Were we to stand still while the Soviets
surpassed us—or even appeared to surpass us—the Free World's ability to deter, to survive and to respond to an all-out attack would be
seriously weakened.

So, in the absence of a prompt agreement to cease all tests, the
United States in April would once again explode nuclear weapons
in the air. "I have no doubt that most of our friends around the
world have shared my own hope that we would never find it necessary to test again—and my own belief that, in the long run, the
only real security in this age of nuclear peril rests not in armament
but in disarmament."

But I am equally certain that they would insist on our testing once
that is deemed necessary to protect free world security. They know
we are not deciding to test for political or psychological reasons—and
they also know that we cannot avoid such tests for political or psychological reasons.

The leaders of the Soviet Union are also watching this decision.
Should we fail to follow the dictates of our own security, they will
chalk it up, not to goodwill, but to a failure of will—not to our confidence in Western superiority, but to our fear of world opinion, the
very world opinion for which they showed such contempt. They
could well be encouraged by such signs of weakness to seek another
period of no testing without controls—another opportunity for stifling
our progress while secretly preparing, on the basis of last fall's experiments, for the new test series which might alter the balance of power.
With such a one-sided advantage, why would they change their strategy, or refrain from testing, merely because we refrained? Why would

they want to halt their drive to surpass us in nuclear technology? And why would they ever consider accepting a true test ban or mutual disarmament?

Our reasons for testing and our peaceful intentions are clear—so clear that even the Soviets could not objectively regard our resumption of tests, following their resumption of tests, as provocative or preparatory for war. On the contrary, it is my hope that the prospects for peace may actually be strengthened by this decision—once the Soviet leaders realize that the West will no longer stand still, negotiating in good faith, while they reject inspection and are free to prepare further tests. As new disarmament talks approach, the basic lesson of some three years and 353 negotiating sessions at Geneva is this—that the Soviets will not agree to an effective ban on nuclear tests as long as a new series of offers and prolonged negotiations, or a new uninspected moratorium, or a new agreement without controls, would enable them once again to prevent the West from testing while they prepare in secret.

But inasmuch as this choice is now no longer open to them, let us hope that they will take a different attitude on banning nuclear tests—that they will prefer to see the nuclear arms race checked instead of intensified, with all the dangers that intensification is likely to bring: the spread of nuclear weapons to other nations; the constant increase in world tensions; the steady decrease in all prospects for disarmament; and, with it, a steady decrease in the security of us all.

In the event the Soviets changed their position, we could know it immediately and would be prepared to act accordingly, the President promised.

On the 14th of March, in Geneva, Switzerland, a new 18 power conference on disarmament will begin. A statement of agreed principles has been worked out with the Soviets and endorsed by the U.N. In the long run, it is the constructive possibilities of that conference—and not the testing of new destructive weapons—on which rest the hopes of all mankind. However dim those hopes may sometimes seem, they can never be abandoned. And however far-off most steps toward disarmament appear, there are some that can be taken at once.

The United States will offer at the Geneva conference—not in the advance expectation they will be rejected, and not merely for purposes of propaganda—a series of concrete plans for a major "breakthrough to peace." We hope and believe that they will appeal to all nations opposed to war. They will include specific proposals for fair and enforceable agreements: to halt the production of fissionable materials and nuclear weapons and their transfer to other nations—to convert them from weapon stockpiles to peaceable uses—to destroy the warheads and the delivery systems that threaten man's existence—to check the dangers of surprise and accidental attack—to reserve outer space for peaceful use—and progressively to reduce all armed forces in such a way as ultimately to remove forever all threats and thoughts of war.

And of greatest importance to our discussion tonight, we shall, in association with the United Kingdom, present once again our proposals for a separate comprehensive treaty—with appropriate arrangements for detection and verification—to halt permanently the testing of all nuclear weapons, in every environment: in the air, in outer space, underground or under-water. New modifications will also be offered in the light of new experience.

The essential arguments and facts relating to such a treaty are well-known to the Soviet Union. There is no need for further repetition, propaganda or delay. The fact that both sides have decided to resume testing only emphasizes the need for new agreement, not new argument. And before charging that this decision shatters all hopes for agreement, the Soviets should recall that we were willing to work out with them, for joint submission to the U.N., an agreed statement of disarmament principles at the very time their autumn tests were being conducted. And Mr. Khrushchev knows, as he said in 1960, that any nation which broke the moratorium could expect other nations to be "forced to take the same road."

Our negotiators will be ready to talk about this treaty even before the Conference begins on March 14th—and they will be ready to sign well before the date on which our tests are ready to begin. That date is still nearly two months away. If the Soviet Union should now be willing to accept such a treaty, sign it before the latter part of April, and apply it immediately—if all testing can thus be actually halted—then the nuclear arms race would be slowed down at last—the security of the United States and its ability to meet its commitments would be safeguarded—and there would be no need for our tests to begin.

But this must be a fully effective treaty. We know enough now about broken negotiations, secret preparations and the advantages gained from a long test series never to offer again an uninspected moratorium. Some may urge us to try it again, keeping our preparations to test in a constant state of readiness. But in actual practice, particularly in a society of free choice, we cannot keep top-flight scientists concentrating on the preparation of an experiment which may or may not take place on an uncertain date in the future. Nor can large technical laboratories be kept fully alert on a stand-by basis waiting for some other nation to break an agreement. This is not merely difficult or inconvenient—we have explored this alternative thoroughly, and found it impossible of execution.

In short, in the absence of a firm agreement that would halt nuclear tests by the latter part of April, we shall go ahead with our talks—striving for some new avenue of agreement—but we shall also go ahead with our tests. If, on the other hand, the Soviet Union should accept such a treaty in the opening month of talks, that single step would be a monumental step toward peace—and both Prime Minister Macmillan and I would think it fitting to meet Chairman Khrushchev at Geneva to sign the final pact.

This, the President reiterated, was the course of affairs we would welcome most.

For our ultimate objective is not to test for the sake of testing. Our real objective is to make our own tests unnecessary, to prevent others from testing, to prevent the nuclear arms race from mushrooming out of control, to take the first steps toward general and complete disarmament. And that is why, in the last analysis, it is the leaders of the Soviet Union who must bear the heavy responsibility of choosing, in the weeks that lie ahead, whether we proceed with these steps—or proceed with new tests.

If they are convinced that their interests can no longer be served by the present course of events, it is my fervent hope that they will agree to an effective treaty. But if they persist in rejecting all means of true inspection, then we shall be left no choice but to keep our own defensive arsenal adequate for the security of all free men.

It is our hope and prayer that these grim, unwelcome tests will never have to be made—that these deadly weapons will never have to be fired—and that our preparations for war will bring us the preservation of peace. Our foremost aim is the control of force, not the pursuit of force, in a world made safe for mankind. But whatever the future brings, I am sworn to uphold and defend the freedom of the American people—and I intend to do whatever must be done to fulfill that solemn obligation.

Thank you—and good night.

In his March 2 address the President succeeded where he had failed after his first unhappy meeting with Chairman Khrushchev. He talked to the American people frankly, took them into his confidence, made them his partners. The President had found the way to communicate the seriousness and the challenge of our situation, informing his listeners without overalarming them.

After a year of trial and error, Kennedy was at home with the American people. He himself was confident of what we must do and where we must go, and the country and our allies were confident of his leadership as they had not been since his election.

Six months of increasingly heavy pressure to resume nuclear tests had not swerved the President from his determination to stand firm on the principle of negotiation as the only way to the larger goal of general disarmament with controls. The personal political risk he ran did not dismay Kennedy any more than the risk he ran in deciding to send American astronauts deep into space in full public view.

This was a time suited to the man. "Daring in the face of great odds is the single quality that John F. Kennedy has always most admired," James MacGregor Burns, the President's biographer, tells us. Here, more than at any other point in his first year in the White House, Mr. Kennedy himself demonstrated that quality.

Index

Cosman, Bernard, 17
Cosmos Club, 126
Council of Economic Advisers,
President's, 146, 149, 150, 151,
160, 161, 171, 172, 173, 177,
186, 191
Council of the Federation of American Scientists, 288-89
Cox, Archibald, 117
Cox, Eugene, 80
Credit, tight vs. easy, 171-73
Cuba, 18, 26, 59, 60, 62, 90, 95,
160, 193, 200, 201, 204, 226,
236, 271, 272; invasion of,
52, 54-58, 209; post-mortems on,
211; Russian response to failure
of invasion of, 160, 161, 209
Cummings, Homer S., 66

Daniel, Price, 9
Dean, Arthur H., 202, 204, 206,
207, 208, 209, 211, 212, 213, 275
Defense Department, 49, 63, 65,
221, 225, 247, 248
De Gaulle, Charles, 165, 227, 230,
231, 234, 245, 250, 251, 253
Delaney, James J., 102, 103
Democratic National Convention
(1936), 80
Democratic National Convention
(1960), 3
Democratic Study Group, 81, 86,
89, 94, 104
Depressed-areas legislation, 73, 95,
96, 99, 148
Depression, Great, 189
Desegregation, 122, 123, 125, 136,
138-39, 141, 142
Development Loan Fund, 255, 259
Diefenbaker, John G., 230
Dillon, C. Douglas, 44, 69, 146,
150, 151, 152, 154, 159, 164, 165,
172, 178, 179, 190, 191, 255, 269;
influence on President Kennedy,
169-71; tax rise urged by, 177
Dirksen, Everett M., 78, 90, 97,
100, 246, 265; quoted, 98
Disarmament, President Kennedy's
views on, 197-211 passim, 213,
286, 289, 290; and negotiations
with Soviet Union, 194-200

passim, 202-11 passim, 213;
Stevenson's report on, 194-95
Disarmament Administration, 196
Disarmament and Arms Control
Agency, 104, 287
Dixon-Yates contract, 270
Dodd, Thomas J., 78
Dolan, Joseph, 128
Dominican Republic, 59
Donahue, Richard K., 41
Doty, Paul Mead, Jr., 198, 199, 200
Dougherty, Bill, 87
Douglas, Paul H., 19, 98, 99, 157;
quoted, 189, 190
Douglas, William O., 110
Dowling, Walter C., 234
DuBridge, Lee A., 215
Dulles, Allen, 36, 55, 65, 247, 271
Dulles, John Foster, 27, 33, 202,
247, 260
Dungan, Ralph A., 41, 262
Dutton, Frederick G., 64

Eastland, James O., 15, 75, 118,
121, 132, 181; Marshall questioned by, 118-20
Education Bill, 73-74, 98, 100-04,
262, 264
Eisenhower, Dwight D., 21, 37, 52,
68, 69, 142, 143, 159, 165,
168, 286, 287; and Congress,
70, 72, 82; Kennedy's call on,
192; Kennedy warned by, on
Passman, 265
Eisenhower Administration, 19,
20, 22, 29, 30, 40, 43, 44, 155,
160, 177, 183, 202; budget in,
175-76, 179; on civil defense,
224-25; committees and boards
of, 48, 49, 50; and Cuba, 52,
53, 54, 55; foreign-aid program
of, 259, 261, 269; Kennedy's
campaign criticisms of, 192-93,
214; gold outflow during, 163;
and space race, 214, 215, 216,
218
Elliott, Carl, 88
Ellis, Frank Burton, 225, 237, 238,
239, 240
Emancipation Proclamation Association, 114